Shakespeare's book

MANCHESTER
1824

Manchester University Press

Shakespeare's book

Essays in reading, writing and reception

Edited by

RICHARD MEEK, JANE RICKARD
AND RICHARD WILSON

Manchester
University Press

Manchester and New York

distributed in the United States exclusively by Palgrave Macmillan

Published by Manchester University Press
Oxford Road, Manchester M13 9NR, UK
and Room 400, 175 Fifth Avenue, New York, NY 10010, USA
www.manchesteruniversitypress.co.uk

Distributed in the United States exclusively by
Palgrave Macmillan, 175 Fifth Avenue, New York,
NY 10010, USA

Distributed in Canada exclusively by
UBC Press, University of British Columbia, 2029 West Mall,
Vancouver, BC, Canada V6T 1Z2

British Library Cataloguing-in-Publication Data
A catalogue record for this book is available from the British Library

Library of Congress Cataloging-in-Publication Data applied for

ISBN   978 07190 7905 4   *hardback*

First published 2008

17 16 15 14 13 12 11 10 09 08   10 9 8 7 6 5 4 3 2 1

Contents

Part III Readers

Acknowledgements

The editors would like to thank the contributors for their hard work and patience. We are also grateful to the anonymous readers for the press for their helpful suggestions. Some of the material in this collection develops work published elsewhere. Chapter 1 draws upon material from Patrick Cheney, *Shakespeare's Literary Authorship* (Cambridge: Cambridge University Press, 2008). Chapter 6 is a revised version of Duncan Salkeld, 'The Texts of *Henry V*', *Shakespeare*, 3: 2 (August 2007), 161–82, reprinted by permission of the publisher (Taylor & Francis Ltd). Chapter 7 is a development of E. A. J. Honigmann, 'Shakespeare's Deletions and False Starts', *The Review of English Studies*, 56 (2005), 37–48. Chapter 10 is a revised version of Stanley Wells, 'By the Placing of His Words', *Times Literary Supplement*, no. 5243, 26 September 2003, pp. 14–15. We are grateful to the publishers and editors for permission to reprint.

Notes on contributors

Patrick Cheney, Pennsylvania State University

George Donaldson, University of Bristol

Gabriel Egan, University of Loughborough

Lukas Erne, University of Geneva

E. A. J. Honigmann, University of Newcastle

John Lyon, University of Bristol

Richard Meek, University of York

Jane Rickard, University of Leeds

Duncan Salkeld, University of Chichester

Helen Smith, University of York

Stanley Wells, Shakespeare Institute, University of Birmingham

Richard Wilson, University of Cardiff

Introduction
'Th'world's volume': printer, page and the literary field

Richard Wilson, Jane Rickard and Richard Meek

> This was my master,
> A very valiant Briton, and a good . . .
> Alas,
> There is no more such masters. I may wander
> From east to occident, cry out for service,
> Try many, all good; serve truly, never
> Find such another master.
> *(Cymbeline,* 4.2.370–6)

When the boy Fidele played by Imogen is asked to identify the 'valiant Briton' he mourns as his lost master, the time-frame of *Cymbeline* is broken by one of Shakespeare's most localised and self-reflexive allusions, with an anachronistic reply, 'Richard du Champ', a play on *page*, and a disclaimer of untruth: 'If I do lie and do / No harm by it, though the gods hear I hope / They'll pardon it' (4.2.379–81). As editors note, the French name translates as that of Richard Field, first printer of *Venus and Adonis* and *The Rape of Lucrece*, and the dramatist's slightly older Stratford-upon-Avon schoolmate, while Field is itself a near anagram of the *faithful* Fidele.[1] 'Thy name well fits thy faith, thy faith thy name', the Roman Lucius assures the page (4.2.383). But Shakespeare only ever named one other Stratford contemporary, with a joke about 'lousy' Sir Thomas Lucy that kick-starts *The Merry Wives*; and the hostility of that allusion makes the *fidelity* of this apparent tribute to the one and only missing master the more patent and affecting.

At the time of *Cymbeline* Shakespeare's company had just moved into the Blackfriars playhouse, slap beside Field's printing house in the Blackfriars Liberty, and only yards from the book-trade offices

at Stationers' Hall and the booksellers' stalls in St Paul's Churchyard
Thomas Nashe called the 'Exchange of All Authors'.[2] As Adrian
Johns writes in *The Nature of the Book: Print and Knowledge in the
Making*, 'Virtually every building in this precinct', where in 1613
Shakespeare would himself buy the Gatehouse, 'had a role to play
in the making and moving of words. In this area the topography of
print could be measured in feet'.[3] With shop-frontages of thirty foot,
the St Paul's book trade was, in Peter Blayney's words, 'an advanced
industry of mass-production'.[4] There is, then, a poignant irony to
the picture these lines suggest, of the writer scouring London's
twenty printing-houses and fifty presses, from Aldersgate in the east
to Holborn in the west, in a mythic quest for an equal of the irre-
placeable master from whom he has split, like the minstrel Blondel
searching for *his* King Richard.[5] For if they share a space, Richard
and Fidele live in different eras; and, as with the anagram, their
anachronistic master–page relation hints at a story of textual desire
and disappointment, and the tantalising *untimeliness* of the fidelity
between Shakespeare's stage and page, player and printer, in the city
of the first literary field and dawning age of mechanical reproduction. In their address 'To the great Variety of Readers' prefacing the
1623 Folio, Shakespeare's colleagues Heminge and Condell would
ruefully record that 'It had bene a thing . . . worthie to haue bene
wished, that the Author himselfe had liu'd to haue set forth, and
ouerseen his owne writings'.[6] Yet what the haunting testimonial to
the absent master printer in *Cymbeline* suggests is that it was not
simply Shakespeare's untimely demise that prevented him seeing his
writings through the press, but rather the fact that, when it came to
publication to his satisfaction in his own lifetime, the 'page' would
'cry out for service' sufficient to produce 'Shakespeare's Book'.

'I may . . . Try many': Shakespeare's frustrated search for the
perfect printer provides a textual corroboration and aspirational
context for a starting-point of the present *Shakespeare's Book*: the
theory floated by Lukas Erne in his 2003 *Shakespeare as Literary
Dramatist* that Shakespeare always desired publication of his words,
and had his texts printed as expertly as possible, until some point in
1602 when he began to *authorise* the novel idea of a bound collected
Works, which would take definitive shape as 'Shakespeare's Book'.[7]
In particular, the despair at finding a printing-press to equal Field's at
which *Cymbeline* may hint supports Erne's image of Shakespeare as
a literary writer who wished to publish plays with the same textual

fidelity as he had his poems. Indeed, one implication of the lament for the faithful master is that Erne may *underrate* Shakespeare's early desire to reproduce 'a certain text' (*Romeo and Juliet*, 4.1.21), when he follows John Roe, a recent editor of the poems, in assuming that once the manuscript was in Field's hands Shakespeare 'entrusted the enterprise to the professional competence of others, pausing over the printed copy only long enough to make sure that all was well with the dedication'.[8] For Laurie Maguire counters that 'it was usual for authors to correct proofs' in 'some little Closet adjoining to the Composing room'.[9] Since *Venus and Adonis* and *Lucrece* are impeccably printed compared to the later playtexts, and so carefully proofread, biographers have in fact long imagined a primal scene of proofing, as the rapt poet 'stood in Field's shop in Blackfriars and corrected the sheets, taking care to iron out idiosyncratic spelling'.[10] The 1593 title-page of *Venus and Adonis* reveals how the master also 'corrected' Shakespeare as this was the first time the name was ever spelt with an 'e' between syllables, an insertion prompted by a tendency for the Tudor letters 'k' and 's' to break if set together.[11] And it was Field who to squeeze stanzas into the pagination spoiled the rhyme by docking Warwickshire spellings.[12] Yet that emotive declaration, 'This was my master', does invoke apprenticeship; and rumour even had it that as the professional partnership developed the 'page-boy' performed Field's 'office 'twixt his sheets when his old friend was on trips to Stratford'.[13] As Samuel Schoenbaum tactfully put it, 'there would be speculation about how well they were acquainted', after critics thought they glimpsed the Dark Lady of the Sonnets in Field's wife: 'a Frenchwoman, likely to have dark eyes, and that indefinable *charm* so much alluded to'.[14] The fantasy may be far-fetched, but it encapsulates a typographic saga of textuality and sexuality to rival legends of the Bard of Bankside, with a Shakespeare-as-page immersed in the inky milieu of the Blackfriars printers' precinct, and intimately *pressed* into the homosocial metier of the book. More generally, what the romance of Shakespeare in love with Jacqueline Field illustrates is the argument that, as Erne puts it, 'the institutions of the printing press and modern theatre "grew up together"'.[15]

'Mr Shaxpere one book': a memorandum made by Richard Field's sister Margery lists among items later valued at £5 9s 4d, which on July 20 1595 fell 'deceitfully' into the grasp of another Stratford widow, a volume that hints that, contrary to tales of illiteracy, Shakespeare's father John was one of those able to read but not to write.[16] And it is tempting to guess that on this occasion 'Shakespeare's Book' was an inscribed copy, despatched to his father hot from Field's press, of *Venus and Adonis*, which the author boasted in the dedication to be 'the first heir of my invention'. In any case, Mr Shakespeare's purloined book situates the families of the poet and printer side-by-side in the sociable 'Little World of the Book' where knowledge was made and identity fashioned.[17] The Fields and Shakespeares were, in fact, neighbours from the outset, Richard being born in 1561 in the Bridge Street house where in 1592 John Shakespeare appraised his deceased father's worldly possessions at a meagre £14.[18] Henry Field had been a tanner, sued by Shakespeare the glover in 1556 for 144 bushels of barley.[19] But trade in leather was what united these craftsmen in the malodorous industry the dramatist would for ever connect with the material conditions of writing, and shock that 'the skin of an innocent lamb should be made parchment' (*2 Henry VI*, 4.2.70). Shakespeare never forgot the instinct to judge a book well if 'fairly bound', nor lost a shrewd sense that a 'precious book . . . To beautify him only lacks a cover' (*Romeo and Juliet*, 1.3.89; 3.2.84). So, we could infer self-interest was why Stratford's leather-workers apprenticed so many boys to London printers, including Jasper, a second of Field's sons, and John Lock, the son of another glover. In 1602 they were joined by Richard, son of Shakespeare's Henley Street next-door neighbour, George Badger.[20] And if Shakespeare, for all his teasing of 'book-men' (*Love's Labour's Lost*, 2.1.227), was indeed one of the first poets since Chaucer to wish to purge the 'stigma of print' and make print culture the royal road to social *distinction*, then this paternally approved local career-path might provide some explanation.[21] For, with a clown such as Jack Cade, the writer turned aristocratic print-phobia upside-down, to denigrate peasants who alleged that grammar schools 'corrupted youth' or paper mills were 'contrary to the king' (*2 Henry VI*, 4.7.27–31).[22] This petit-bourgeois revenge of the clerks was sparked by the Tudor 'reading revolution' when one grammar school was erected for every 4400 persons.[23] But no wonder, with Richard Field for role-model and printing as a potential profession, that the glover's son became one of the earliest to have his characters voice the desire to 'speak in print' (*Two Gentlemen of Verona*, 2.1.151), nor that such desire was flaunted from the start in the ambition to, as Armado puts it, 'Devise, wit!

Write, pen! For I am for whole volumes, in folio' (*Love's Labour's Lost*, 1.2.163–4). Yet no surprise either that with such artisanal origins this yearning for the printed page was indelibly 'branded' by the stain of ink:

> Thence comes it that my name receives a brand,
> And almost thence my nature is subdued
> To what it works in, like the dyer's hand.
> Pity me then, and wish I were renewed,
> Whilst like a willing patient I will drink
> Potions of eisel 'gainst my strong infection;
> No bitterness that I will bitter think,
> Nor double penance to correct correction.
>
> (Sonnet 111, 5–12)

'If I do lie and do / No harm': the page's defence of white lies comes in a text fixated on textual corruption, and the need to 'correct' 'this fair paper, this most goodly book', of the inky blot of 'whore' (*Othello*, 4.2.73–4), to 'wash clean' the adulterating stigma of the 'pit of ink' (*Much Ado About Nothing*, 4.1.139).[24] For, like all the romances, *Cymbeline* is fraught with a sexualised anxiety that 'To write and read [is] henceforth treacherous' (4.2.316), owing to the promiscuous relations of a bastard industry, and the uncertainty about textual origins, betrayed in his name, Posthumus vents when he fears his own father 'was I know not where / when I was stamped' (2.5.4).[25] These are the paternal insecurities over unauthorised epitomes, imitations, piracies and translations that climax in Leontes' refusal, seemingly justified by Autolycus' illegitimate ballads 'in print', to believe that 'although the print be little', his daughter is 'the whole matter / And copy of the father' (*The Winter's Tale*, 2.3.99; 4.4.251). Shakespeare's last pages respond in this way to a legitimacy crisis in early modern thinking about paternity and printing; a crisis only intensified, Margreta de Grazia explains, by the pornographic mechanics of a *press* built from eroticised parts 'performing virtual copulative acts'.[26] Yet, as Ann Thompson points out, *Cymbeline* marks a major shift in this phallocentric discourse of printing and parenting, when Posthumus reverses the question, 'Is this an *authorized* copy?' to condemn *his own falsity* in doubting Imogen's truth: ''Tween man and man they weigh not every stamp; / Though light, take pieces for the figure's sake.'[27] This act of faith cues Jupiter's gift of a 'rare' book which Posthumus trusts will not have a jacket 'Nobler than that it covers'. As Robert Knapp remarks in *Shakespeare: The Theater and the Book*, henceforth these plays depend upon what he calls the 'bookish authority' of texts such as this, 'whose containing / Is so from sense' (*Cymbeline*, 5.5.118–19, 227–9; 5.6.431–2) but whose contents have to be trusted even if 'the text is foolish' (*King Lear*, 4.2.38).[28] Thus, Shakespeare's most 'impure' work prefigures the 'containing' of the Folio as an aggregation of 'six hundred typefaces, non-uniform spelling and punctuation, erratic divisions, mispaging and irregular proofing', of which no two copies are the same.[29] And a story about following a page in good faith contributes to the epistemic change Johns describes when the credibility gap was bridged by 'intersubjective trust'. For the real 'print revolution', Johns stresses, was when 'questions of credit took the place of assumptions of fixity'. This is a recognition – that 'fixity lies in the eye of the beholder' – Leontes affirms when, punning on the 20 by 25 inch paper size for *royal prints*, he tells Florizel, 'Your mother was most true to wedlock, Prince, / For she did print your royal father off' (*The Winter's Tale*, 5.1.123). So, it cannot be mere verbal luck when, on the page that makes this leap of faith, Shakespeare provides a local habitation and a name for the new literary faithfulness which in *The Nature of the Book* validates the world of print, and that he calls this *fidelity* Field.[30]

'It is required / You do awake your faith' (*The Winter's Tale*, 5.3.94–5): in plays written for Blackfriars Shakespeare staged the revolution when faith in books eclipsed the dream of the perfect text. And in his most localised of tributes he attributed this epochal shift to trust in the master who faithfully – 'even slavishly' – followed the author's page.[31] For 'behind the scenes', in Johns's account, the master printers of the Liberty were 'manufacturers of credit', the guarantors of the 'civility' and 'collective morality' that underlay London's emerging 'literary life'. In a culture where 'books trumpeted their provenance on their title pages', where 'locations had cultural consequences' and the social characteristics attributed to different areas affected the epistemic status of printed texts, it was these masters who ensured the credibility which was a precondition of the literary field. Thus, it is only when the 'benefit of being close to the social centre of the book world', and a habit of 'attributing trust to a book on the basis of evaluation of a person', are appreciated that the implications for 'Shakespeare's book' of his promoting a printer 'dwelling in the Blackfriars' can be grasped.[32] For if he did not expressly nominate the Blackfriars maestro for the contract to print his collected Works,

Shakespeare may have hinted in *Cymbeline* that Field was the only printer he could trust. He knew, that is to say, what Roger Chartier reminds us in *The Order of Books*: that there is no text 'apart from the physical support it offers for reading (or hearing), hence there is no comprehension of any written piece that does not . . . depend upon the forms in which it reaches the reader'.[33] Early modern Londoners were in fact confused about the authorising yet supporting role of the printer, seeing him as both server and boss, or a 'Master Page' (*The Merry Wives of Windsor*, 1.1.116). So the printing-house was 'a blank slate to be inscribed with their aims, prejudices and predilections'.[34] But since Field may be recommended in *Cymbeline* as the one printer by whose standards all the others will be judged, it seems important to consider what made him such a paragon Shakespeare could 'never / Find such another master'. In 1610 this unique trade endorsement rang true, because Field, who had been admitted to the Stationers' Company in 1598, had climbed to the prestigious post of Assistant in 1604, and Under Warden in 1605, then Upper Warden, at the summit of London's world of books. Twice, in 1619 and 1622, his professional reputation would be crowned by election to the Mastership of the Company. But if *Cymbeline* was acted at court, as editors suppose, there its salute to literary masters and pages who follow each other so faithfully would have had an extra resonance for the most truly sovereign of authors, because Field was the pupil and chosen heir of the first printer of the poems of King James himself.[35]

'[C]orrected by your Maiest. owne hande': it had been the boy-king James who, according to Thomas Hudson, one of the book-loving 'brethren' around the 'royal Apollo', personally corrected the text of Hudson's *Historie of Judith* published in Edinburgh by the man Field called *his* master, Thomas Vautrollier.[36] Thus the royal author's literary ambitions may account for Shakespeare's product-placement in *Cymbeline*, as Field had been apprenticed to the French émigré printer at the moment in 1579 when Vautrollier travelled to Edinburgh. Vautrollier's Scottish career would peak in 1584 with his publication of the King's own early poems, *The Essayes of a Prentise, in the Diuine Art of Poesie*, which included his work of poetic theory, *Ane Schort Treatise conteining some Reulis and Cautelis to be obseruit and eschewit in Scottis Poesie*. As David Bergeron remarks, to refer to the 'divine art of poesie' in the title of his first volume suggests 'this young writer took himself and his poetry seriously'; and the creation of a 'Castalian band' of writers around him lent an extraordinary prestige to the emerging concept of the rights or 'royalty' of the literary world.[37] As 'a stranger banished for religion', the Huguenot Vautrollier would be tempted by this promise of literary sovereignty, and by his 'licence and privilege' to print books 'to his Majesty's own use by his Highness's special command'.[38] But since James displayed such concern to 'comman[d] . . . the field of writing and print', he would equally relish the technical flair the Frenchman vaunted printing within *Essayes of a Prentise* texts like 'Ane Metaphoricall Inuention of a Tragedie Called Phoenix', the King's elegy to Esmé Stuart, which opened with a column of 18 lines patterned as 'an implausible diamond-shaped votive urn'.[39] This was an expertise Vautrollier learned from his own mentor, the great scholar-printer Christopher Plantin, and displayed in complex jobs like mathematical treatises and Italian madrigals. But Elizabeth Eisenstein also puts Vautrollier in the loop of a European-wide network smuggling 'heterodox, libertine, innovative' books like those of Giordano Bruno; and it was contacts and patents, as well as press and type, that he passed to his apprentice.[40] *Love's Martyr*, the anthology Field printed in 1601 which featured 'The Phoenix and Turtle', seems a coded relic of this ciphered world. And Field's first works under his own imprint were French translations about the Wars of Religion. So, it is hardly necessary to imagine Shakespeare toiling in the workshop 'as a proof reader or typographer' to recognise in these operations 'the ground, the books, the academes' of *Love's Labour's Lost* (4.3.291:8).[41]

When Vautrollier died in 1587 Field lost no time marrying the French widow. And what excited writers, as the reference to 'Richard du Champ' may have reminded the poet-king, was indeed how the 'cross-cultural interchange experienced first by typefounders, correctors, translators, copy editors, illustrators, print dealers, and indexers' connected the local to the *global*; how print, as Imogen reflects, restored the torn page of the little British isles to its proper place in a book so much greater than 'Our Britain':[42]

Hath Britain all the sun that shines? Day, night,
Are they not but in Britain? I'th'world's volume
Our Britain seems as of it but not in't,
In a great pool a swan's nest. Prithee, think
There's livers out of Britain.

(*Cymbeline*, 3.4.136–40)

It was Field's emblem of a phoenix on fire that resembled a nesting swan.[43] And in 1610, when Shakespeare jokingly called this 'valiant Briton' the French 'Champ', the printer was about to relocate to the other St Paul's book enclave of Little Britain, where, if it was like the shops of his European partners, The Splayed Eagle in Wood Street gave him room to host 'an international meeting-house, message-centre, and sanctuary all in one'. So, in his Spanish publications, which included a Bible, Field called himself Ricardo del Campo; and the multi-culturalism of his texts in French, Greek, Hebrew, Italian and even Welsh justifies Eisenstein's metaphor for the Plantin book-exchanging circuit as the 'chief switchboard of the Republic of Letters'.[44]

It seems apt, therefore, that the only book from Shakespeare's library we think we retain is the life of the politique Catherine de Medici by the scholar-publisher Henri Estienne, whose printing dynasty kept open house at the nexus of this polyglot promiscuous system.[45] For if it was his, Shakespeare's volume fits the tolerant Erasmian *Concordia Mundi* dreamed in *Cymbeline*. And if it did come from New Place, Shakespeare's book testifies to the global lines of credit and trust in a 'family of man' that made it possible to conceptualise for the first time a folio volume, such as a Bible or col-lected Works, which would indeed aspire to be 'the world's'. Field's great achievement had in fact been just such a cosmopolitan tome, when Sir John Harington's 1591 translation of Ariosto's *Orlando Furioso* required co-operation by his entire team of typesetters, illus-trators and engravers in correspondence with the publishers of the 1584 Venetian edition. Here too the pressmen had to be reinforced by designers trained in the techniques of perspective, which as Harington had to explain, meant 'that which is nearest seems great-est, and the furthest smallest'. Harington's brag that he 'gave direc-tion for their making' to 'the best workmen that have been in this land', implies that, while his illustrations were engraved by the 'Frenchmen, Dutchmen, or such like', employed by Field, the printer let him, as author, have the last say.[46] Likewise William Bedwell recalled that his 1614 geometry treatise was made viable only by Field bearing the expense, after all other printers, 'seeing in the copy diverse figures and diagrams, refused to meddle with it'.[47] Altogether, 23 of the 295 books produced by Field were folios, including Chapman's *Iliad* and *Odyssey*. Field, whose small house averaged two thousand pages a year, was *champion* of a luxury press that did not count the cost. What graces his imprint is said to be his 'sense of fitness, proportion, discrimination about the final effect of the printed page, and marked skill in handling masses of type'.[48] And it was his 'expensive and beautiful' folio of Plutarch's *Lives* that, after helping him to settle in London, James Shapiro suspects the printer *gave* to Shakespeare.[49] But the questions posed by such fidelity are why, in spite of advertising the master, the Shakespearean 'page' was never pressed by Field again; and why, despite producing fine books right up until his death in 1624, the 'very valiant' printer of *Arcadia* and *The Faerie Queene* would never be the one to print the real 'world's volume' which was 'Shakespeare's Book'.

The hint in *Cymbeline* that Shakespeare wearily hunted for 'such another master' as his first printer offers a counter to the received idea that because he 'never used Field again' he 'showed no interest in publishing'.[50] Recycled in 2001 by David Scott Kastan with *Shakespeare and the Book*, the notion of Shakespeare's lifelong 'lack of interest in publishing' was a target of Erne's study.[51] But the master–page quest further disturbs the Globe-obsessed corollary that he had no 'desire to see his plays in print at all. He might well have brought them to his townsman Field, as he apparently did with his narrative poems, but he did not.'[52] For what this report of consumer dissatisfaction does imply is that by the time of *Cymbeline* Shakespeare felt disappointed by *all* the pressmen he had 'tried' since Field. In 1610 he might have had cause to feel let down by the industry if his *Sonnets* were prepared the year before, as John Kerrigan maintains, with special care to have them 'cleanly printed', when there were such discrepancies between the spelling and punctuation of the two typesetters in George Eld's shop that their work appears to belong to different generations.[53] Katherine Duncan-Jones, who believes that the grasping poet 'sold cheap what is most dear' (Sonnet 110, line 3) by handing the publishing to Thomas Thorpe, who 'gave a good price', rather than Field, thinks the signs of 'haste and carelessness' in the *Sonnets* also resulted from 'a severe shortage of good-quality type'.[54] Ironically, Shakespeare issued the 1609 quarto, editors infer, only after being 'much offended' ten years earlier when, 'altogether unknown to him', William Jaggard 'presumed to make so bold' as to pirate four of his sonnets in *The Passionate Pilgrim*: 'he since, to do himself right', or so Thomas Heywood attested, 'hath published them in his own name'.[55] As Andrew Murphy concludes in his recent *Shakespeare in Print*, 'Looking back on the early history of the publication of his poetry from a twenty-first-century perspective, we may be inclined to feel that, with the possible exception of his fellow-Stratfordian, Richard Field, Shakespeare was singularly poorly served by his publishers and printers'.[56]

When Shakespeare's Sonnets were first reissued in 1640, the publisher John Benson would compound this record of disservice by altering the text, combining individual sonnets, fabricating titles and re-gendering the male recipient. Such highhandedness illustrates how, as Douglas Brooks comments, 'In early modern London, the death of the author was in some sense merely a workaday hazard of publication'.[57] But even with an unintelligible dedication, the printing of the Sonnets was passable beside that of the play quartos, which reached a pitch of incompetence after 1602, mainly at the hands of Thomas Creede and Valentine Simmes, with 'Q1 *Merry Wives*, a text that is bad even in comparison with the other "bad" quartos . . . the "bad" text of *Henry V* . . . and the "bad" quarto of *Hamlet*', followed in 1609 by the 'bad' quarto of *Pericles*. As his theatrical duties increased, 'Shakespeare can hardly be blamed for not having spent time in printing houses' supervising the printing of his plays, reasons Erne.[58] Or perhaps he was just 'sickened with reading proofs'.[59] Yet in *Cymbeline* the dramatist may hint that in 'crying out for service' the printers he 'tried' were 'all good': it was just that none was ever 'such another master'. By 1610 Shakespeare had, in fact, been served by ten printers after Field; most creditably, if Heywood is believed, by Nicholas Okes, who could never be accused of 'misquotations, mistaking of syllables, misplacing of half lines, [or] coinage of strange and never heard words'.[60] Though in reality poorly printed, possibly from a shorthand or private transcript, Blayney confirms how Okes's 1608 *King Lear* required proof-sheets for no fewer than 21 painstaking stages of production.[61] But that the miscreant Heywood contrasted with Okes for committing errata 'without number' was none other than (the now blind) Jaggard, and that this was the very printer who, despite launching the falsely dated, unauthorised, partly apocryphal 'Pavier' Shakespeare series in 1619, would eventually be chosen to press the expensive pages of the Folio, only deepens the mystery why in 1623 'Shakespeare's book' was denied to that year's Master of Stationers, who had served him most faithfully of all.[62]

In *Shakespeare and the Book* Kastan defends the choice of Jaggard and his son Isaac for the Folio on the grounds that, though 'opportunistic and pragmatic', and operating 'at the edge of propriety and legality', they were employed because 'The commitment of resources and impossibility of quick profits would make it an unattractive venture for any but the most ambitious'.[63] Yet Johns dates the literary field precisely to the elimination of such shady deals and sharp practices. So, if Fidele's *fidelity* is indeed the writer's own idealisation of the 'trustworthy realm of printed knowledge', Erne is surely correct to assign the responsibility for the parting of the ways between the printer and the page to Field, rather than Shakespeare.[64] Erne decides that the reason why Field was not 'more hospitable' had nothing to do with money or facilities, but was because he was 'of a conviction that made playbooks unsuitable matter for his printing-house'.[65] This echoes A. E. M. Kirwood who, in his study of Field, presumed that the printer of Puttenham's *Arte of English Poesie* 'was not convinced of the poetic powers of his fellow townsman. Can any good come out of Stratford?'[66] Bergeron draws attention to the doubts, indeed, about the status of playtexts behind the appeal for patronage in the Epistle Dedicatory of the Folio, where Heminge and Condell liken 'these trifles' to the 'milk, cream, fruits' proffered the Herbert Earls by 'country hands'.[67] Such solicitations were fast becoming gestures, and Jonson announced himself to nobles as 'thy servant, but not thy slave'.[68] But if Pembroke and Montgomery were, in Erne's phrase, 'Shakespeare's most important readers', the Blackfriars master's aversion to works which would, after all, be packaged as '"literary" reading texts' suggests it may have been his suspicion of such servile rituals, entangled with Shakespeare's affiliations as a 'company man', that debarred staged plays from the Liberty's independent 'Republic of Letters'.[69] In *Cymbeline* the dramatist pictured the printer within the service economy of his own liveried household. But this might have been his mistake; for, as Pierre Bourdieu detailed, the autonomy of the literary field was conditional on liberation from those very institutions of church and state to which the players paid court. In this respect, the industry in which Field was the new type of 'master' was truly out of sync with Shakespeare, whose work was still grounded, however literary his ambitions, in the logic of a pre-capitalist economy and the socially shared conventions of the oral and rhetorical cultures that preceded print. If the idea of 'literature' was, as some critics have contended, a formation of print, Field's list was a roll-call of authors committed to its 'rules of art': that legitimacy was conferred only by other authors, whose duty was to 'look in thy heart, and write!'[70] Thus, the faithful master would print Sir William Alexander's sonnets and closet plays for the Folio publisher Edward Blount; but not one page of the world's favourite volume would cross the threshold of this literary field.

'Never master had / A page so kind' (5.6.85–6): in what may be Shakespeare's homage to Field we can catch the inverted economic logic, analysed by Bourdieu in *The Field of Cultural Production* and *The Rules of Art*, whereby the modern literary field freed itself by submitting exclusively to the authority of other cultural producers. So, if the purist printer – who sold his rights in the lucrative *Venus and Adonis* after only one of twelve editions in his lifetime and 'did not publish a single play written for a public playhouse' – spurned his chance to print 'Shakespeare's Book', that would have been a sad misrecognition of his friend's game of feudal service, which was kept up precisely to maintain equidistance from both the marketplace and palace.[71] Thus, when the Folio finally appeared its prefaces played off the patrons against the public, which, by being exhorted to 'what euer you do, Buy', was allowed to imagine it now ranked with the nobility in consecrating literary worth.[72] As Bergeron remarks, Heminge and Condell brilliantly 'succeeded in working both sides of the street . . . They skilfully positioned the Folio to reap the advantages of aristocratic *and* market-place patronage.'[73] The 'literary' Field, who never made a profit from poetry, and followed his master Vautrollier in 'the printing of Ovid, and other great works in Latin', in which he did 'neither great good nor harm', and 'other small things wherewith he [kept] his press in work', could not foresee 'Books made of Ballads: Works of Plays'.[74] But Shakespeare's 'Great Book' was, in the end, ahead of his best printer: it introduced a writer for both mass entertainment and elite consumption, for the playhouse and the printing-shop.

The present book, *Shakespeare's Book*, examines Shakespeare's works in relation to these different contexts of production and reception. Several of the chapters that follow explore Shakespeare's relationship with actual printers, patrons and readers, while others consider the representation of writing, reading and print within his works themselves. The collection gives us, then, glimpses into different Shakespeares: Shakespeare the man who lived and worked in Elizabethan and Jacobean London; Shakespeare the author of the works attributed to him; and 'Shakespeare', the construction of his colleagues, printers and readers. In examining these Shakespeares, and the interactions, overlaps and disjunctions between them, the chapters offer different conceptions of Shakespearean 'authorship'. Some chapters try to trace Shakespeare as the creative force behind his works, charting, for example, what variations between different editions of the same play might tell us about his processes of composition. Others focus on the ways in which Shakespeare was the product of a particular historical and cultural moment, and of the processes of publishing and reading. What all of the contributors share, however, is a sense of the importance of books – the books Shakespeare read, the books he represented within his works, the books within which his works were first read – to our understanding of Shakespeare's cultural significance for his contemporaries and for us.

The first part of the book focuses on representations of reading, writing and printing within Shakespeare's plays. Patrick Cheney's opening chapter begins with an overview of the recent critical shift towards consideration of Shakespeare's literary authorship, in which he, along with Erne and others, has been a key figure and to which the present book contributes. Cheney goes on to develop the argument of his 2004 study *Shakespeare, National Poet-Playwright* by focusing on Shakespeare's dramatic works. Throughout his career, Cheney writes, Shakespeare 'rehearses a discourse of the book and a discourse of the theatre, and, more importantly, he combines the two discourses together, letting the terms *book* and *theatre* jostle in historically telling ways'. Cheney offers a wide-ranging exploration of the ways in which Shakespeare's own model of authorship – one divided between the print-author and the play-author – is figured in the plays themselves. Shakespeare emerges as a writer who was as 'troubled by the individuated authorship of the literary print-house' as he was sceptical of the theatre. Cheney suggests that the rhetorical figure of *hendiadys* – in which a single idea is conveyed through two nouns linked by a conjunction – is a suggestive metaphor for Shakespeare's status as a 'poet-playwright' who vacillates between page and stage.

Continuing this exploration of the 'discourse of the book', Helen Smith tests out Erne's claims of Shakespeare's interest in print by examining the representation of books in his plays, arguing that Shakespeare's dramatic works are as much metatextual as metatheatrical. She reminds us, however, that books in Shakespeare's day were not necessarily printed; this was a world in which oral, manuscript and print traditions intersected and overlapped. Focusing on Shakespeare's varied uses of the terms 'print' and 'press', Smith emphasises that these words do not always constitute references to the mechanical means of book production, but retain earlier meanings that our concern with the printed book may lead us to overlook. She thus agrees with Erne that Shakespeare was deeply conscious that his plays would circulate in textual form, yet emphasises that his interest in texts as material objects was not limited to printed books.

Richard Meek's chapter explores the textuality of Shakespeare's plays via a reading of *King Lear*, a play that contains a large number of letters and other stage documents. Meek argues that *Lear* seems especially interested in the relationship between seeing, hearing and reading, and that Shakespeare's presentation of these different modes of perception comments upon our experience of the play. Focusing on Edgar's extended description of Dover cliff, Meek suggests that the blinded Gloucester – who has to 'look with [his] ears' – can be seen as a figure not only for the audience but also for the play's readers. As Meek puts it, 'Shakespeare demonstrates the power of language alone to act upon our imaginary forces, and suggests that – like Gloucester perhaps – we don't need to *see* his plays for this to happen'. These questions are further complicated by the contrast between Gloucester's offstage death – which is narrated to us by Edgar – and the onstage death of King Lear. This contrast, Meek argues, implicitly emphasises the mediatedness of both text *and* performance.

In Chapter 4, Richard Wilson explores the relationship between poetry and theatre in *Richard II*, and reads the opposition between Richard's antiquated model of kingship and Bolingbroke's theatrical reign as an allegory of Shakespeare's transition from the world of aristocratic patronage to the professional stage. Shakespeare's new business venture – becoming a shareholder of the Lord Chamberlain's Men, and thus part of the joint-stock company that was to own the Globe – opened up the playhouse 'to the new commercial monarchy of the mass market'. Wilson invites us to see *Richard II* as a meditation on Shakespeare's ambivalent position between 'crown and crowd, the monarch and the mob'. The irony, of course, is that this 'drama about the defeat of poetry' is itself a masterpiece of Shakespeare's poetic art: it is one of the few plays by Shakespeare written entirely in verse.

The second part of the book turns to the textual history of Shakespeare's plays and asks what this history might tell us about his practice as a writer and his relationship to both stage and page. In an essay that brings together textual scholarship and theatre history, Gabriel Egan interrogates the Foucauldian claim that the early modern sense of 'verbatim repetition' was markedly different from our own. Egan offers a detailed consideration of a moment in *2 Henry VI* when an article of peace is read aloud by two different characters in the same scene, and argues that a single copy of this document would have been produced for use as a stage property. This practice would – at least in performance – have eliminated the discrepancy between the two versions of the document that we find in the Folio text. Egan also argues that the typographical similarity between the two appearances of Posthumus' 'tablet' in the Folio text of *Cymbeline* is due to the printer's use of the same block of type to save time and effort. In these examples we find that an unauthorised 'principle of thrift' introduces regularities into the performances and texts of Shakespeare's plays. Egan's chapter thus prompts us to reconsider both the 'regularising effects of . . . the playhouse and the printing-house' and the collaborative nature of early modern authorship.

Duncan Salkeld offers a detailed examination of editorial theory and practice in relation to the two versions of *Henry V* – the 1600 quarto and the longer version printed in the 1623 Folio. Salkeld engages with some of the issues raised by Erne's *Shakespeare as Literary Dramatist*, in particular the notion that the shorter texts of Shakespeare's plays are oral 'theatrical' texts, while the longer texts correspond to what an 'emergent dramatic author wrote for readers'.[75] Salkeld suggests that some critics may have been too hasty in dismissing the possibility that the quarto text is a memorial reconstruction, arguing that behind its textual transmission lies a 'complex sequence of mediations . . . a sequence difficult to ascertain precisely'. Salkeld regards Q1 as a text produced indirectly from performance rather than a text designed for performance. He proposes evidence to suggest that F's Choruses, though absent from Q1, were performed in 1599. For Salkeld, the complex and often unstable relationship between Q1 and F means that it is hard to maintain any 'neat distinction' between shorter and longer texts as 'literary' and 'theatrical'.

In the third chapter in this section, Ernst Honigmann argues that Shakespeare often failed to delete cancelled passages, with the result that these passages sometimes found their way into the quartos and Folio of his plays. Honigmann proposes that a number of textual cruxes may be explained as 'false starts' or confusions of the printing-house. This argument clearly has important implications for editors and producers of Shakespeare's plays. But it also gives us a tantalising glimpse into 'Shakespeare in the act of composition', making false starts, having second thoughts, and sometimes leaving two alternative versions of the same passage in place so as to keep his options open. Honigmann further suggests that Shakespeare's habit of not marking deleted passages clearly in his foul papers indicates that he expected – even if this did not in fact happen – to have the opportunity to prepare the fair copy himself. This leads Honigmann to share Erne's view that Shakespeare may have intended to oversee the production of a collected edition of his works before his death.

Finally the book turns to assumed and actual readers of Shakespeare's works. Reflecting the centrality of the First Folio to the early construction of Shakespeare as an author, two chapters take this book as their focus. George Donaldson offers a close examination of the ways in which the prefatory materials construct Shakespeare, paying particular attention to the notion of Shakespeare as a dramatist to be read on the page as well as seen on the stage. He argues that while Jonson's contributions represent Shakespeare as a poet to be admired for his wit and Heminge and Condell represent him as a playwright of popular success, this does not equate to a contention between the stage and the page. Rather, the First Folio audaciously claims to give its readers access to a point of origin that lies beyond previous printings or performances, and thus works to collapse the difference between the two.

In the following chapter, Jane Rickard examines the First Folio in relation to two other important folio collections of the Jacobean period: the *Workes* of Ben Jonson of 1616 and the *Workes* of King James of the same year. Through this comparison, Rickard not only shows how the 1623 collection grew out of earlier developments and innovations but also highlights specific ways in which it was unprecedented. Focusing on the ways in which authors, readers and the relationship between them are represented in each collection, the chapter emphasises how much more open the First Folio is to its readers and to a commercial market, and suggests that this difference in turn reflects how much less concerned to control interpretation Shakespeare was than were his rival Jonson or his monarch James. At the same time the chapter argues that – paradoxically – this folio more fully achieves the effect Jonson and James had sought in their earlier folios: that of the self-authorising author.

While these two chapters consider representations of and addresses to readers, Stanley Wells's chapter gives us a rare glimpse into an actual early reader of Shakespeare. Wells discusses a recently discovered manuscript by William Scott, written between 1599 and 1601, the title of which is '[The Model] of Poesy or the Art of Poesy drawn into a short or summary discourse'. This scholarly treatise discusses the relative merits of poets such as Sidney, Spenser and Daniel. Most striking for our own purposes, however, are Scott's references to Shakespeare. Scott offers detailed readings of Shakespeare's style in *The Rape of Lucrece* and *Richard II*, describing both works as 'well-penned'. What we find is an astute reader of Shakespeare – perhaps even, as Wells puts it, Shakespeare's 'first serious critic' – closely analysing the language of his poems *and* plays alongside the work of other literary artists of the period. Wells's chapter thus offers us further evidence that a 'readerly attention' to Shakespeare's plays is 'not a modern anti-social aberration but an authentic Jacobethan experience'.[76]

In the last chapter, John Lyon offers further reflection on the relationship between the stage and the page that is addressed in a range of ways throughout the book, considering the qualities of the plays that seem to transcend or exceed both media. Throughout his career Shakespeare produces works that are, in the words of Biron in *Love's Labour's Lost*, 'too long for a play'. Noting Shakespeare's fascination with elsewheres, befores, afterwards, gaps and absences, Lyon suggests that Shakespeare's fictional worlds extend *beyond* the spatial and temporal limits of his plays: 'Shakespeare's imagination', he writes, 'though clearly affected by the contingencies of both text and performance, is finally constrained by neither'. The Shakespearean author, Lyon argues, is not only a literary dramatist but also a kind of proto-novelist; one whose imagination is 'bafflingly profligate', and who is decidedly *un*anxious about the multiplicity of interpretations that his works elicit.

As Lukas Erne's 'Afterword' reflects, the present collection thus joins other recent work in engaging with questions that, as the result of a lack of communication between different areas in Shakespeare studies and a widespread critical insistence on Shakespeare's indifference to the printing of his plays, have been given insufficient attention. What was Shakea̤ re's attitude to his printers and readers, and to the bibliograp   presence he had already gained in his own lifetime? Did he ever ᴠ rite plays with readers in mind? Had he lived longer would he have overseen the publication of the First Folio? How were his printed plays regarded by his contemporaries? In short, how far and in what ways should we regard Shakespeare as – to borrow from the title of Smith's chapter – 'a man in print'? Not all of these questions are capable of definitive answers and yet, as the chapters below demonstrate, asking them sheds fresh light on how we interpret, edit and perform the works of the author whose colleagues enjoined us to 'Reade him . . . againe, and againe'.

Notes

All quotations of Shakespeare are from the Norton edition, based on the Oxford edition, ed. Stephen Greenblatt, Walter Cohen, Jean Howard and Katharine Eisaman Maus (New York: Norton, 1997).

1 See J. M. Nosworthy (ed.), *Cymbeline*, The Arden Shakespeare (London: Methuen, 1955), note to 4.2.377, p. 138; and Robert Kane, '"Richard du Champ" in *Cymbeline*', *Shakespeare Quarterly*, 4 (1953), p. 206.

2 Thomas Nashe, *The Works of Thomas Nashe*, ed. R. B. McKerrow, rev. F. P. Wilson, 5 vols (Oxford: Oxford University Press, 1958), vol. 1, p. 278. For Nashe's own embeddedness in the milieu of the printers' precinct see Charles Nicholl, *A Cup of News: The Life of Thomas Nashe* (London: Routledge and Kegan Paul, 1984), pp. 42–3.

3 Adrian Johns, *The Nature of the Book: Print and Knowledge in the Making* (Chicago and London: University of Chicago Press, 1998), p. 68.

4 Peter Blayney, 'The Publication of Playbooks', in John D. Cox and David Scott Kastan (eds), *A New History of Early English Drama* (New York: Columbia University Press, 1997), pp. 413–14.

5 The locations and figures for the number of printing-houses and licensed presses are those provided in Mark Bland, 'The London Book-Trade in 1600', in David Scott Kastan (ed.), *A Companion to Shakespeare* (Oxford: Blackwell, 1999), pp. 450, 459.

6 John Heminge and Henry Condell, 'To the great Variety of Readers', reprinted in Greenblatt et al. (eds), *The Norton Shakespeare*, p. 3350.

7 Lukas Erne, *Shakespeare as Literary Dramatist* (Cambridge: Cambridge University Press, 2003).

8 John Roe (ed.), *The Poems*, The New Cambridge Shakespeare (Cambridge: Cambridge University Press, 1992), p. 291, quoted in Erne, *Shakespeare as Literary Dramatist*, p. 97.

9 Laurie Maguire, 'The Craft of Printing (1600)', in Kastan (ed.), *A Companion to Shakespeare*, pp. 443–4; 'Some little Closet': Joseph Moxon, *Mechanick Exercises on the Whole Art of Printing* (1693–94), ed. Herbert Davis and Harry Carter (Oxford: Oxford University Press, 1958), p. 247. For the debate about authorial proofreading see Peter Blayney, *The Texts of 'King Lear' and Their Origins: Nicholas Okes and the First Quarto* (Cambridge: Cambridge University Press, 1982), pp. 188–218.

10 Michael Wood, *In Search of Shakespeare* (London: BBC, 2003), p. 148. The theory that Shakespeare spent his 'lost years' assisting Field, or even apprenticed to another London printer, Henry Denham, was first proposed by William Blades in *Shakespeare and Typography* (London: Trübner, 1872), and elaborated in a lecture delivered at Stationers Hall by the uncannily named William Jaggard: *Shakespeare: Once a Printer and Bookman* (Stratford-upon-Avon: Shakespeare Press, 1911). The theory is humorously discussed in Andrew Murphy, *Shakespeare in Print: A History and Chronology of Shakespeare Publishing* (Cambridge: Cambridge University Press, 2003), pp. 15–16.

11 Park Honan, *Shakespeare: A Life* (Oxford: Oxford University Press, 1998), pp. 172–3.

12 Edgar Fripp, *Shakespeare: Man and Artist*, 2 vols (Oxford: Oxford University Press, 1938), vol. 1, pp. 379–84. Field imposed the same rigorous standards of spelling and punctuation on even Sir Philip Sidney: see William Ringler (ed.), *The Poems of Sir Philip Sidney* (Oxford: Clarendon Press, 1962), pp. 535–6; and W. W. Greg, 'An Elizabethan Printer and His Copy', *The Library*, 4th series, 4 (1923–24), 102–18.

13 Anthony Holden, *William Shakespeare: His Life and Work* (London: Little, Brown, 1999), p. 114.

14 Samuel Schoenbaum, *Shakespeare's Lives* (Oxford: Clarendon Press, 1970), p. 64; *William Shakespeare: A Documentary Life* (Oxford: Oxford University Press, 1975), p. 130.

15 Erne, *Shakespeare as Literary Dramatist*, p. 7, quoting Julie Stone Peters, *Theatre of the Book, 1480–1880: Print, Text, and Performance in Europe* (Oxford: Oxford University Press, 2000), p. 1. For a suggestive discussion of the ways in which '*Cymbeline* joins a host of other texts that represent infidelity through reference to blackness and ink' see Wendy Wall, 'Reading for the Blot: Textual Desire in Early Modern English Literature', in David M. Bergeron (ed.), *Reading and Writing in Shakespeare* (Newark: University of Delaware Press, 1996), p. 137.

16 Mark Eccles, *Shakespeare in Warwickshire* (Madison: University of Wisconsin Press, 1961), p. 35. For the early modern distinction between illiteracy and the capacity to read without writing see Keith Thomas, 'The Meaning of Literacy in Early Modern England', in Gerd Baumann

(ed.), *The Written Word: Literacy in Transition* (Oxford: Clarendon Press, 1986), pp. 97–131. Schoenbaum, however, contends that the memorandum suggests John Shakespeare 'may have mastered reading *and* writing' (*William Shakespeare: A Documentary Life*, p. 36).

17 'The Little World of the Book': Lucien Febvre and Henri-Jean Martin, *The Coming of the Book: The Impact of Printing, 1450–1800*, trans. David Gerard (London: Verso, 1976), pp. 136–8. For the importance of the reading circle in book culture see Roger Chartier, 'Leisure and Sociability: Reading Aloud in Early Modern Europe', in Susan Zimmerman and Ronald F. E. Wiseman (eds), *Urban Life in the Renaissance* (Newark: University of Delaware Press, 1989), pp. 103–20.

18 A. E. M. Kirwood, 'Richard Field, Printer, 1589–1624', *The Library*, 4th series, 12 (1931), 1–39.

19 Schoenbaum, *William Shakespeare: A Documentary Life*, p. 27.

20 Eccles, *Shakespeare in Warwickshire*, p. 60.

21 For a definitive account see J. W. Saunders, 'The Stigma of Print: A Note on the Social Bases of Tudor Poetry', *Essays in Criticism*, 1 (1951), 139–64. For Chaucer's assertion of his own printed status above Lydgate, with his 'penner' and 'ynkehorne', and the argument that Chaucer celebrates the mechanical 'grind' of Caxton's shop see Alexandra Gillespie, *Print Culture and the Medieval Author: Chaucer, Lydgate and Their Books, 1473–1557* (Oxford: Oxford University Press, 2006).

22 This is the argument of Richard Wilson in *Will Power: Essays in Shakespearean Authority* (Hemel Hempstead: Harvester, 1993), pp. 23–46. But for the opposite reading – that Shakespeare identifies with Cade in his 'revolution to combat literacy and the tyranny it represents' – see Geraldo de Sousa, 'The Peasant's Revolt and the Writing of History', in Bergeron (ed.), *Reading and Writing in Shakespeare*, pp. 178–93 (p. 187); and Annabel Patterson, 'Popular Culture and Popular Pressure', in *Shakespeare and the Popular Voice* (Oxford: Basil Blackwell, 1989), pp. 36–51. For a discussion that emphasises the (anachronistic) introduction of a printing press into the play see Helen Smith, Chapter 2, below. For an overview of the debate see Sharon O'Dair, *Class, Critics, and Shakespeare: Bottom Lines on the Culture Wars* (Ann Arbor: University of Michigan Press, 2000).

23 Keith Thomas, *Religion and the Decline of Magic: Studies in Popular Beliefs in Sixteenth- and Seventeenth-Century England* (Harmondsworth: Penguin, 1973), p. 4. For the long-term political implications see Kevin Sharpe, *Reading Revolutions: The Politics of Reading in Early Modern England* (New Haven: Yale University Press, 2000). For the impact of the Tudor education reforms on Shakespeare see the classic studies by T. W. Baldwin: *William Shakspere's Petty School* (Urbana: University of Illinois Press, 1943) and *William*

Shakspere's Small Latine and Lesse Greeke, 2 vols (Urbana: University of Illinois Press, 1944).

24 For the printing press as a bastardising 'whore' see Wendy Wall, *The Imprint of Gender: Authorship and Publication in the English Renaissance* (Ithaca: Cornell University Press, 1993), p. 169, and passim. And for Shakespeare's countermodel, and desire to purge the sexualised stigma of print with 'a scene of eroticized reading that does not tap into the possibilities of sinful ink', see Wall, 'Reading for the Blot', pp. 145–55.

25 Wilson, *Will Power*, p. 165.

26 Douglas Brooks, 'Introduction' to Brooks (ed.), *Printing and Parenting in Early Modern England* (Aldershot: Ashgate, 2005), p. 9; Margreta de Grazia, 'Imprints: Shakespeare, Gutenberg, and Descartes', ibid., p. 43.

27 Ann Thompson and John Thompson, 'Meaning, "Seeing", Printing', in Brooks (ed.), *Printing and Parenting*, pp. 59–86 (p. 71).

28 Robert S. Knapp, *Shakespeare: The Theater and the Book* (Princeton: Princeton University Press, 1989), p. 241; and see David Bergeron, 'Treacherous Reading and Writing in Shakespeare's Romances', in Bergeron (ed.), *Reading and Writing in Shakespeare*, pp. 160–77.

29 Johns, *The Nature of the Book*, p. 31; Margreta de Grazia, *Shakespeare Verbatim: The Reproduction of Authenticity and the 1790 Apparatus* (Oxford: Clarendon Press, 1991), pp. 15–19.

30 Johns, *The Nature of the Book*, pp. 31, 35, 58.

31 See Maguire, 'The Craft of Printing', p. 442.

32 Ibid., pp. 33, 35, 73–4 and 95: 'Discussion in terms of these areas is both useful and warranted, because the trade itself divided its practitioners in terms of six districts . . . Contemporaries knew very well the differences and similarities between such zones' (p. 66); for 'dwelling in the Blackfriars' (1610) see Kirwood, 'Richard Field, Printer', p. 12.

33 Roger Chartier, *The Order of Books: Readers, Authors, and Libraries in Europe Between the Fourteenth and Eighteenth Centuries*, trans. Lydia G. Cochrane (Stanford: Stanford University Press, 1994), p. 9.

34 Johns, *The Nature of the Book*, p. 75.

35 Kirwood, 'Richard Field, Printer', p. 11. For the debate about a possible court performance see John Pitcher's account of '*Cymbeline* and the Court of King James', in Pitcher (ed.), *Cymbeline*, New Penguin Shakespeare (Harmondsworth: Penguin, 2005), pp. 155–9.

36 Thomas Hudson, *The Historie of Judith in forme of a poeme. Penned in French, by the Noble Poet, G. Salust, Lord of Bartas. Englished by Tho. Hudson* (Edinburgh: Thomas Vautrollier, 1584), sig. A3r. It is unclear whether Hudson means that James corrected his work in manuscript before it went to press, or that he corrected proofs from the

press. The latter seems less likely; but the former still suggests a hands-on involvement in the publication process.

37 David M. Bergeron, *King James and Letters of Homoerotic Desire* (Iowa City: Iowa University Press, 1999), p. 53; Sharpe, *Reading Revolutions*, pp. 29–31. For the most recent consideration of James's literary ambitions see Jane Rickard, *Authorship and Authority: The Writings of James VI and I* (Manchester: Manchester University Press, 2007). For James as literary author see also G. P. V. Akrigg, 'The Literary Achievement of King James I', *University of Toronto Quarterly*, 44 (1975), 115–29; Jonathan Goldberg, *James I and the Politics of Literature: Jonson, Shakespeare, Donne, and Their Contemporaries* (Stanford: Stanford University Press, 1983), pp. 17–27; R. D. S. Jack, 'James VI and Renaissance Poetic Theory', *English*, 16 (1967), 208–11; and 'Poetry under King James VI', in R. D. S. Jack (ed.), *The History of Scottish Literature: Origins to 1660* (Aberdeen: Aberdeen University Press, 1987), p. 125.

38 Quoted in Kirwood, 'Richard Field, Printer', p. 4.

39 'Commanding the field of writing and print': Sharpe, *Reading Revolutions*, p. 30; for 'an implausible diamond' see Alan Stewart, *The Cradle King: A Life of King James* (London: Pimlico, 2004), p. 70. See also David M. Bergeron, *Royal Family, Royal Lovers: King James of England and Scotland* (Columbia: Missouri University Press, 1991), pp. 33–4.

40 Kirwood, 'Richard Field, Printer', p. 2; Elizabeth L. Eisenstein, *The Printing Press as an Agent of Change*, single volume edition (1979; Cambridge: Cambridge University Press, 1980), p. 417. For Vautrollier's clandestine trade see also Denis B. Woodfield, *Surreptitious Printing in England, 1550–1690* (New York: Bibliographical Society of America, 1973), pp. 415–17.

41 Clara Longworth de Chambrun, *Shakespeare: A Portrait Restored* (London: Hollis and Carter, 1957), p. 68.

42 Eisenstein, *The Printing Press*, p. 75.

43 Kirwood, 'Richard Field, Printer', pp. 26–7 (illustration on p. 27): 'A device of the figure of a bird standing erect with outspread wings. I am in some doubt what this bird is: it may be a phoenix rising from its nest of flames, or it may be the "splayed eagle" which was the sign of Field's shop.'

44 Eisenstein, *The Printing Press*, p. 448.

45 Ibid., p. 447; Schoenbaum, *William Shakespeare: A Documentary Life*, p. 249. On the Estienne dynasty see also Elizabeth Armstrong, *Robert Estienne: Royal Printer* (Cambridge: Cambridge University Press, 1954); and Natalie Zemon Davis, *Society and Culture in Early Modern France* (Cambridge: Polity Press, 1987), p. 238.

46 Sir John Harington, 'Advertisement to the Reader', *Orlando Furioso* (1591), quoted Kirwood, 'Richard Field, Printer', p. 21; 'Frenchmen, Dutchmen, or such like', ibid., p. 4. Harington's manuscript contains numerous complicated instructions to Field about layout and ornamentation, e.g.: 'Mr ffeld I dowt this will not come in in the last page, and thearfore I wowld have yow immedyatly in the next page after the fynyshinge of this last booke, with some pretty knotte to set down the tytle' (quoted and discussed in Murphy, *Shakespeare in Print*, p. 18).

47 Kirwood, 'Richard Field, Printer', pp. 23–4.

48 Ibid., pp. 20, 25–6.

49 James Shapiro, *1599: A Year in the Life of William Shakespeare* (London: Faber and Faber, 2005), p. 150.

50 Samuel Schoenbaum, 'Shakespeare and the Book', in *Shakespeare and Others* (Washington DC: Folger Shakespeare Library, 1988), p. 24.

51 David Scott Kastan, *Shakespeare and the Book* (Cambridge: Cambridge University Press, 2001), p. 15. Cf. Douglas A. Brooks, *From Playhouse to Printing House: Drama and Authorship in Early Modern England* (Cambridge: Cambridge University Press, 2000): 'Shakespeare seems to have been singularly indifferent about whether and how the plays he wrote made it into print' (p. 55).

52 David Scott Kastan, *Shakespeare After Theory* (London: Routledge, 1999), p. 77.

53 John Kerrigan (ed.), *'The Sonnets' and 'A Lover's Complaint'*, The New Penguin Shakespeare (Harmondsworth: Penguin, 1986), p. 431.

54 Katherine Duncan-Jones (ed.), *Shakespeare's Sonnets*, The Arden Shakespeare (London: Nelson, 1997), pp. 37–8. Duncan-Jones pushes the argument that Shakespeare was directly involved in the publication of the Sonnets in 'Was the 1609 *Shakespeares Sonnets* Really Unauthorized?', *Review of English Studies*, 34 (1983), 151–71.

55 Thomas Heywood, *An Apology for Actors* (1612), repr. in Schoenbaum, *William Shakespeare: A Documentary Life*, p. 219.

56 Murphy, *Shakespeare in Print*, p. 21.

57 Brooks, *From Playhouse to Printing House*, p. 10.

58 Erne, *Shakespeare as Literary Dramatist*, pp. 96, 109.

59 Blades, *Shakespeare and Typography*, p. 35.

60 Quoted in Maguire, 'The Craft of Printing', p. 446.

61 Peter Blayney, *The Texts of 'King Lear' and Their Origins*, pp. 188–218; 'shorthand or private transcript': Erne, *Shakespeare as Literary Dramatist*, pp. 106–7, 185–6. But cf. Kastan, *Shakespeare and the Book*: 'It is a poorly printed play (indeed the first that its printer, Nicholas Okes, had ever undertaken), and Shakespeare did not oversee its publication or concern himself with the imperfect results' (p. 33).

62 Quoted in Maguire, 'The Craft of Printing', p. 446.

63 Kastan, *Shakespeare and the Book*, pp. 59–60. Peter Blayney proposes that Jaggard was preferred precisely because he had the complicated web of theatre connections which was vital in negotiating permissions: *The First Folio of Shakespeare* (Washington DC: Folger Shakespeare Library, 1991), p. 4.

64 'Trust-worthy realm': Johns, *The Nature of the Book*, p. 34.

65 Erne, *Shakespeare as Literary Dramatist*, p. 98.

66 Kirwood, 'Richard Field, Printer', p. 14.

67 David Bergeron, *Textual Patronage in English Drama, 1570–1640* (Aldershot: Ashgate, 2006), pp. 141–54.

68 Ben Jonson, *Epigram*, 18:2, in *Ben Jonson*, ed. C. H. Herford and Percy and Evelyn Simpson, 11 vols (Oxford: Clarendon Press, 1925–52), vol. 4, p. 33. For the classic analysis of this proclamation of artistic independence see Thomas Greene, 'Ben Jonson and the Centered Self', *Studies in English Literature*, 10 (1970), 325–48.

69 Erne, *Shakespeare as Literary Dramatist*, p. 112; for 'literary reading texts' see Jonathan Bate, 'The Folio Restored', *Times Literary Supplement*, 30 April 2007, pp. 11–13 (p. 13). In an influential essay Richard Dutton has proposed that the reason 'why Shakespeare never published his own plays is quite likely that he was a company man, too identified with an ethos in which any removal of company property warranted expulsion from its ranks, too bound to a small group by ties that went beyond a mere contractual framework' ('The Birth of the Author', in R. B. Parker and S. P. Zitner (eds), *Elizabethan Theater: Essays in Honor of S. Schoenbaum* (Newark: University of Delaware Press, 1996), pp. 71–92; repr. and rev. in Cedric C. Brown and Arthur F. Marotti (eds), *Texts and Cultural Change in Early Modern England* (Basingstoke: Macmillan, 1997), pp. 153–78 (p. 161)).

70 Pierre Bourdieu, 'The Market of Symbolic Goods', trans. R. Swyer, in *The Field of Cultural Production: Essays on Art and Literature*, ed. Randal Johnson (Cambridge: Polity Press, 1993), pp. 112–41 (pp. 113–14), orig. pub. as 'Le marché des biens symboliques', in *L'Année Sociologique*, 22 (1971), 49–126; *The Rules of Art: Genesis and Structure of the Literary Field*, trans. Susan Emanuel (Cambridge: Polity Press, 1996), orig. pub. as *Les Règles d l'art* (Paris: Éditions du Seuil, 1992); Sir Philip Sidney, *Astrophil and Stella*, in Ringler (ed.), *The Poems of Sir Philip Sidney*, p. 165, 1:14. For 'literature' as a formation of 'high print culture' see especially the important essay by Walter Ong, 'Romantic Difference and the Poetics of Technology', in *Rhetoric, Romance, and Technology: Studies in the Interaction of Expression and Culture* (Ithaca: Cornell University Press, 1971), pp. 276–9; and *Orality and Literacy: The Technologizing of the Word* (London: Methuen, 1982).

71 See Erne, *Shakespeare as Literary Dramatist*, p. 98; and Pierre Bourdieu, 'Intellectual Field and Creative Project', trans. Sian France, in Michael F. D. Young (ed.), *Knowledge and Control: New Directions in the Sociology of Education* (London: Collier-Macmillan, 1971), pp. 161–188 (pp. 162–3); originally pub. as 'Champ intellectual et projet créatur', *Les Temps Modernes*, 246 (1966), 865–906 (pp. 868–9).

72 Heminge and Condell, 'To the great Variety of Readers', reprinted in Greenblatt et al. (eds), *The Norton Shakespeare*, p. 3350.

73 Bergeron, *Textual Patronage in English Drama*, pp. 153–4.

74 'The griefs of the printers, glass sellers, and cutlers' (1577), quoted in Kirwood, 'Richard Field, Printer', p. 3; Henry Fitzjeffrey, 'Satyra Prima', in *Satyres and Satyricall Epigrams* (London, 1617), sig. A8r, quoted in Kastan, *Shakespeare and the Book*, p. 63. Cf. Bourdieu, 'The Field of Cultural Production, or: The Economic World Reversed', trans. Richard Nice, in Bourdieu, *The Field of Cultural Production*, ed. Johnson: 'The more autonomous the field becomes, the more favourable the symbolic power balance is to the most autonomous producers . . . But lack of [economic] success is not in itself a sign and guarantee of election . . . while some box-office successes may be recognised, at least in some sections of the field, as genuine art' (p. 39).

75 Erne, *Shakespeare as Literary Dramatist*, p. 220.

76 Nicholas Robins, 'The Script's the Thing', review of *Shakespeare as Literary Dramatist*, *Times Literary Supplement*, 7 November 2003, p. 10.

Part I
Books

1

'An index and obscure prologue': Books and theatre in Shakespeare's literary authorship

Patrick Cheney

Lechery, by this hand; an index and obscure prologue to the history of lust and foul thoughts.

(*Othello*, 2.1.257–8)[1]

The epigraph to this chapter, taken from a speech by Iago on the companionate marriage of Othello and Desdemona, speaks to a historic divorce in Shakespeare studies: between theatre criticism and criticism on the materiality of the book. Theoretically, these two forms of criticism seem to have little to do with each other, for indeed the expertise required for each tends to be quite different. *Theatre* criticism, as we might term it, is more diverse and complex, but those who practise it tend to be concerned with questions of theatre history, with performance, with metatheatre, and thus with viewing Shakespeare as a consummate 'man of the theatre': a playwright, actor and shareholder in the Chamberlain's Men and later the King's Men, committed to the economy of the new commercial theatre in London.[2] In contrast, the much more recent bibliographical criticism, not as diverse but none the less complex, tends to focus on the history of the book, on print culture and on a material model of cultural collaboration that underlies the production of printed books by William Shakespeare.[3]

Despite obvious differences with theatre criticism, *bibliographical* criticism (as we might call it) grows out of, bonds itself with and remains complicit in the dominant twentieth-century model of Shakespeare as the arch-theatrical man. In the words of one of its leading practitioners, 'Shakespeare had no obvious interest in the printed book. Performance was the only form of publication he sought for his plays.'[4] For the majority of critics today, the divorce between theatre and bibliographical criticism exists in practice (as perhaps in training). Yet during the past few years a new field has sought to mend the divorce: 'stage to page' criticism. According to a practitioner in 2004, 'As a movement . . . the stage-to-page field combin[es] . . . theatre history and book history, reaching towards a "Shakespeare" defined by multiple contexts, rather than authorial intention . . . [This] critical movement . . . concentrates not on "Shakespeare" the individual author but on the collaborative, multilayered, material, historical world that fashioned the Shakespeare canon.'[5] As this formulation makes clear, stage-to-page criticism joins bibliographical and theatrical criticism in benefiting from recent historical criticism to respond to the older, traditional or Romantic model of Shakespeare famously articulated by Milton in *L'Allegro*: 'sweetest Shakespeare, fancy's child', 'Warbl[ing] . . . his native Wood-notes wild'.[6] Most recent historical criticism rightly resists this *poetic* view of Shakespeare because it is fanciful and thus unhistorical.[7]

Yet the present volume testifies to an even newer phase of criticism, which acknowledges the revisionist principle of collaboration but simultaneously grants Shakespeare's *literary authorship*. The leading spokesman of this new phase has been Lukas Erne, whose groundbreaking 2003 monograph, aptly titled *Shakespeare as Literary Dramatist*, resists the overreaching conclusions of bibliographical, theatre and stage-to-page criticism in order to find space for the literary author:

> Shakespeare, 'privileged playwright' that he was, could afford to write plays for the stage *and* the page . . . From the very beginning, the English Renaissance plays we study had a double existence, one on stage and one on the printed page . . . The long texts of plays such as *Hamlet* (Q2, 1604 and Folio, 1623) and *Henry V* (Folio 1623) . . . tend to function according to a 'literary' logic, while the short texts of the same plays (*Hamlet* Q1, 1603; *Henry V*, Q1 1600) reflect their oral, theatrical provenance . . . Printed playbooks became respectable reading matter earlier than we have hitherto supposed, early enough for Shakespeare to have lived through and to have been affected by this process of legitimation . . . The assumption of Shakespeare's indifference to the publication of his plays is a myth.[8]

By seeing Shakespeare as a 'literary dramatist' composing scripts both for performance and for publication within his own moment, Erne constructs a historical model that coalesces the best energies of poetic, theatrical and bibliographical criticism; most emphatically, he alters 'stage to page' to 'stage *and* page'.

In the present chapter, I would like to suggest, first, that Erne's model of the literary dramatist is not quite accurate, since it remains unconsciously circumscribed by the 'dramatic' terms of the previous phases, and thus neglects to account for the five freestanding poems that this author saw published during his own lifetime.[9] In 1593 and 1594, Shakespeare published two Ovidian narrative poems, complete with dedicatory epistles to the earl of Southampton: *Venus and Adonis* and *The Rape of Lucrece*. By 1599, Shakespeare's reputation as a nondramatic author was so marketable that William Jaggard, who in 1623 would bring out the First Folio of the plays, printed *The Passionate Pilgrim*, whose title page falsely ascribed the collection of lyric poems to 'W. Shakespeare'. Then in 1601 Shakespeare himself contributed a 67-line philosophical hymn, known today as 'The Phoenix and Turtle', to Robert Chester's *Love's Martyr*, which also printed poems by Ben Jonson, John Marston and George Chapman. Finally, in 1609 *Shake-speares Sonnets* appeared, printing both the Sonnets and a third narrative poem, *A Lover's Complaint* – whether authorized by him or not, we are still debating.[10] Ever since Charles Gildon in 1710, critics have been trying to account for the fact that the world's most famous playwright ended up producing a substantial body of poetic verse.[11] By benefiting from Erne's pioneering work, we may re-classify Shakespeare as an early modern author: he is a *literary poet-playwright*.

Second, we may find evidence for this revised classification *in the discourse of Shakespeare's plays themselves*.[12] In other words, the literary poet-playwright recurrently puts his model of authorship centre-stage. From early in his career till late, across the genres of comedy, history, tragedy and romance, he rehearses a discourse of the book and a discourse of the theatre, and, more importantly, he combines the two discourses together, letting the terms *book* and *theatre* jostle in historically telling ways. The epigraph from *Othello* supplies a succinct example, and intimates how Shakespearean authorship often interlaces the language of books and the language of theatre to voice subjective vectors – here 'lust' and 'thought', or desire and consciousness, as well as their social dynamics, since Iago is objecting to the marriage of a Moor with a racially white woman. Recently, Margreta de Grazia has resisted the widespread notion that Shakespeare uses soliloquies (notably in *Hamlet*) to depict 'consciousness', arguing instead that Shakespearean discourse represents 'mind' as material object, and thereby 'collaps[ing] ... the distinction between inner and outer'.[13] I wish to argue that Shakespeare does represent consciousness, but that at this time he represents consciousness as *literary*, a bibliographical and theatrical phenomenon composed of and represented by a professional discourse of authorship. Moreover, the author William Shakespeare, rather than being simply 'reconstituted as an "AVTHOR" in the commercial desires of the early modern book trade', *participates in his own historical making*.[14] The 'fantasy of literary autonomy' is not simply Jaggard's and his colleagues' but a deep structure in the Shakespearean texts themselves.[15] In making it so, this author linguistically registers the historic founding of Elizabethan England's two professional institutions as the premier sites of a nascent literary authorship: the theatre and the print shop.[16]

For Shakespeare, Iago's word 'index' is rare, occurring only four other times – and only in his plays (*Richard III*, 2.2.149, 4.4.185; *Hamlet*, 3.4.52; *Troilus and Cressida*, 1.3.343). According to the *OED*, Shakespeare uses the term in *Othello* under definition 5a: 'A table of contents prefixed to a book, a brief list or summary of the matters treated in it'. All of Shakespeare's other uses subscribe to this textual definition; for instance, in *Troilus and Cressida*, Nestor remarks to Ulysses, 'And in such indexes (although small pricks / To their subsequent volumes) there is seen / The baby figure of the giant mass / Of things to come at large' (1.3.343–6). When Iago uses the term, he also does so metaphorically, to mean that Desdemona's public display of affection for her husband is a summary of her unruly desire. More often, Shakespeare uses the word 'prologue' – 25 times in his canon, and again only in his plays. Not surprisingly, he almost always connects the term to theatre, as appears in the *OED*'s definition 2: 'One who speaks or recites the prologue to a play on the stage'. In his plays, Shakespeare does not simply use the word 'prologue', or occasionally preface his drama with formal prologues (as in *Henry V* and *Troilus and Cressida*); he also stages metaprologues, fictions rehearsing a formal prologue (as in *Love's Labour's Lost*, *A Midsummer Night's Dream* and *Hamlet*), often with characters commenting on them. For his part, Iago uses the term 'prologue' metaphorically, to see Desdemona's physical affection as a sign of her interior corruption.

It is true that the *OED* does indicate slippage for both terms. An *index* can mean 'a preface, prologue' (*OED*, 5a), while a *prologue* can mean 'The preface or introduction to a discourse or performance; a preliminary discourse, proem, preface, preamble; esp. a discourse or poem spoken as the introduction to a dramatic performance' (*OED*, 1). During the period, then, each term could have both a textual and a theatrical resonance. At one point in his canon, in the first quarto of *Romeo and Juliet*, Shakespeare appears to elide the distinction between *book* and *prologue*, when Benvolio turns up the curious phrase 'without-book prologue' (1.4.7) – referring to a prologue delivered extemporally, without a promptbook. In fact, then, Benvolio's book is not printed but a tool of the playhouse. Acknowledging this instance of potential slippage, we can summarise that Shakespeare tends to select out the textual meaning of *index* and the theatrical meaning of *prologue*. Usefully, in the New Cambridge edition of *Othello*, Norman Sanders glosses Iago's 'index' as 'indicator; lit. "table of contents prefacing"', and he leaves 'prologue' unglossed, presumably because its theatrical meaning is clear.[17]

Iago's superbly conjunctive phrase 'index and . . . prologue' yokes a textual with a theatrical term in order to get, not at Desdemona's literary consciousness, but inadvertently at his own. This ambitious military man purports to rely on a combined discourse of books and theatre to interpret the physical action of a beautiful young woman in relation with her husband, when in fact he unwittingly conveys the terms of his own (literary) agency. If we look further into the Shakespeare canon, we see that very often 'books' turn out to be books of poetry, more so than past criticism avers. Iago, as we shall see, is more than a dark model for the Shakespearean man of books and theatre; he is also a shrewd practitioner of the art of poetry. In his deployment of poetic books, as in his staged theatre, Iago joins a whole host of other figures in the Shakespeare canon. In *The Merry Wives of Windsor*, Abraham Slender could well speak for many when he says, 'I had rather than forty shillings I had my Book of Songs and Sonnets here' (1.1.198–9) – a reference to one of the most important publications of the era, Tottel's *Miscellany* (1557), which first published the collected poems of Wyatt, Surrey and contemporaries, and was known by the title Slender supplies.[18]

In the remainder of this chapter, I would like to look further into Shakespeare's authorial discourse of books and theatre in order to outline a rubric that might be useful for subsequent research. In the following section, I recall Shakespeare's discourse of the theatre briefly in order to attend more fully to his neglected discourse of the book, including printed books and books of poetry. Next, I concentrate on key passages that conjoin the two discourses in a single utterance. Then, in a concluding section, I return to the significance of this analysis for this volume's presentation of Shakespearean authorship; I suggest that we may find a frame for viewing the conjunction of books and theatre (as well as the subindustries commenting on them) in the rhetorical figure called *hendiadys*. Throughout, I rely on a post-revisionist model of authorship, which acknowledges the revisionist model of the social constructedness of all texts but allows for a traditional model by granting agency to the author. In Richard Helgerson's succinct formulation, Shakespeare 'helped make the world that made him'.[19]

In *Troilus and Cressida*, Shakespeare seems to anticipate this post-revisionist model, when Achilles asks Ulysses, 'What are you reading?' (3.3.95), and Ulysses reports on the contents of his book, twice using the theatrical concept of the actor's 'part':[20]

> A strange fellow here
> Writes me that man, how dearly ever parted,
> How much in having, or without or in,
> Cannot make boast to have that which he hath,
> Nor feels not what he owes, but by reflection;
> . . .
> I do not strain at the position –
> It is familiar – but at the author's drift,
> Who in his circumstance expressly proves
> That no man is the lord of any thing,
> Though in and of him there be much consisting,
> Till he communicates his parts to others.
>   (*Troilus and Cressida*, 3.3.95–117)

We do not know who the 'strange fellow' or 'author' is (Plato has been the main candidate), and the topic being discussed is the nature of perception – 'that the eye could not see itself except by reflection'[21] – but the 'drift' that Ulysses reads into his author's text bears usefully on the question of authorial agency. Especially in the last three lines, Ulysses anticipates a post-revisionist model when he locates agency in the reciprocity between self and other: 'man' cannot own (be 'lord of') 'any thing', 'though' he himself possesses much value ('consisting').

As in Ulysses' phrase 'author's drift', Shakespeare often uses the word 'author' and its cognates: a total of 24 times, across both poems and plays, from beginning to end.[22] Half of these instances appear to refer to a nonliterary cause or agency, as when Ursula in *Much Ado About Nothing* says, 'Don John is the author of all' (5.2.98–9), meaning the cause of the turmoil. But the other half of the instances clearly refer to a literary 'author' – whether the author of a printed book, as in Ulysses' phrase, or the author of a staged play, as in the final Chorus to *Henry V*: 'Thus far, with rough and all-unable pen, / Our bending author hath pursued the story' (Epilogue 1–2). As such, Shakespeare's own definition of authorship is divided, not merely between the conceptual and the literary (the causal and the creative) but between the print-author and the play-author. As we shall see, even though Shakespeare uses the word 'author' to emphasise a character's agency and intention, inside his fictions he tends to represent authorship itself more enigmatically. In effect, his plays stage a historic dialogue about the meaning of the 'author' and thus of Shakespearean literary authorship.

'Find delight writ there with beauty's pen': books or theatre

Shakespeare's discourse of the theatre is so well known that it has become virtually equated with the name 'William Shakespeare', and not surprisingly a small industry on 'metadrama' was a major form of twentieth-century criticism. Recurrently, Shakespeare makes the theatre an integral part of his fiction, as when he stages a play-within-a-play in *The Taming of the Shrew*, *Love Labour's Lost*, *A Midsummer Night's Dream* and *Hamlet*, or such masques as that of Hymen in *Much Ado*, of the Fairy Queen in *Merry Wives*, of Ceres and Juno in *The Tempest* or of the shepherds in *Henry VIII*. Most dramatically, he inserts the fiction of the strolling players into *Hamlet*, leading the Prince to produce his famous instructions on 'the purpose of playing' (3.2.20). More often, Shakespeare presents characters who turn to the theatre as a metaphor, as when Jacques reports humorously in *As You Like It*, 'All the world's a stage, / And all the men and women merely players' (2.7.139–40); or Macbeth laments hauntingly, 'Life's but a walking shadow, a poor player, / That struts and frets his hour upon the stage, / And then is heard no more' (5.5.24–6). The effect is to render character *theatrical* – lending to us one of this author's most historic accomplishments. Thus, Hamlet is commonly viewed as 'the English Renaissance's greatest tribute to the theatrical man'.[23] Indeed, the Shakespearean discourse of the theatre is so rich and famous that we hardly need to remind ourselves of it.[24]

In contrast, Shakespeare's discourse of the book has not been studied in sufficient detail. Yet with the recent advent of bibliographical criticism, we can expect any number of studies to emerge shortly.[25] Until such studies emerge, we might wish to recall some further statistics. The word *book* and its cognates occurs over 130 times in the Shakespeare canon, spread over nearly all of his works, from early to late. Allied words and cognates include *volume* (15 times); *text* (13); and *library* (3), this last revealing the author's occasional reference to the architectural place of the book, as in Prospero's recollection of his 'library', which contains 'books' and 'volumes' that he once 'prize[d] above . . . [his] dukedom' (1.2.166–8). More rarely, Shakespeare uses such words as *folio* (1 instance) and *edition* (1), while other terms from print culture pepper his plays: *character*, *binding*, *copy*, *press*, *print* and of course *publish*.[26] From the plays, we hear about a lot of different types of books; we have mentioned historical books of poetry like Tottel's 'Book of Songs and Sonnets'. Other historical books include the Bible, called 'God's book' (*2 Henry VI*, 2.3.4), or even specific books of Scripture such as the 'book of Numbers' (*Henry V*, 1.2.98); a 'book of prayer' (*Richard III*, 3.7.98), perhaps the *Book of Common Prayer*; the 'Book of Riddles' (*The Merry Wives of Windsor*, 1.1.201–2); and the 'Absey book' (*King John*, 1.1.196), a book of ABCs or primer. Still others include a 'note-book' (*The Merry Wives of Windsor*, 1.1.145), a 'table-book' (*The Winter's Tale*, 4.4.598), a 'copy-book' (*Love's Labour's Lost*, 5.2.42); and 'lenders' books' (*King Lear*, 3.4.97). Shakespeare even manages to come up with a single phrase to circumscribe them all: 'all the books in / England' (*1 Henry IV*, 2.4.49).

Yet many of the 'books' exist as figures of speech, and of every imaginable variety: a 'book of memory' (*1 Henry VI*, 2.4.101); a 'book of life' (*Richard II*, 1.3.202); a 'book of heaven' (*Richard II*, 4.1.236); a 'book of beauty' (*King John*, 2.1.485); a 'lawless bloody book / Of forg'd rebellion with a seal divine' (*2 Henry IV*, 4.1.91–2); a 'beggar's book' (*Henry VIII*, 1.1.122); a 'book of love' (*The Two Gentlemen of Verona*, 1.1.20); a 'book of words' (*Much Ado About Nothing*, 1.1.307); a 'book for good manners' (*As You Like It*, 5.4.91); a 'book of sport' (*Troilus and Cressida*, 4.5.239); a 'book of all that monarchs do' (*Pericles*, 1.1.93); a 'book of virtue' (*The Winter's Tale*, 4.3.122); a 'book / Of arithmetic' (*Romeo and Juliet*, 3.1.102); 'sour misfortune's book' (*Romeo and Juliet*, 5.3.82); a 'saw of books' (*Hamlet*, 1.5.100); a 'book of bloody law' (*Othello*, 1.3.67); 'nature's book of infinite secrecy' (*Antony and Cleopatra*, 1.2.10); a ' book of . . . good acts' (*Coriolanus*, 5.2.15); and 'Jove's own book' (*Coriolanus*, 3.1.291) – this last being the book of fame, which names the telos of the Shakespearean book itself.[27]

Occasionally, Shakespeare even appears to eye early modern printed books in his plays. In *As You Like It*, for instance, Touchstone can quip, 'we quarrel in print, by the book – as you have books for good manners' (5.4.90–1). According to the *Riverside Shakespeare*, 'There were, in fact, such books, hardly less fantastic than Touchstone's . . . One which may be glanced at here is Vincent Savillo's *Practice of the Rapier and Dagger* (1594–5).'[28] At least twice, Shakespeare intimates that the printed books he has in mind are quartos. In *2 Henry IV*, near the middle of his career, the Earl of Northumberland says of his retainer Morton,

> Yea, this man's brow, like to a title-leaf,
> Foretells the nature of a tragic volume.
>
> (*2 Henry IV*, 1.1.60–1)

The Earl likens the face of his retainer – literally, his forehead – to a book, as the technical words 'title-leaf' and 'volume' indicate, but he particularises the printed book as a tragedy in his phrase 'tragic volume'. Similarly, in *Pericles* the King of Pentapolis, Simonides, addresses the knights who have just come to a banquet from a tilting tournament:

> To say you're welcome were superfluous,
> [To] place upon the volume of your deeds,
> As in a title-page, your worth in arms,
> Were more than you expect, or more than's fit,
> Since every worth in show commends itself.
>
> (*Pericles*, 2.3.2–6)

Rather than a tragedy, the chivalric discourse suggests a book of epic romance, fitting the genre being staged.[29] Here Simonides refers to the early modern printing convention of detailing the contents of a book on its 'title-page', which he declares 'superfluous', and then adds a rationale based on a metaphor from the theatre: 'Since very worth in show commends itself.'[30]

Just as Shakespeare often stages plays-within-plays, so he recurrently brings books on to the stage as a prop. Hamlet is the

Renaissance's greatest tribute not merely to the theatrical man but also to the bookish man; this may be his ultimate signature. For instance, in Act 2, scene 2, the Prince enters '*reading on a book*', prompting his mother to exclaim, 'look where sadly the poor wretch comes reading' (2.2.168 and stage direction preceding). Perhaps because of Hamlet's commitment to books, in Act 3, scene 1, Polonius sets Ophelia up as a decoy by instructing her, 'Read on this book' (3.1.43). In both cases, the actors read printed books on stage, making the process of printing and reading part of the fiction. In the case of the book Hamlet 'read[s]', we know it is printed because Polonius asks the Prince what its 'matter' is, prompting Hamlet to retort, 'Slanders, sir; for the satirical rogue says here that old men have grey beards' (191–7). The Prince's wry reference to the author of the book as a 'satirical rogue' indicates most likely that he reads a volume of printed poetry from the genre of satire, and long ago William Warburton even identified a particular poetic book: Juvenal's tenth *Satire*.[31]

This sort of fiction also emerges early in Shakespeare's career. The opening scene of *Two Gentlemen of Verona* sets the pace:

> *Valentine.* And on a love-book pray for my success?
> *Proteus.* Upon some book of love I'll pray for thee.
> *Valentine.* That's on some shallow story of deep love –
>   How young Leander crossed the Hellespont.
>   (*Two Gentlemen of Verona*, 1.1.19–22)

Shakespeare does not reveal which 'love-book' about Hero and Leander the young men discuss, but almost certainly it is the version by Christopher Marlowe.[32] Similarly, in *The Taming of the Shrew* Shakespeare quotes Ovid's *Heroides* (3.1.28–9; see *3 Henry VI*, 1.3.48), while the trickster Tranio pulls out a 'small packet of Greek and Latin books' (2.1.100) in a play that seems to be as much about the erotic work of books as it is about eros. In *Love's Labour's Lost*, Shakespeare constructs a plot that is more formally about book-learning, as the four 'book-men' (2.1.227, 4.2.34) retire from public life to form an academy organised around scholarship: 'Our court shall be a little academe, / Still and contemplative in living art' (1.1.12–13). Among Shakespeare's kings, Henry VI is particularly prone to scholarship: his 'bookish rule hath pull'd fair England down' (*2 Henry VI*, 1.1.259). Equally tragic, in Act 4, scene 1, of *Titus Andronicus* young Lucius runs on stage with a book in his hand, chased by his aunt Lavinia, who has been raped and dismembered by the sons of the Gothic queen, Tamora. When Titus asks the boy, 'what book is that she tosseth so?' (4.1.41), Lucius replies, 'Grandsire, 'tis Ovid's Metamorphosis, / My mother gave it me' (4.1.42–3). As we next learn, Lavinia has chased the book-bearing boy to 'turn . . . the leaves' to 'the tragic tale of Philomela' (4.1.45–7) in order to communicate the 'root' of her 'annoy' (4.1.48) – the cause of her tragic rape.

At the end of his career, Shakespeare returns the book of Ovid's *Metamorphoses* to the stage. In Act 2, scene 2, of *Cymbeline*, Iachimo pops out of the trunk in Imogen's bedchamber to spy for her husband, Posthumus, only to discover that before she fell asleep the princess 'hath been reading late / The tale of Tereus: here the leaf's turn'd down / Where Philomela gave up' (2.2.44–7). Like Marcus Brutus on campaign (*Julius Caesar*, 4.3.252–74), Imogen at home is in the habit of reading a book before falling asleep. Later in this romance, Posthumus awakens from his dream of the Leonati to discover a 'book' lying on his chest (5.4.133), the detailed contents of which he then reads out loud on stage (5.4.138–50). In *The Tempest*, the books of the magician Prospero become an important feature in the plot. Like Henry VI, Brutus and Hamlet, Prospero is a bookish man. Not simply does he locate the origin of his fall in his obsession with 'the liberal arts', as he recalls to Miranda: 'those being all my study, / The government I cast upon my brother, being transported / And rapt in secret studies' (1.2.73–7). Also, Prospero tells his daughter of the good services of his counsellor Gonzalo: 'Knowing I lov'd my books, he furnish'd me / From mine own library with [prized] volumes' (166–7). Accordingly, in the subplot Caliban fixates on getting hold of Prospero's books as the key to his revolt: 'first seize . . . his books . . . First . . . possess his books . . . Burn but his books' (3.2.89–95). Finally, at the end of the play Prospero decides to abandon his bookish art as a prelude to his return home to Milan: 'I'll drown my books' (5.1.57). To a remarkable extent, from Henry VI to Hamlet to Prospero, the Shakespearean dramatic canon can be said to be *about scholarship*.[33]

One of the most intriguing sites for viewing Shakespeare's authorial discourse of scholarship emerges in his recurrent representation of the *body* as a *text* – or more precisely, the seemingly gratuitous conceit of *the human face as a book*. In *Macbeth*, for instance, Lady Macbeth says to her husband, 'Your face . . . is as a book, where men / May read strange matters' (1.5).[34] Othello himself deploys the conceit when confronting his wife; touching Desdemona's beautiful face, he says, longingly, 'Was this fair paper, this most goodly book, / Made to write "whore" upon?' (4.2.70–1).[35] Although the conceit may be conventional, we might wonder whether the following lines from the opening scene of *Pericles* were written by the author of such passages: 'Her face the book of praises, where is read / Nothing but curious pleasures' (1.1.15–16). Underlying the equation may be a term from the culture of books, and perhaps the printing house, for, according to the *OED*, a *face* could also be 'a leaf in a book' (*OED*, 11b), citing as the first example Fulke Greville in 1575.[36]

Following from Shakespeare's body-as-face conceit is his conceit of identity – inwardness, subjectivity, consciousness – as a book. In *Twelfth Night*, for instance, Duke Orsino tells Viola, in disguise as Cesario, 'I have unclasp'd / To thee the book even of my secret soul' (1.4.13–14). The equation here between a material object, the 'book', and consciousness, the 'secret soul', speaks to a rather precise relation between 'subject and object in Renaissance culture' and more particularly in Shakespearean culture.[37] In Shakespeare's lexicon, the 'soul' has a textual and thus a literary character, composed of books, made up from books, and expressive of books.[38] Occasionally, Shakespeare puts together an articulation that operates along the border of subject and object. In *Richard II*, for instance, the King defends himself against accusation: 'I'll read enough, / When I do see the very book indeed / Where all my sins are writ, and that's myself' (4.1.263–5). Similarly, in *1 Henry IV* the Earl of Worcester tells his rebel relatives, 'now I will unclasp a secret book, / And to your quick-conceiving discontents / I'll read you matter deep and dangerous' (1.3.186–8).

Yet Shakespeare's most detailed figural representation of the book comes from *Romeo and Juliet*; it deploys the face-as-book conceit and gathers in several of the conceptual leaves we have perused. In Act 1, scene 3, Lady Capulet tries to persuade her daughter to marry the County Paris:

> Read o'er the volume of young Paris' face,
> And find delight writ there with beauty's pen;
> Examine every married lineament,
> And see how one another lends content;
> And what obscur'd in this fair volume lies
> Find written in the margent of his eyes.

This precious book of love this unbound lover,
To beautify him, only lacks a cover.
. . .
That book in many's eyes doth share the glory,
That in gold clasps locks in the golden story.
                                        (*Romeo and Juliet*, 1.3.81–92)

Shakespeare brings considerable ingenuity to the conceit – too much, thought Alexander Pope, who omitted the 'ridiculous speech' in his 1725 edition, with modern directors and critics following suit.[39] In his New Cambridge edition, G. Blakemore Evans calls Lady Capulet's praise of Paris 'precious and nonsensical' and its results 'unhappy'[40] – without recognising that this mode is characteristic of the *self-effacing Shakespearean literary*. If we deride or omit the speech, we miss not only a textbook example of the Shakespearean 'conceit' but also an unusual model of Shakespearean authorship.

Juliet, her mother advises, is to read Paris as a book – in particular, the physical beauty of his face as its 'content[s]'. But the young girl is also to look into Paris' eyes to find a marginal gloss on the 'obscure' terms of his outward appearance, the inner truth to his beauty and heart. Perhaps referring to early modern printing practices, Lady Capulet identifies Paris as an 'unbound' book, in need of the 'cover' that Juliet can supply by becoming his wife. Juliet can 'share the glory' through this 'married' act, just as a book acquires beauty and fame when the act of binding completes the process of printing.

The book in question may be the 'book of love', but Shakespeare goes further: it is a book of poetry. Thus, Lady Capulet in the third line moves into rhymed couplets to describe the 'content' of the book, while Evans helps us see that Shakespeare might allude to a particular book: Ovid's *Ars Amatoria*.[41] Not simply a conceit, Lady Capulet's trope is a moment of intertextuality, linking Shakespeare's Renaissance stage play with a famous book of classical love poetry. Additional book-learning goes into the conceit, for, as Jill L. Levenson observes, line 90, 'For fair without the fair within to hide', refers to the 'Neoplatonic concept of *fair* outside reflecting *fair* inside'.[42] Underlying Lady Capulet's 'ridiculous' conceit, then, is a rather ingenious gloss on the philosophical Shakespearean book of consciousness.

Yet most striking is what remains unseen: the very author of the book. Shakespeare may attend to the book's material make-up – its

'writ[ing]', its 'content[s]' and even the 'pen' that 'writ' it – but
nowhere does he identify the author behind the book: 'find delight
writ there with beauty's pen'. The disembodied action of a pen
writing a book with delight rather *conceals* the author.[43] We might
wonder, then, whether we can find here a model of Shakespeare's
own authorship, as described recently by Stephen Greenblatt in *Will
in the World*: 'Shakespeare was a master of double consciousness . . . [H]e contrived . . . to hide himself from view . . . [he had
an] astonishing capacity to be everywhere and nowhere, to assume
all positions and to slip free of all constraints.'[44] Evans anticipates
this idea when he identifies the speech as 'an ornamental set-piece
calculated to display the writer's wit rather than a character's
feeling'.[45] In sum, from the beginning to the end of his professional
career Shakespeare seeks innovative ways to bring both books and
plays on to the stage as part of the historic making of the London
theatre itself. Yet even more historic are moments that conjoin a discourse of the book with a discourse of the theatre.

'He reads much . . . He loves no plays': books and theatre

The divided literary man in question is 'spare Cassius' (1.2.200), as
reported by Julius Caesar to Mark Antony near the beginning of
their tragedy:

> He reads much,
> He is a great observer, and he looks
> Quite through the deeds of men. He loves no plays,
> As thou dost, Antony; he hears no music.
>
> (*Julius Caesar*, 1.2.201–4)

Here Shakespeare uses the discourse of books and theatre to portray
Cassius as private, introspective and socially penetrating. In contrast
to his love of reading, Cassius' lack of love for the theatre marks him
out as a distinct (patently flawed) breed of literary man – different,
say, from Hamlet, or even from his own best friend, Brutus, or from
his future arch-enemy, Antony, and presumably from Caesar
himself. David Daniell, in his note on this passage in his recent Arden
edition, remarks that Caesar's criticism of Cassius 'puts positively
what Brutus . . . dismissed as superficial in Antony' earlier in the
scene, when Brutus told Cassius that he was not interested in
running in the race that Caesar sponsors: 'I am not gamesome. I do

lack some part / Of that quick spirit that is in Antony' (1.2.28–9).[46] However we interpret the Cassius portrait, through it Shakespeare voices one of his primary inventions for dramatic character, cut from the discourse of his professional career.

One of the most graphic of such literary couplings appears in *Richard III*, when Richard sees the head of the recently executed Hastings:

> I took him for the plainest harmless creature
> That breath'd upon the earth a Christian;
> Made him my book, wherein my soul recorded
> The history of all her secret thoughts,
> So smooth he daub'd his vice with show of virtue.
>
> (*Richard III*, 3.5.25–9)

To borrow Buckingham's phrase a few lines earlier (for what he mistakenly thinks is his own agency in the historical action), Richard here 'counterfeit[s] the deep tragedian' (3.5.5), charging Hastings with deceiving him as a true Christian when in fact he has merely played a part – daubed his vice with 'show' of virtue. Yet Richard's exquisite lines about making Hastings his 'book' are important, and anticipate Iago's formulation: Richard has made Hastings a book in that he recorded the 'history' of his 'secret thoughts' – expressed the truth of his inward 'soul'. As clearly as any passage in the Shakespeare canon, this one reveals how Shakespeare understands the 'book': not simply as a material object but also as a site of theatrical consciousness.

As the examples from *Titus* and *Two Gentlemen* earlier indicate, often the books referred to or brought on stage are books of poetry. In *The Taming of the Shrew*, Tranio makes the identification explicit: 'we'll read in poetry / And other books, good ones' (1.2.169–70). In *As You Like It*, Orlando enters to declaim, 'Hang there, my verse . . . / O Rosalind, these trees shall be my books, / That in their barks my thoughts I'll character' (3.2.1–6). Similarly, in *Love's Labour's Lost*, Don Adriano de Armado rhapsodizes,

> Assist me, some extemporal god of rhyme, for I am sure I shall turn sonnet. Devise, wit, write, pen, for I am for whole volumes in folio.
>
> (*Love's Labour's Lost*, 1.2.183–5)

While 'rhyme' and 'sonnet' refer to Elizabethan poetry, 'volumes' and 'folio' locate the poetry in printed books.[47] Armado's final line indeed captures the entire process of early modern print-authorship, from invention ('Devise, wit'), to composition ('write, pen'), to publication itself ('volumes in folio'). Yet, as his word 'extemporal' indicates, Armado also understands his utterance – his poetic print-authorship – as a form of theatre.[48]

We can even find Shakespeare's poetic theatre in the most unusual places – such as Juliet's confused indictment of Romeo after she learns that he has killed her cousin Tybalt:

> O serpent heart, hid with a flowering face!
> Did ever dragon keep so fair a cave?
> Beautiful tyrant! fiend angelical!
> Dove-feather'd raven! wolvish ravening lamb!
> Despised substance of divinest show!
> Just the opposite to what thou justly seem'st,
> . . .
> Was ever book containing such vile matter
> So fairly bound? O that deceit should dwell
> In such a gorgeous palace.
>
> (*Romeo and Juliet*, 3.2.73–85)

If Romeo had earlier 'kiss[ed] by the book' (1.5.110), here Juliet *storms* by the book: the book of Petrarch, as the heavy articulation of erotic oxymoron reveals.[49] On the surface, Juliet's conceit of the beloved as a book looks merely conventional, but it is more engaging than its appearance shows.

For one thing, the conceit turns the convention on its head, exchanging Petrarchan praise for Shakespearean dispraise (on display, for instance, in the dark lady sonnets); for another, it deploys Shakespeare's famed theatrical trope of *inner* and *outer*, contrasting Romeo's physical beauty and his 'gorgeous' person with the ugly character of his inward identity. As a book, Romeo is 'fairly bound', but inside the attractive cover he is 'vile matter'. Yet what is especially notable is the surge of theatrical terms surrounding the discourse of the book: not simply 'seem'st' and 'deceit' but more formally 'divinest show'. In her anger, Juliet jumbles book and theatre, accusing Romeo of falsely staging a religious play of affection and writing a deceitful book of companionate love. In attacking his agency as a lover, she inadvertently casts up the literary terms of her creator's own authorship.

That Shakespeare is thinking of his own authorship here emerges through the likelihood of a self-allusion in the passage's opening line:

'O serpent heart, hid with a flowering face!' This is as fine a rendering as any of a line then infamous: 'O tiger's heart wrapp'd in a woman's hide' (*3 Henry VI*, 1.4.137). As readers will recall, the line had been rewritten before – by Robert Greene in 1592, when he criticised Shakespeare as 'an upstart Crow, beautified with our feathers, that with his *Tygers hart wrapt in a Players hyde*, supposes he is as well able to bombast out a blanke verse as the best of you: and being an absolute *Iohannes fac totum*, is in his owne conceit the onely Shake-scene in a country'.[50] Importantly, Greene reads the Shakespearean author *into* the 'blank verse' of a dramatic text, turning York's savage indictment of Queen Margaret into an attack against a fellow writer, a misogynistic cut at the cruel hypocrisy of a woman into a homosocial jab at a colleague's professional impersonation (whether Shakespeare's skill at literary plagiarism, his role as an actor or more likely both).

Shakespeare's terms of indictment in both speeches are eerily similar, including when York calls Margaret 'She-wolf of France, but worse than wolves of France' (111), but more notably when he uses the metaphor of the theatrical face – twice iterated: 'thy face is vizard-like, unchanging . . . / And yet be seen to wear a woman's face?' (116, 140). Let us put the two lines together:

> O tiger's heart wrapp'd in a woman's hide!
> > (*3 Henry VI*, 1.4.137)

> O serpent heart, hid with a flowering face!
> > (*Romeo and Juliet*, 3.2.73)

Not simply do both lines put a powerful exclamation in a single blank-verse line, and use the same cadence, but both begin with the exclamatory 'O', use the word 'heart' as a noun modified by an adjectival beast, and include cognates of the theatrically ringing word *hide*, in order to get at an individual's false concealment of an ugly identity. The phrase at the end of the line, 'flowering face', merely looks innocuous; Levenson's gloss reads, 'face serving as a floral cover'.[51] While it might be too much to see a reference to printer's flowers ornamenting title-pages of early modern books, 'flowers' were a conventional metaphor for poetry during the period, while 'face' (as we have seen) is a theatrical word, making 'flowering face' a fine metonymy for the poetry–theatre conjunction. If this self-reference has not made it into annotation on *Romeo and Juliet*, perhaps it is because we have neglected the signature terms of Shakespearean authorship.[52]

Levenson has suggested that in this play 'Shakespeare created a new genre . . . a unique arrangement of tragedy, comedy, and sonnet sequence' (p. 49), and she reminds us that, in addition to its famed dramatic hybridity of 'comedy' and 'tragedy', *Romeo and Juliet* features a wide array of poetic forms: 'sonnets . . . quatrains, octaves, an aubade, an epithalamion, a duet, a quartet, and . . . rhymed passages' (p. 52). Levenson situates Shakespeare's generic experimentation within both the English Petrarchan movement of the 1590s and his own sonnet sequence (pp. 54–5), and she speculates on his purpose: 'Perhaps he meant to dignify his theatrical craft by fusing it with the art of lyric' (p. 55). She concludes, 'Whatever his purpose, Shakespeare has deconstructed the poetic form and distributed it throughout the tragic-comic structure', ensuring that 'the lyric form loses some of its affect' (p. 55). Whether we agree with this conclusion (or not), we might wish to recall the wider context for Shakespeare's generic experiment: the sixteenth-century invention of a new form of authorship that combines poems with plays in a single literary career.[53] Once we do, we may be prepared to acknowledge the radical success of the experiment – the play's stunning invention of an art-form out of the strange yoking of lyric and dramatic forms.

Individuation and/or collaboration: Shakespeare's hendiadys-authorship

In the later tragedy of *Othello*, Iago represents the dark underside of the Shakespearean poet-playwright, as if the author were here imagining or perhaps processing his fear of what his art could perform civically. Iago is most often remembered as a man of the theatre. Near the beginning, he informs Roderigo that he has a theatrical 'soul' (1.1.54), a performed consciousness: 'trimm'd in forms and visages of duty', he keeps his 'heart' attending on himself, 'throwing but shows of service' on his lord, does 'well' by him, and when he has 'lin'd' his 'coat', does himself 'homage' (1.1.50–4). Later, in soliloquy, he tells the audience, 'I play the villain': 'When devils will the blackest sins put on, / They do suggest at first with heavenly shows, as I do now' (2.3.336, 351–3).

Yet less discussed is Iago's role as the author of poetry. In Act 2, scene 1, he insinuates himself into the consciousness of Desdemona by performing the role of a Petrarchan poet, after she asks him, coyly, 'What wouldst write of me, if thou shouldst praise me' (2.1.117). '[M]y invention', he replies,

> Comes from my pate as birdlime does from frieze,
> It plucks out brains and all. But my Muse labours,
> And thus she is deliver'd.

(Othello, 2.1.125–8)

At this point, he lapses into a 14-line extemporal verse in rhymed couplets, the opening lines of which read, 'If she be fair and wise, fairness and wit, / The one's for use, the other useth it' (2.1.29–30). Iago redeploys Sidney's metaphor of invention from Sonnet 1 of *Astrophil and Stella* – that of pregnancy and childbirth – showing that for early modern writers invention was not merely a technique but a topic, a dramatic representation in a fiction about authorship. What is noteworthy in *Othello* is Shakespeare's transposition of Petrarchan invention from printed poetry to the place of the stage.[54] In short, Shakespeare presents Iago not merely as a malicious villain but as a literary man practised in the compound art of his own creator, yet removed to the very edge of evil, that fathomless cult of the self, organized powerfully to 'plume up . . . [the] will' (1.3.393): ''tis in ourselves that we are thus or thus' (1.3.319–20). Perhaps authorship is evil because Iago so powerfully locates agency in the hands of the self, detached from the other or the community.

Consequently, when Iago charges Desdemona with 'Lechery' – an 'index and obscure prologue to the history of lust and foul thoughts' – he expresses the terms of his own dark consciousness, and locates the literary as its primary 'content'. Indeed, half of Iago's key vocabulary – 'obscure', 'lust', 'thoughts' – indicate that he gives verbal rather than 'ocular proof' (3.3.360) to the hidden nature of female consciousness. The word 'obscure' means 'unclearly expressed, hidden',[55] underscoring perhaps the sense that, in the depths of Iago's authorship, consciousness is merely a form of concealment, secrecy, disguise, and thus theatricality.

Yet we cannot come to terms with the most perplexing part of Iago's vocabulary, the conjunction of 'index and . . . prologue', until we identify it as one of Shakespeare's most enigmatic uses of hendiadys. George Wright, and more recently Frank Kermode and James Shapiro, have all written invaluably on this rhetorical figure, which 'means, literally, "one through two"'.[56] In particular, Wright marks the development of Shakespeare's language by tracking the presence of hendiadys: at the beginning of his career, Shakespeare employs the device sparingly, but 'in the great plays of his middle career' he uses it 'with some frequency', in two plays centrally: *Hamlet* (66 times) and *Othello* (28 times).[57]

Although Wright's essay is on *Hamlet*, he discusses *Othello* briefly (pp. 175–6), and although he does not cite 'index and obscure prologue' as an example he does create a frame by which we might do so. Tracing the origins of hendiadys to Servius' commentary on Virgil's *Aeneid* (p. 168) – an epic poem – he emphasises that 'the device is appropriate to the "high style"', since it appears in 'passages of a certain elevation, dignity, or remoteness from ordinary experience' (p. 173). Moreover, Wright shows how Shakespeare suits the device to 'character', to 'theme', to 'story', to 'setting' (p. 176) and even to 'the problematic depths of thought and feeling' (p. 173): 'The device is always somewhat mysterious and elusive, and its general appropriateness to . . . *Hamlet* is obvious' (p. 176). Wright does not identify hendiadys as Shakespeare's premier figure for theatre, but he comes close: 'hendiadys is a stylistic means of underlining the play's themes of anxiety, bafflement, disjunction, and the falsity of appearances . . . A miniature stylistic play within the play, hendiadys holds its mirror up to *Hamlet*' (pp. 178, 181).

According to Shapiro, in *Hamlet*

> Shakespeare clearly wanted audiences to work hard and one of the ways he made them do so was by employing an odd verbal trick called hendiadys . . . a single idea conveyed through a pairing of nouns linked by 'and'. When conjoined in this way, the nouns begin to oscillate, seeming to qualify each other as much as the term each individually modifies.[58]

Shapiro adds, 'The more you think about examples of hendiadys, the more they induce a kind of mental vertigo', and, like Wright, he finds the superabundance of the figure in *Hamlet* 'suit[ing] the mood of the play perfectly': 'an acknowledgement of how necessary and impossible it is to suture things together'.[59] Kermode, who discusses *Othello* in the most detail, notes the examples of hendiadys in such phrases as 'loving his own pride and purposes', 'trimm'd in forms and visages of duty', and 'flag and sign of love', but does not mention 'index and obscure prologue'. Well we may, because it is in this hendiadys alone that we can locate an accurate model of Shakespearean literary authorship. The vertigo is not only mental but professional; the necessary and impossible suture, authorial. In other words, because hendiadys is such a self-conscious, stylised rhetorical device, we can view its use as a concentrate of Shakespearean authorship itself.

We might conclude, then, by suggesting that hendiadys offers a clear frame for bridging the gap between criticism on Shakespeare's literary authorship and that on Shakespearean textuality, theatre and 'page to stage'. Above all, hendiadys is a principle that asserts conjunction and *thwarts* it.[60] We need such a principle to explain the conjoined presence of 'books and theatre' in Shakespeare's career *and* their 'opposition, disequilibrium'.[61] According to David Scott Kastan, through the 1623 printing of the First Folio,

> if Shakespeare cannot with any precision be called the creator of the book that bears his name, that book might be said to be the creator of Shakespeare. Ben Jonson, driven by a powerful literary ambition, actively sought his role as an author. Shakespeare . . . was largely indifferent to such individuation, comfortably working in the collaborative ethos of the theater.[62]

Kastan slots 'Shakespeare' into the received story about the invention of early modern authorship – as told, for instance, by Wendy Wall in 'Authorship and the Material Conditions of Writing', from the recent *Cambridge Companion to English Literature 1500–1600*: 'When Spenser and Jonson used the book format to generate the author's laureate status . . . they produced . . . modern and familiar images of literary authority – classically authorized writers who serve as the origin and arbiter of a literary monument that exceeds its place in everyday cultural transactions'.[63] According to this narrative, Spenser and Jonson, not Shakespeare, transact the large-scale cultural shift from the older notion of authorship to the one held widely today: the author as a self-shaping agent in the production of his own literary oeuvre and fame.[64] Kastan's formulation helps us understand why Shakespeare has been excised from the story: indifferent to the 'individuated authorship' (p. 16) of Jonson (and Spenser), Shakespeare took comfort in the collaborative authorship that has been the hallmark of criticism about the materiality of the book.[65]

Individuation and/or collaboration: these are the terms of the battle early in the twenty-first century. Neither party seems quite willing to imagine a Shakespeare who was at once comfortable with the 'collaborative ethos of the theater' *and* troubled by the 'individuated authorship' of the literary print-house. Yet Shakespeare's use of hendiadys helps us to imagine a 'Shakespeare' wearing precisely this strange authorial yoke. Accordingly, the 'Shakespeare' presented here has been that of a *hendiadys-author*, for whom the boundary between conjunction and disjunction virtually disappears. Disturbingly, this author is a poet and a playwright, yet always seeming to evade easy classification; he is interested in page and stage, yet famous for expressing the stigma of both; he is intent to represent books and theatre, in his staged plays as in his printed poetry, yet forever resisting the singular authorship of either. In the end, it is Shakespeare's unsettling literary authorship that serves as a profound index and clear prologue to the history not of lust and foul thoughts but of English literature.

Notes

1 All quotations of Shakespeare come from *The Riverside Shakespeare*, 2nd edn, ed. G. Blakemore Evans (Boston: Houghton Mifflin, 1997).

2 Without question, theatre criticism cuts across areas of specialisation, but it will prove useful here to designate a larger class. For instance, in an important 1986 essay, Harry Levin identifies theatre criticism as the major accomplishment of the twentieth century: 'Our century . . . has restored our perception of him to *his genre, the drama*, enhanced by increasing historical knowledge alongside the live tradition of the performing arts.' See Levin, 'Critical Approaches to Shakespeare from 1660–1904', in Stanley Wells (ed.), *The Cambridge Companion to Shakespeare Studies* (Cambridge: Cambridge University Press, 1986), pp. 213–29 (p. 228, emphasis added). The showpiece for this accomplishment is Stanley Wells and Gary Taylor (eds), *The Oxford Shakespeare. William Shakespeare: The Complete Works* (Oxford: Clarendon Press, 1988), which aims to present Shakespeare as 'supremely, a man of the theatre' (p. xxxvi) and his texts as they were originally performed: 'It is in performance that the plays lived and had their being. Performance is the end to which they were created' (p. xxxviii). See also Stephen Greenblatt et al. (eds), *The Norton Shakespeare: Based on the Oxford Edition* (New York: Norton, 1997), which institutionalises this methodology for the American academy. For important 'performance criticism' see Anthony Dawson, *Watching Shakespeare* (London: Macmillan, 1988); Robert Hapgood, *Shakespeare the Theatre-Poet* (Oxford: Oxford University Press, 1988); Alan C. Dessen, *Recovering Shakespeare's Theatrical Vocabulary*

(Cambridge: Cambridge University Press, 1995); Barbara Hodgon, *The Shakespeare Trade: Performances and Appropriations* (Philadelphia: University of Pennsylvania Press, 1998); and Andrew Gurr, *The Shakespeare Company, 1594–1642* (Cambridge: Cambridge University Press, 2004). For a recent overview see Miriam Gilbert, 'Performance Criticism', in Stanley Wells and Lena Cowen Orlin (eds), *Shakespeare: An Oxford Guide* (Oxford: Oxford University Press, 2003), pp. 550–67; and its companion piece, Patricia Tastpaugh, 'Performance History: Shakespeare on the Stage, 1660–2001', pp. 525–49.

3 For a superb model of this criticism see Peter Stallybrass, Roger Chartier, J. Franklin Mowery and Heather Wolfe, 'Hamlet's Tables and the Technologies of Writing in Renaissance England', *Shakespeare Quarterly*, 55 (2004), 379–419. This form of criticism does not show up in (for instance) Wells and Orlin (eds), *An Oxford Guide*, which inventories twelve forms of criticism, ranging from 'Humanist interpretations', 'Character criticism' and 'Source study', to 'Post-colonial criticism', 'Deconstruction' and 'Performance criticism'. The ninth form, 'Materialist criticisms', discusses only the 'three most influential strands – Marxism, new historicism, and cultural materialism'. See Jonathan Gill Harris, 'Materialist criticisms' (pp. 472–84, 472).

4 David Scott Kastan, *Shakespeare and the Book* (Cambridge: Cambridge University Press, 2001), p. 6. Kastan voices the received wisdom; see, e.g., Stephen Orgel and A. R. Braunmuller (eds), *Pelican Shakespeare*, 'The Texts on Shakespeare' (New York: Penguin, 2002): 'Shakespeare always had performance, not a book, in mind' (p. 1); and Jonathan Bate (ed.), *Titus Andronicus*, Arden 3 (London: Thomas Nelson, 1995): 'Shakespeare wrote his plays as scripts for performance, not as texts for publication' (p. 97). For other important textual criticism see Stephen Orgel, 'What Is a Text?' (1981), rpt. in David Scott Kastan and Peter Stallybrass (eds), *Staging the Renaissance: Reinterpretations of Elizabethan and Jacobean Drama* (New York: Routledge, 1991), pp. 83–87; Margreta de Grazia and Peter Stallybrass, 'The Materiality of the Shakespearean Text', *Shakespeare Quarterly*, 44 (1993), 255–83; Laurie E. Maguire, *Shakespearean Suspect Texts: The 'Bad' Quartos and Their Contexts* (Cambridge: Cambridge University Press, 1996); Peter W. M. Blayney, 'The Publication of Playbooks', in John D. Cox and David Scott Kastan (eds), *A New History of Early English Drama* (New York: Columbia University Press, 1997), pp. 383–422; Jeffrey B. Masten, *Textual Intercourse: Collaboration, Authorship, and Sexualities in Renaissance Drama* (Cambridge: Cambridge University Press, 1997); Andrew Murphy (ed.), *The Renaissance Text: Theory, Editing, Textuality* (Manchester: Manchester University Press, 2000); and Andrew Murphy, *Shakespeare in Print: A History and Chronology*

of Shakespeare Publishing (Cambridge: Cambridge University Press, 2003). The origin lies in D. F. McKenzie, esp. 'The Printers of the Mind: Some Notes on Bibliographical Theories and Printing-House Practices', in D. F. McKenzie, *Making Meaning: 'Printers of the Mind' and Other Essays*, ed. Peter D. McDonald and Michael F. Suarez, S.J. (Amherst: University of Massachusetts Press, 2002), pp. 13–85.

5 Tiffany Stern, *Making Shakespeare: From Stage to Page* (London: Routledge, 2004), pp. 5–6. Stern cites two 'recent books' as 'principal' instigators of the new field: Cox and Kastan (eds), *A New History of Early English Drama*; and David Scott Kastan (ed.), *A Companion to Shakespeare* (Oxford: Blackwell, 1999). Two older books (cited by Orgel, 'What Is a Text?', p. 83) are E. A. J. Honigmann, *The Stability of Shakespeare's Text* (London: Edward Arnold, 1965); and G. E. Bentley, *The Profession of Dramatist in Shakespeare's Time, 1590–1642* (Princeton: Princeton University Press, 1971). More recently see also W. B. Worthen, *Shakespeare and the Authority of Performance* (Cambridge: Cambridge University Press, 1997); Robert Weimann, *Author's Pen and Actor's Voice: Playing and Writing in Shakespeare's Theatre* (Cambridge: Cambridge University Press, 2000); and Douglas A. Brooks, *From Playhouse to Printing House: Drama and Authorship in Early Modern England* (Cambridge: Cambridge University Press, 2000).

6 Milton, *L'Allegro*, 134–5, in Merritt Y. Hughes (ed.), *John Milton: Complete Poems and Major Prose* (Indianapolis: Odyssey, 1957). For details see Levin, 'Critical Approaches'.

7 On how textual criticism differs (in particular) from performance criticism see Kastan, *Shakespeare and the Book*, pp. 6–9; for his critique of the (Miltonic) 'literary' as a category see esp. pp. 14–49. For evidence that the Romantic view can still be practised with power and influence see Harold Bloom, *Shakespeare: The Invention of the Human* (New York: Riverhead-Penguin Putnam, 1998).

8 Erne, *Shakespeare as Literary Dramatist* (Cambridge: Cambridge University Press, 2003), pp. 20, 23, 25–6. As progenitors of his project, Erne cites Harry Berger, Jr, *Imaginary Audition: Shakespeare on Stage and Page* (Berkeley: University of California Press, 1989); and Julie Stone Peters, *Theatre of the Book, 1480–1880: Print, Text, and Performance in Europe* (Oxford: Oxford University Press, 2000).

9 For an overview explaining this process of reception history for the poems see Sasha Roberts, 'Reception and Influence', in Patrick Cheney (ed.), *The Cambridge Companion to Shakespeare's Poetry* (Cambridge: Cambridge University Press, 2007), pp. 260–80.

10 For chapters on all five poems and *The Passionate Pilgrim* see Patrick Cheney, *Shakespeare, National Poet-Playwright* (Cambridge: Cambridge University Press, 2004); on the question of the Sonnets'

authorisation see ch. 8. Formally, the founding texts of the back-to-the-poems movement are Colin Burrow, 'Life and Work in Shakespeare's Poems', Chatterton Lecture on Poetry, *Proceedings of the British Academy*, 97 (1998), 15–50; and Colin Burrow (ed.), *The Complete Sonnets and Poems* (Oxford: Oxford University Press, 2002). For additional commentators see Cheney, *Poet-Playwright*, esp. p. 4 note 6.

11 Gildon, *The Works of Mr. William Shakespear. Volume the Seventh. Containing, Venus & Adonis. Tarquin & Lucrece And His Miscellany of Poems. With Critical Remarks on his Plays, &c. to which is Prefix'd an Essay on the Art, Rise and Progress of the Stage in Greece, Rome, and England* (London, 1710). See also Paul D. Cannan, 'Early Shakespeare Criticism, Charles Gildon, and the Making of Shakespeare the Playwright-Poet', *Modern Philology*, 102 (2004), 35–55.

12 Such critics as Erne and Kastan tend to stick to textual and historical scholarship, yet they thereby open the gate to literary criticism.

13 De Grazia, 'Soliloquies and Wages in the Age of Emergent Consciousness', *Textual Practice*, 9 (1995), 67–92 (p. 81). 'Consciousness' is the term that many critics now use to describe Shakespeare's representation of mental action, thought or inwardness. De Grazia traces the concept to Hegel, to Marx and to Burckhardt, emphasising that Foucault influentially resists the nineteenth-century invention of the 'Renaissance' as the birth of modern consciousness (pp. 70–3).

14 Kastan, *Shakespeare and the Book*, p. 78. On 'Shakespeare' as made by others in subsequent centuries see, for example, Michael Dobson, *The Making of the National Poet: Shakespeare, Adaptation, and Authorship, 1660–1769* (Oxford: Clarendon Press, 1992); and Margreta de Grazia, *Shakespeare Verbatim: The Reproduction of Authenticity and the 1790 Apparatus* (Oxford: Clarendon Press, 1991).

15 Kastan, *Shakespeare and the Book*, p. 5.

16 Michael Bristol, *Big-Time Shakespeare* (New York: Routledge, 1996), identifies 'two different and in some sense fundamentally opposed forms of production [in Shakespeare's career]: theatrical performance and printed books' (p. 30). He reminds us that the two institutions were not separate: 'members of the repertory companies themselves invested in theater buildings and eventually even formed partnerships with book-sellers for the distribution and sale of printed editions of selected plays' (p. 31).

17 Norman Sanders (ed.), *Othello* (1984; Cambridge: Cambridge University Press, 2003), p. 105. In his Arden 3 edition, E. A. J. Honigmann glosses 'index' as 'table of contents prefixed to a book; preface; prologue', and similarly leaves 'prologue' un-glossed (London: Thomson Learning, 1997), p. 179.

18 Theresa M. Krier, *Birth Passages: Maternity and Nostalgia, Antiquity to Shakespeare* (Ithaca: Cornell University Press, 2001), sees Shakespeare's 'career' as 'creat[ing] . . . for himself' a place between 'a specific poetic history and the radically developing institution of the theater' (p. 162). James P. Bednarz, *Shakespeare and the Poets' War* (New York: Columbia University Press, 2000), reminds us how Renaissance treatises tended to see the relation between poetry and theatre: 'Sidney's *Apology for Poetrie* and Heywood's *Apology for Actors* are linked by the proposition that drama is a subset of "poetry" that deploys a wide range of fictional constructs to move an audience to moral action' (p. 253).

19 Richard Helgerson, *Forms of Nationhood: The Elizabethan Writing of England* (Chicago: University of Chicago Press, 1992), p. 215. Discussing the question of 'Shakespeare's individual agency' (p. 215), Helgerson joins many leading Renaissance critics in moving us into a post-revisionist phase. See, for example, Bristol, *Big-Time Shakespeare*, pp. 49–58; Leah S. Marcus, *Puzzling Shakespeare: Local Reading and Its Discontents* (Berkeley: University of California Press, 1988), pp. 19, 42, 68–70; and, for a thrilling indictment of Foucault and social construction, Louis Montrose, 'Spenser's Domestic Domain: Poetry, Property, and the Early Modern Subject', in Margreta de Grazia, Maureen Quilligan and Peter Stallybrass (eds), *Subject and Object in Renaissance Culture* (Cambridge: Cambridge University Press, 1996), pp. 83–130, esp. p. 92. The revisionist (post-structuralist) model to which these critics respond derives most famously from Roland Barthes, 'The Death of the Author', in Vincent B. Leitch et al. (eds), *The Norton Anthology of Theory and Criticism* (New York: Norton, 2001), pp. 1466–70; and Michel Foucault, 'What Is an Author?', in *The Foucault Reader*, ed. Paul Rabinow (New York: Pantheon Books, 1984), pp. 101–20.

20 On the word 'part' in Shakespeare's acting vocabulary see Cheney, *Poet-Playwright*, pp. 120, 123–4, 141, 170.

21 Kenneth Muir (ed.), *Troilus and Cressida* (1982; Oxford: Oxford University Press, 1998), p. 126.

22 He also uses words like 'authority' (56 times) and 'authorities' (6).

23 Richard Helgerson, *Self-Crowned Laureates: Spenser, Jonson, Milton, and the Literary System* (Berkeley: University of California Press, 1983), p. 159.

24 The ground-breaking study is by Anne Righter (later Anne Barton), *Shakespeare and the Idea of the Play* (London: Chatto and Windus, 1962). Subsequently, see, for example, James L. Calderwood, *Metadrama in Shakespeare's Henriad: 'Richard II' to 'Henry V'* (Berkeley: University of California Press, 1979) and *To Be and Not to Be: Negation and*

Metadrama in 'Hamlet' (New York: Columbia University Press, 1983).
Metatheatrical criticism also informs the work of Stephen Greenblatt;
see, for example, 'Invisible Bullets', in *Shakespearean Negotiations: The
Circulation of Social Energy in Renaissance England* (Oxford: Clarendon
Press, 1988), pp. 21–65 (esp. pp. 64–5).

25 The present material extends that from Cheney, *Poet-Playwright*. Since
being published, this book has been cited as a precedent in Charlotte
Scott, *Shakespeare and the Idea of the Book* (Oxford: Oxford University
Press, 2007). Scott identifies her study as the first to examine fully
Shakespeare's use of the book in his plays. Her analysis is invaluable, but
neglects the emphasis of the present chapter, the conjunction between
books and theatre in the discourse of the plays. For related criticism see
Heidi Brayman Hackel, 'The "Great Variety" of Readers and Early
Modern Reading Practices', in Kastan (ed.), *A Companion to
Shakespeare*, pp. 139–57, and *Reading Material in Early Modern
England: Print, Gender, and Literacy* (Cambridge: Cambridge University
Press, 2005); Frederick Kiefer, *Writing on the Renaissance Stage: Written
Words, Printed Pages, Metaphoric Books* (Newark: University of
Delaware Press, 1996); David M. Bergeron (ed.), *Reading and Writing in
Shakespeare* (Newark: University of Delaware Press, 1996).

26 On such terms see Cheney, *Poet-Playwright*, esp. chs. 1, 4, and 8. On
Shakespeare worrying about print publication see, for example, Burrow,
'Life and Work'. Thus, Kastan is, if not mistaken, at least misleading:
'Shakespeare was, for the most part, uninterested in print' (*Shakespeare
and the Book*, p. 136).

27 The claim that Shakespeare 'never admitted' to 'literary ambition'
(Kastan, *Shakespeare and the Book*, p. 135) is belied everywhere in the
Shakespearean text – including in the Sonnets, where the poet, as J. B.
Leishman long ago observed, 'has written both more copiously and
more memorably [on the idea of poetic immortality] than any other son-
neteer' (*Themes and Variations in Shakespeare's Sonnets* (New York:
Harper and Row, 1963), p. 22), as Sonnet 55 alone testifies. See also
Katherine Duncan-Jones, *Ungentle Shakespeare: Scenes from His Life*
(London: Thomson Learning, 2001), for the Shakespearean commitment to fame in the Sonnets coming from 'the printed book' (p. 177);
and Cheney, *Poet-Playwright*, for index entries under the following:
'eternity', 'fame', 'glory, Christian', 'immortality' and 'oblivion'.

28 *Riverside*, p. 433. Other editions cite other books printed at the time,
including specific 'books of good manners'.

29 Some editors now believe that George Wilkins wrote Acts 1–2 of
Pericles and that Shakespeare wrote Acts 3–5 (Brian Vickers,
*Shakespeare as Co-Author: A Historical Study of Five Collaborative
Plays* (Oxford: Oxford University Press, 2002), pp. 292–332). None the

less, Shakespeare may have added 'touches' to the opening acts (*Riverside*, p. 1528), and this passage may be one of them, as its similarity with that in *2 Henry IV* suggests. For recent scepticism about collaboration in *Pericles* see Kastan, *Shakespeare and the Book*, pp. 64–6.

30 On Shakespeare's use of 'show' as his habitual term for theatre see Cheney, *Poet-Playwright*, pp. 108–13, 240–2, citing esp. *Hamlet*, 3.2.140–6.

31 *A New Variorum Edition of Shakespeare: 'Hamlet'*, ed. Horace Howard Furness, 2 vols (1877; New York: Dover, 1963), vol. 1, p. 151. The genre of satire was especially in vogue around the turn of the seventeenth century.

32 See Cheney, *Poet-Playwright*, p. 79; and *The Norton Shakespeare*, p. 85.

33 On scholarship as a 'form of nationhood' for viewing the Marlowe corpus see Patrick Cheney, *Marlowe's Counterfeit Profession: Ovid, Spenser, Counter-Nationhood* (Toronto: University of Toronto Press, 1997), esp. p. 23.

34 In his poems Shakespeare deploys the conceit several times. See, for example, *The Rape of Lucrece*, lines 99–105, 615–16, 806–12, 1183, 1195; and Sonnet 77, lines 1–4. On the Tudor 'aesthetics of the body' see Clark Hulse, 'Tudor Aesthetics', in Arthur F. Kinney (ed.), *The Cambridge Companion to English Literature 1500–1600* (Cambridge: Cambridge University Press, 2000), pp. 29–63 (p. 30).

35 See Honigmann (ed.), *Othello*, p. 277.

36 The word *face* is a term from the printing house, the surface of a piece of type (= typeface), but the *OED* does not record the first example until 1683. The *OED* also has 'Of a document: The inscribed side' (*OED*, 'face', 13c), tracing to 1632. As we shall see, *face* also has a theatrical meaning.

37 For a different model see Margreta de Grazia's 'Introduction' to De Grazia, Quilligan and Stallybrass (eds), *Subject and Object in Renaissance Culture*, which emphasises the primacy of 'object' over 'subject'.

38 Cf. Alison Findlay, '*Hamlet*: A Document in Madness', in Mark Burnett and John Mannery (eds), *New Essays on Hamlet* (New York: AMS Press, 1994), pp. 189–205: Hamlet's '"distracted" speeches [including on "the book and volume of my brain" at 1.5.103] suggest that it is language as much as female sexuality, neglected love, or grief that has made him mad' (p. 194).

39 Pope, quoted in Jill L. Levenson (ed.), *Romeo and Juliet* (Oxford: Oxford University Press, 2000), p. 177. The following analysis is indebted to Levenson's detailed annotation, as well as to Brian Gibbons (ed.), *Romeo and Juliet*, Arden 2 (London: Methuen, 1980), p. 104; and

to G. Blakemore Evans (ed.), *Romeo and Juliet* (Cambridge: Cambridge University Press, 1984). Levenson points out that Shakespeare's main source for the play, Arthur Brooke's poem *Romeus and Juliet* (1562), 'mentions only that Capulet's wife "paints" an impression of Paris "with curious words" (1893–6)' (p. 176).

40 Evans (ed.), *Romeo and Juliet*, p. 73.
41 Ibid.
42 Levenson, (ed.), *Romeo and Juliet*, p. 177.
43 See Cheney, 'The Epic Spear of Achilles: Self-Concealing Authorship in *The Rape of Lucrece, Troilus and Cressida*, and *Hamlet*', in *Shakespeare's Literary Authorship* (Cambridge: Cambridge University Press, 2008), which also discusses the disembodied spear-as-pen in the Shakespeare family coat of arms (see pp. 34–7).
44 Greenblatt, *Will in the World: How Shakespeare Became Shakespeare* (New York: Norton, 2004), p. 155.
45 Evans (ed.), *Romeo and Juliet*, p. 17.
46 Daniell (ed.), *Julius Caesar*, Arden 3 (London: Thomson Learning, 1998). The characterisation does not come from Plutarch.
47 See Wendy Wall, 'Turning Sonnet', in *The Imprint of Gender: Authorship and Publication in the English Renaissance* (Ithaca: Cornell University Press, 1993), pp. 23–109.
48 For Shakespeare, 'extemporal' is a theatrical term; see, for example, *1 Henry IV*, 2.3.280: 'a play extempore'.
49 Cf. Romeo at 1.1.175–81. On the Petrarchan idiom see Gayle Whittier, 'The Sonnet's Body and the Body Sonnetized in *Romeo and Juliet*', *Shakespeare Quarterly*, 40 (1989), 27–41; Heather Dubrow, *Echoes of Desire: English Petrarchism and its Counter-discourses* (Ithaca: Cornell University Press, 1995), pp. 262–7; Diana E. Henderson, *Passion Made Public: Elizabethan Lyric, Gender, and Performance* (Urbana: University of Illinois Press, 1995), pp. 1–7; and Levenson (ed.), *Romeo and Juliet*, pp. 52–61.
50 *Greenes Groats-Worth of witte*, quoted in *Riverside*, p. 1959.
51 Levenson (ed.), *Romeo and Juliet*, p. 268.
52 The annotated editions of Levenson, Evans and Gibbons pass the self-reference by.
53 This is the historical context proposed in Cheney, *Poet-Playwright*, esp. ch. 1.
54 On the metaphor during the period see Katherine Eisaman Maus, 'A Womb of His Own: Male Renaissance Poets in the Female Body', in *Inwardness and Theater in the English Renaissance* (Chicago: University of Chicago Press, 1995), pp. 182–209.
55 Honigmann (ed.), *Othello*, p. 179.
56 Wright, 'Hendiadys and *Hamlet*,' *PMLA*, 96 (1981), 168–93 (p. 168);

Kermode, *Shakespeare's Language* (London: Allen Lane-Penguin, 2000), esp. pp. 101–2 and 167–9 (on *Othello*); and James Shapiro, *1599: A Year in the Life of William Shakespeare* (London: Faber and Faber, 2005), pp. 321–2.

57 See Wright, 'Hendiadys', pp. 168, 173.

58 Shapiro, *1599*, p. 321.

59 Ibid., p. 322.

60 Wright, 'Hendiadys', pp. 169, 181.

61 Ibid., p. 181.

62 Kastan, *Shakespeare and the Book*, p. 78.

63 Wall, 'Authorship and the Material Conditions of Writing', in Kinney (ed.), *The Cambridge Companion to English Literature 1500–1600*, pp. 64–89 (p. 86). Wall maps recent work on authorship and print culture on to Helgerson's model of the laureate or national poet from *Self-Crowned Laureates*.

64 Wall refers to Shakespeare only once in passing ('Authorship', p. 83). Similarly, in *Self-Crowned Laureates*, Helgerson makes only intermittent remarks about Shakespeare (e.g., pp. 4, 10, 39–40, 48–9), as does Colin Burrow in the orienting essay to *The Cambridge Companion to English Literature 1500–1600*, titled 'The Sixteenth Century' (pp. 11–28). Burrow argues that the 'chief legacy' of the period was the 'development of a form of authorship which was located in London life and articulated through the medium of print'. Like Wall and Helgerson, Burrow foregrounds Spenser (p. 22) and Jonson (pp. 25–6) in his narrative about 'the emergence of a dignified profession of literary authorship which worked in collaboration with the medium of print' (pp. 25–6), but mentions only the 'name of Shakespeare' once (p. 22). Thus, all three critics miss an opportunity to slot Shakespeare into a fuller story about the emergence of the modern English author.

65 See another overview essay, by Jeffrey B. Masten, 'Playwrighting: Authorship and Collaboration', in Cox and Kastan (eds), *A New History of Early English Drama*, pp. 357–82.

2

'A man in print'? Shakespeare and the representation of the press

Helen Smith

'[I]t is well', Francis Bacon reminded readers of his 1620 *Novum Organon*,

> to observe the force and virtue and consequences of discoveries, and these are to be seen nowhere more conspicuously than in those three which were unknown to the ancients, and of which the origin, though recent, is obscure and inglorious; namely, printing, gunpowder, and the magnet. For these three have changed the whole face and state of things throughout the world; the first in literature, the second in warfare, the third in navigation; whence have followed innumerable changes, insomuch that no empire, no sect, no star seems to have exerted greater power and influence in human affairs than these mechanical discoveries.[1]

Bacon's endorsement of the transformative power of print has been re-enacted in recent years by a number of historians of the book, who argue that the early modern period witnessed a profound shift from an oral to a literate, and particularly to a print-literate, culture.[2] In her recent study of *Reading and Writing in Seventeenth-Century England*, Cecile Jagodzinski reproduces this view, explaining that 'it is no coincidence that a technological innovation – the printing press – created a sociological revolution'.[3] In line with a number of recent revisionist accounts which argue against any radical shift from an oral or manuscript culture to a putative 'age of print', this chaper seeks to test early modern understandings of print culture by asking whether Bacon's almost exact contemporary, William Shakespeare, shared his belief in the epoch-defining impact of the press.[4]

This is a question grounded in the debate about the status of Shakespeare's plays prompted by the publication of Lukas Erne's *Shakespeare as Literary Dramatist*. Erne's detailed and provocative argument, along with the earlier work of scholars including Peter Blayney, Richard Dutton, Laurie Maguire and Paul Werstine, has called into question the popular conception of Shakespeare's plays as essentially theatrical texts, which appeared in print only as butchered shades of their former selves.[5] Gone is our picture of early quarto editions as pirated texts, patched together by ill-remembering actors and unskilled shorthand reporters. Gone are, in Nicholas Robins's words, the 'obscure cliques of sneaking actors and devious printers, their inky faces set in expressions of blunt greed, their slack hands botching and mutilating their way through the canon of the world's greatest theatrical literature'.[6] Instead, Erne argues, we should see the shorter 'bad' quartos as theatrical versions, designed for the playhouse, while the later folio texts and some of the 'good' quartos represent self-consciously literary versions of the plays, prepared for print by an author contemplating the possibility of a collected works, neither negligent of publication nor a victim of the playing company's determination to prevent their property circulating in the marketplace of print.

Erne argues against an editorial and bibliographical tradition that has sought to establish a Shakespeare exclusively concerned with the stage versions of his dramatic works, and careless of their appearance on the printed page. This is a tradition bolstered during the last decades of the twentieth century by a corresponding critical emphasis on metatheatre, a tradition which stresses the plays' repeated and self-reflexive acknowledgement of their condition as acted contracts between audience, players and playwright.[7] As Anne Righter puts it in one of the earliest critical works to address the self-consciously theatrical nature of the plays:

> From the very beginning, Shakespeare seems to have been concerned with the play metaphor to a degree unusual even among his contemporaries. Gradually, the association of the world with the stage fundamental to Elizabethan drama built itself deeply into his imagination, and into the structure of his plays. There it acquired dimensions and a sensitivity which were quite unique. Essentially a technique for maintaining contact with the spectators, the play image also became in mature Shakespearian drama a meditation upon the nature of the theatre.[8]

Yet while Bottom in *A Midsummer Night's Dream* is a keen actor, he is also an engaged member of a textual culture hovering on the boundary of print and orality, declaring 'I will get Peter Quince to write a ballad of this dream: it shall be called "Bottom's Dream", because it hath no bottom' (4.2.212–14). While Cleopatra imagines the future moment when 'I shall see / Some squeaking Cleopatra boy my greatnesse / I'th' posture of a Whore' (5.2.228–30), she also, like Caesar, Pompey, Romaine and Antony, engages in a frenzy of writing, whether to serve her personal ends in communicating with her lover, or her diplomatic ends in the pursuit of war.[9] And while Hamlet famously talks of players and reproduces the theatrical world in miniature in his play within a play, *The Murder of Gonzago*, he also, like Ophelia, walks on stage reading, and reaches for his tables to 'set it down, / That one may smile, and smile, and be a villain' (1.5.107–8). Even Hamlet's cloak is 'inky', saturated in the materials of his scholarly life at Wittenberg. We soon learn that it is as much Hamlet's habit to anatomise himself in the terms of the written word as in the terms of the playhouse:

> Yea, from the table of my memory
> I'll wipe away all trivial fond records,
> All saws of books, all forms, all pressures past
> That youth and observation copied there,
> And thy commandment all alone shall live
> Within the book and volume of my brain,
> Unmix'd with baser matter.
>
> (1.5.98–104)

Punning on 'form' as university course, his previous learning, and 'forme' as a body of type set for printing under pressure, Hamlet swears to reprint his palimpsestic mind, showing himself to have internalised the vocabulary of literacy and of print culture as a way of thinking about himself and his actions.[10] As well as being metatheatrical, Shakespeare's plays are deeply metatextual, as much aware of their incarnation as material objects circulating in manuscript and print as of their inherently dramatic concerns.

A number of critics have identified and attempted to catalogue the numerous books and papers that populate the Shakespearean stage, from Tranio's 'small packet of Greek and Latin Books' in *The Taming of the Shrew* to the table-books and ballads Autolycus sells in *The Winter's Tale*, and from Slender's copy of the *Book of Songs and Sonnets* in *The Merry Wives of Windsor* to the book of prayers that lies on the pillow of the two princes murdered by Tyrrel in *Richard II*.[11] For John Pitcher, meditating upon the fateful copy of Ovid's

Metamorphoses seized by the handless Lavinia in *Titus Andronicus*, this mass of textual matter is intimately identified with a nascent print culture, one that sits uneasily alongside the world of the theatre:

> The most troubling aspect of the public stage as hybrid . . . was in its shameless joining of knowledges, vulgar with arcane, and high with low . . . [I]n this the theatres were allied to the other great agent for cultural and imaginative upheaval at this time, the printed book. It is characteristic of Shakespeare that he should be prescient enough to recognize this conjunction (and confrontation) of stage and book from the outset of his career, in one of his plays from the early 1590s, *Titus Andronicus*.[12]

Perhaps, however, Shakespeare's recognition of the epoch-shaping novelty of print is not as self-evident as Pitcher claims. Shakespeare and his fellows were not immune to anachronism, and it is possible that on the Renaissance stage the Roman Lavinia did leaf through a printed, rather than manuscript, book, particularly as the *Metamorphoses* was widely available in printed editions, and familiar to most schoolboys through its inclusion in Erasmus's *De Copia*. None the less, many of the other printed texts that appear in Shakespeare's plays, including Marlowe's *Hero and Leander*, Norton and Sackville's *Gorboduc*, and the jestbook *A Hundred Merry Tales* allegedly possessed by Beatrice in *Much Ado About Nothing*, also circulated in manuscript, and the plays are heavily populated with handwritten letters, and with manuscript books and tables.[13] Even Prospero's 'own library with volumes that / I prize above my dukedom' (1.2.167–8), was probably, as Barbara Mowat has recently pointed out, stocked with manuscript grimoires, since it was from the owner's laborious handwriting that these texts were believed to derive their magical power.[14] The critical role of scripted texts on the Shakespearean stage reminds us that manuscript circulation did not cease with the advent of print, and that the texts issuing from the presses of early modern London circulated alongside the products of both a continuing scribal tradition and networks of coterie manuscript exchange. Shakespeare repeatedly addresses questions of the status of the text, of the promises and dangers of a bookish existence, and of exegesis, but in doing so he invokes a textual economy in which print, manuscript and oral tradition overlap, and are often difficult to distinguish.[15]

Even when Shakespeare seems specifically to invoke the early modern printing press, as he does in *The Winter's Tale*, *The Merry*

Wives of Windsor and *2 Henry VI*, there is a productive ambiguity in his descriptions which serves to remind us that the press had by no means become either the standard mechanism of textual production or the normalised mode for conceiving of books and texts. By interrogating the multiple connotations of 'print' and 'press' in the plays of Shakespeare, we can at once call into question the assumptions of our own print-centred ontology, and extend our understanding of how print overlapped and interacted with other modes of textual production.

'Behold, my lords', instructs Paulina in *The Winter's Tale*, brandishing the baby Perdita as she asserts Hermione's faithfulness and the child's legitimacy: 'Although the print be little, the whole matter / And copy of the father' (2.3.97–9). For readers caught up in our own print-conscious concerns, it is easy to seize upon this moment as a tongue-in-cheek invocation of the mechanical means of textual production, with the infant Perdita represented as the cheaper octavo derivative of her father's royal folio, or perhaps as the print version of Leontes' manuscript 'copy', faithfully transcribed by the compositor. Such an interpretation is bolstered by Leontes' later observation to Florizel: 'Your mother was most true to wedlock, prince; / For she did print your royal father off, / Conceiving you' (5.1.123–5). In this context, 'royal' can be read as a pun on the size of paper used in prestigious folio volumes. To assert this as the sole, or even the primary, meaning of Paulina's words, however, is to forget that, before it gained its current overriding connotations of typology, 'to print' bore the more general meaning 'to impress or stamp (a form, figure, mark, etc.) in or on a yielding substance' (*OED*, 'print', *v.*, 2a).

Thus, when, in *Henry VI, Part 2*, Queen Margaret wishes her kiss could be 'printed in [Suffolk's] hand / That thou mightst think upon these lips by the seal' (3.2.343–4), 'print' is used to invoke the mark of a signet or medal pressed into wax to secure a letter or to stamp a royal or noble patent.[16] The same meaning is expressed in Sonnet 11 when Shakespeare instructs the young man that nature 'carved thee for her seal, and meant thereby / Thou shouldst print more, not let that copy die' (ll. 13–14). Despite the tempting connotations of both 'print' and 'copy', and the injunction to repeated reproduction, the poem makes reference not to the dissemination of a text but to the inverted reproduction of a signet or seal.[17] In the case of both Sonnet 11 and *The Winter's Tale*, our understanding of the implications of the term 'print' is enriched by the connotations of rigid die and yielding wax, invoking both the sexual act and the early modern understanding of conception as the point at which the father's features were impressed upon the foetus.[18] In *Hamlet*, however, the prince's description of printing a seal reminds us of the possibility of forgery or deception that haunted the wax imposition of royal authority as well as the experience of paternity:

> I had my father's signet in my purse,
> Which was the model of that Danish seal,
> Folded the writ up in the form of th'other,
> Subscrib'd it, gave't th'impression, plac'd it safely,
> The changeling never known.
>
> (5.2.49–53)

In early modern England, 'print' or 'impression' was also used as a term to describe the marking of a coin, an application that adds a further fiscal layer to Costard's declaration in *Love's Labour's Lost* that he will deliver Berowne's letter 'sir, in print' (3.1.171) in return for a financial reward (*OED*, 'print', *v.*, 1a). As Wendy Wall has pointed out, the dream of being 'a man in print', invoked by Antony Scoloker in the preface to his *Daiphantus* of 1604, could be used as a punning representation of the author's decision to publish, to put himself through the press.[19] Something of this bookish connotation is evident in *As You Like It*, in Touchstone's insistence that he and an unnamed courtier quarrel 'in print, by the book' (5.4.88–90). Both Costard and Touchstone, however, also draw upon an older sense of the term with a somewhat obscure origin, surviving now only in dialect forms, in which to do something 'in print' means to do it in 'in a precise and perfect way or manner; in exact order, with exactness or preciseness; to a nicety' (*OED*, 'print', *n.*, 15a). In particular, to wear one's ruff 'in print' meant to have it well-starched and neatly presented, as in Middleton's 1602 *Blurt Master Constable*, when the melancholy Lazarillo tells his audience of ladies 'Your ruff must stand in print; and for that purpose, get poking-sticks'.[20] Bringing together the sense of impression and accuracy, printed coin and acting 'in print', Costard's vow to complete his commission becomes a punning play on his own fashionable neatness, and on the printed coin with which he is presented by Berowne, and whose value – elevenpence farthing more than the remuneration he has just received from Armado – inspires his precise service.

In *The Two Gentlemen of Verona* Valentine's page, Speed, also declares his exact obedience in a rhetorical play, explaining, as he reads, 'All this I speak in print, for in print I found it' (2.1.164). Using antanaclasis, Speed repeats 'in print', altering the meaning of this brief phrase which in the first instance encapsulates his neatness and efficiency, and in the second lays the emphasis squarely upon the mechanics of textual production.[21] Yet Speed's printed document is a manuscript letter, written by Valentine at Silvia's command. The verb 'to print', in this instance, means simply to write clearly or plainly, to mark the paper with a firm hand. Thus in *Titus Andronicus* Marcus hopes that the Gods will guide Lavinia's 'pen' 'to print [her] sorrows plain, / That we may know the traitors and the truth' (4.1.75–6). Similarly, in *Much Ado About Nothing*, Leonato claims to be able to read the guilty story that is 'printed' in Hero's blood (4.1.120–21). Rather than suggesting that his daughter's tainted bodily fluids have yielded to the pressure of a platen or seal, Hero's father implies that her blushes tell a clearly written tale, available for ready interpretation. This repeated etymological ambiguity, the possibility that print may refer to a page marked not by type but by a pen or pencil, makes it difficult to preserve the distance we often enact in our studies between the world of the printing press and the world of manuscript exchange.

If we retain these multiple connotations while returning to the brief passage from *The Winter's Tale* quoted above, it remains possible to read Perdita as a textual reproduction of her father, either written or printed. At the same time, however, Paulina equates Leontes' daughter with a royal patent legitimated by her father's seal, with the print of her father's head marking a genuine coin of the realm (a 'royal'), and with a certain degree of neatness and precision. Set within its 1623 Folio context, the phrase may also suggest a printed likeness that is pictorial rather than typographical. The well-known Droueshout engraving that fronts the First Folio features a fine example of a ruff standing 'in print', and facing Jonson's accompanying verse address 'to the reader'.

Where Jonson's verse invokes the world of print, it does so not to describe the roman and italic fonts of the First Folio but to bemoan the inability of 'the print' to capture Shakespeare's wit, as well as to delineate his likeness: a problematic distinction given that it is precisely Shakespeare's wit which *is* imprinted upon the pages that follow. Both print and writing ('all, that was ever writ in brasse') refer here to the art of the engraver, and are set in opposition to the book they preface: a book to which the reader is asked to turn only when the representative powers of print, as exemplified in an engraved portrait, fail. Paulina, then, may even be describing the baby Perdita as a brass etching of her father's royal countenance. Whether patent, coin or portrait, Paulina's invocation of print raises crucial issues of legitimacy and reliability, particularly in the latter two cases, as the phrase 'to present a copy of one's countenance' meant, until the late eighteenth century, 'to put on a false face, to deceive' (*OED*, 'copy', *n.* 11c). Viewed in the context of the problematic connotations of authority and authenticity, deception and forgery embedded in her chosen metaphor, Paulina's confident declaration of Leontes' paternity becomes a complex attempt to establish legitimacy in terms that consistently cast doubt on the trustworthiness of even the most faithful reproduction. Hers is not a self-evident declaration of truth but a reminder of the difficulty of identifying and testing the illegitimate, making Leontes' continuing jealousy and distrust a dramatically coherent reflection on the potential duplicity of any reproduction.

As well as informing our reading of this small section of *The Winter's Tale*, these connotations can helpfully illuminate our understanding of the ways in which the early modern printing community struggled to establish the faithfulness of its own reproductions. As Adrian Johns has influentially established, early modern stationers were engaged in a difficult series of negotiations around readerly understandings of credit and reliability.[22] The dynamics of Paulina's statement in *The Winter's Tale* suggest that these concerns derived in part from the tensions of a moment of linguistic shift, as the competing meanings of print, with their existing associations of royal authority, the protection of sensitive or dangerous information, economic value, precision, and accurate or inaccurate copying, collided with the new, but related, concerns of the press.

Despite this, two Shakespearean readers, Mistresses Page and Quickly, the eponymous *Merry Wives of Windsor*, do seem to believe that print is a technology of precise and accurate, though not necessarily trustworthy, reproduction. Confessing to each other that they are the recipients of love letters from the lustful Falstaff, the wives quickly realise that their epistles are identical. As Mistress Page complains, in a passage filled, as Patricia Parker points out, 'with figures of reduplication as well as specific invocation of the

geminating power of print': 'I warrant he hath a thousand of these
letters, writ with blank space for different names – sure, more, and
these are of the second edition. He will print them, out of doubt –
for he cares not what he puts into the press when he would put us
two' (2.1.66–70).[23]
Falstaff's handwritten letters to the two wives are so alike that
they might as well be the products of a hand-press as of his hand. As
Elizabeth Pittenger, following Parker, puts it, 'Falstaff's desire, represented by his love letters, runs like a machine, a printing press,
producing identical copies of indiscriminate and unaddressed pro-
posals'.[24] Yet it is not, as Pittenger suggests, the opposition between
duplicitous print and 'the singularity of a love letter written by hand'
which angers the two wives; it is, rather, that no reliable opposition
can be established.[25] The handwritten letter cannot be distinguished
from the typographical epistle. Both operate in a persuasive textual
economy which is suddenly revealed to be capable of endless reproduction, multiplying, and thereby negating, its affective powers.
In the culture of the copy, the category of the genuine has been
collapsed. The divorce revealed between the personal letter and the
undistinguished recipient perhaps reveals a sensitivity to early
modern dedicatory practices that forced a divide between the constructed intimacy of the letter and the publicity of its inclusion in a
printed text: a divide especially apparent in the existence of early
modern printed dedications that could be and were addressed to
more than one recipient. The dedicatory epistle to Walter Baley's
medicinal New-Year's gift book, his *Discourse of Peppers*, was even
printed with blank spaces in which he could later insert, in pen, the
appropriate names and titles of its several recipients.[26]
    Within this scene, the printing press is also sexualised, as the act
of pressing becomes the physical act of love: Falstaff's desire to 'press
us two'. The equation of the operation of the printing press with the
sexual act brings us back to Wendy Wall's influential identification
of the rhetorical strategies by which male prefatory writers femi-
nised the technologies of publication in order to displace class-based
anxieties about the propriety of print on to the already suspect
female form.[27] The male author who 'undergoes a pressing' is tem-
porarily placed in the position of the labouring woman in order to
produce his paper children. In this instance, Falstaff, whose gender
is called into question at numerous points in this play in which he
appears twice as a woman, gets mixed up with the laundry, and is

soundly beaten by Master Ford, attempts to displace the threat of effeminacy on to the bodies of the merry wives, using the strategies of print to try and 'press' them, and, conversely, transforming the threat of a mechanical pressing into the weighty pressure of his own body.

The wives' discussion of the letters appears only in the Folio version of the play, and not in the 1602 quarto printed by Thomas Crown for Arthur Johnson, the second of the quartos to be labelled as 'bad' by W. W. Greg in his 1910 edition of the play.[28] While there are many substantial differences between the two texts, with the quarto standing at roughly half the length of the later Folio edition, it is at least suggestive that it is in its longer, more 'literary' version that the play draws readerly attention to the conditions of its own reproduction, and to the persuasive dangers of print. As *The Winter's Tale* did not appear in print until its 1623 inclusion in the First Folio, we cannot know whether Paulina and Leontes' meditations on print were also prompted by the prospect of folio publication. Hamlet's meditation on his bookish brain contains, in quarto, references to 'the tables of my memory' and 'all sawes of Bookes', but does not invoke the technologies of print, as the Prince swears to wipe away not 'all forms, all pressures past' but 'all triuiall fond conceites / That euer youth, or else obseruance noted'.[29]

Shakespeare's most explicit reference to the social and economic realities of the printing press appears in both quarto and folio versions of *2 Henry VI*. Confronting Lord Saye, the rebel Jack Cade complains: 'Thou hast most traitorously corrupted the youth of the realm in erecting a grammar school; and whereas before our forefathers had no other books but the score and the tally, thou hast caused printing to be used, and contrary to the King his crown, and dignity, thou hast built a paper-mill' (4.7.29–34). By this point in the play, Cade has already attacked the Clerk of Chatham for his activities as a schoolmaster, his ability to sign his name and his possession of a bible, or possibly a school-book, mistaken for a conjuring book because of the red ink used in its printing, and has ordered him to be hanged 'with his pen and inkhorne about his neck' (4.2.102–3). In his prosecution of Saye, Cade goes on to protest that literacy is a tool used to prosecute and punish the poor, turning on its head the benefit of clergy, by which those who could read a verse of the Bible could escape hanging: 'Thou hast appointed justices of peace, to call poor men before them, about matters they were not able to answer.

Moreover, thou hast put them in prison, and because they could not read thou hast hanged them, when indeed only for that cause they have been most worthy to live' (4.7.37–42).

Where Geraldo U. de Sousa argues that 'Shakespeare conflated Jack Cade's Rebellion of 1450 with the Peasant's Revolt of 1381 . . . because he found in the Peasant's Revolt an examination of the power of writing', the introduction of a printing press into a play about an English king who died in 1471, five years before Caxton brought the first press to England, suggests that Shakespeare's Cade is more concerned with the England of the early 1590s than of the 1450s or the 1380s.[30] His anger brings together Elizabethan concerns about the uses of print to regularise education, to impose particular forms of religion through the use of printed bibles and homilies, and to exclude the poor from their traditional rights through a newly literate legalism ('Is this not a lamentable thing', he asks, anticipating Hamlet, 'that of the skin of an innocent lamb should be made parchment; that parchment, being scribbled o'er, should undo a man?' (4.2.73–6)).[31] The play, probably written in 1591, appeared at a point of particular public awareness about issues of print reproduction, following close upon the heels of the flurry of pamphlets penned by the pseudonymous Martin Marprelate to attack church censorship and control of print.[32] These pamphlets also made reference to the Earl of Arundel's manipulation of the press through the offices of John Charlewood, who on several occasions signed himself 'printer to the Earl of Arundel'. Arundel and his wife, like Saye, sponsored a press, though theirs was hidden because of their Catholic sympathies, probably in Spitalfields, where several works of the Jesuit missionary Robert Southwell were printed.

Cade's lines reflect a distinctly Elizabethan sensibility that recognises the structures of power and control inherent in the patronal acts of sponsoring education and promoting a religious vernacular literacy, or of the contemporary impulse toward formalisation and dissemination of key texts. Cade's violent plebeian distrust of the products of the printing press reflects the extent to which books could be and were used as tools of authority and exclusion as much as of education and emancipation, and enrols him in the ranks of those who distrust the bookishness and love of learning that so often characterises Shakespeare's weak rulers. Earlier in the play, York has already anticipated Cade's angry anti-literacy campaign with his own statement 'And force perforce I'll make him yield the crown, / Whose bookish rule hath pulled fair England down' (1.1.256–7), while in *1 Henry VI*, the King himself shies away from the responsibilities of a politic marriage, somewhat prudishly reminding his uncle, 'Alas, my years are young, / And fitter in my study and my books / Than wanton dalliance with a paramour' (5.1.21–3).

Shakespeare draws much of Henry's devotion to religious learning from his chronicle sources, and from the popular representations of the sanctified king as a devout reader that contributed to the sixteenth-century 'cult of Henry VI'.[33] In the chronicles, Cade is himself suspected of a suspicious textual intimacy, being 'suborned by techers', and 'enforced by pryvye scholemasters', and using conjuring books to further his cause, but Shakespeare removes these associations to make his rebel leader thoroughly unlettered.[34] In placing his most virulent attacks upon learning in the mouth of the violent, cruel and ultimately unsuccessful Cade, he is aligning both York and the Elizabethan censors with ignorant plebeian instincts, and with the disorder and brutality of rebellion.

Elsewhere in the plays, however, it is the term 'press' that carries the overtones of violence and crowd movement that are here displaced on to those who distrust the world of print. *Julius Caesar* describes the Roman crowds as 'the Press' (1.2.15) while the third gentleman in *Henry VIII* uses the same term to describe the mass of people who come to Westminster Abbey to observe Anne Boleyn (4.1.78). Conversely, the term 'press' also implies secrecy: both objects and people, like Giacomo in *Cymbeline*, are concealed within presses, large wooden chests. Press or impress also describes the unpopular practice of forced conscription, bringing together Bacon's concern with literary innovation and with the art of war. In *1 Henry IV*, Falstaff ruefully admits 'I pressed me none but such toasts and butter, with hearts in their bellies no bigger than pin's heads, and they have bought out their services' (4.2.20–2). In a cognate sense, to press may also mean violent persuasion, exemplified in Portia's exclamation 'You press me far and therefore I will yield' (*The Merchant of Venice*, 4.1.423). As the punning of the merry wives suggests, pressing may refer to sexual reproduction but it may also mean a pressing to death, two senses brought playfully together in Pandarus' darkly prophetic promise to Troilus and Cressida: 'I will show you a chamber, with a bed; which bed, because it shall not speak of your pretty encounters, press it to death' (3.2.204–5).

A potentially violent move into fixity and closure is similarly mocked by Hero when she complains in *Much Ado* that Beatrice 'would laugh me / Out of myself, press me to death with wit' (3.1.75–6), but is given more pathos in *Richard II* when the dispossessed Queen reflects on her impotency and powerlessness, complaining 'O, I am pressed to death through want of speaking' (3.4.72). The inability to express oneself becomes a pressure from without; the inability to produce a verbal text transforms the act of pressing into a cruel and sterile act of torture.

The vocabulary of the printing press in early modern England occupied the same linguistic space as a number of persistent earlier meanings: meanings which continued to inform the terms of textual production, and which complicate our understanding of early modern textual cultures. While the vocabulary of mechanical reproduction undoubtedly added to the linguistic field of the terms 'print' and 'press', it did not immediately or entirely displace earlier connotations which continued to shadow the terms of the typographic process. The connection made in the examples above between pressing and a violent death is one that haunts early modern thinking about textual production. Besides the (sometimes problematic) promise of birth and parental continuity identified by critics like Douglas Brooks, textual reproduction threatens stillness and fixity: a violent pressing that kills the text as it brings it into being.[35]

More than this, the connection between textual reproduction and death or decay is one embedded in the very materials of textual creation, whether manuscript or print, in the repeated invocation of the ineradicable darkness of ink. In *Cymbeline*, Pisanio curses Leonatus' letter ordering him to murder Imogen, describing it as a 'damn'd paper / Black as the ink that's on thee' (3.2.19–20). In *Much Ado About Nothing*, the seemingly dead and dishonoured Hero has, we are told, 'fall'n / Into a pit of ink, that the wide sea / Hath drops too few to wash her clean again' (4.1.138–40). Middleton describes his woes as 'the blotty inky lines of sin', and complains 'Black sins, I dim you all with inky smother'.[36] As a material of absolute blackness, ink is inevitably imbued with the hues of mourning and loss – it is the fabric of Hamlet's 'inky cloak', and it is inescapably connected to notions of poison, tarnish and decay.

In part, this may be a result of ink's material make-up, compounded as it was of gall and wormwood, and, as De Grazia and Stallybrass remind us, sometimes of even less pleasant ingredients:

'the words of what was to become a classic text were printed in an ink that mingled not only ingredients like juniper gum, linseed oil, and lampblack but also the residual traces of the urine of the printshop workers, who each night used urine to soak the leather casing of the balls that inked the press'.[37] These unpleasant ingredients tainted the word they went to produce, as the gall and acid of the ink became associated with the vitriol of the author. Thus Sir Toby in *Twelfth Night* encourages Sir Andrew Aguecheek, 'Let there be gall enough in thy ink, though thou write with a goose pen, no matter: about it' (3.2.47–9).

In *Cymbeline*, Posthumus anticipates his own bitterness, itself the product of misreading, telling Imogen: 'write, my queen, / And with mine eyes I'll drink the words you send, / Though ink be made of gall' (1.2.30–2). Later in the play, this imagined poison is literalised when Pisanio notes, in fear, 'the paper / Hath cut her throat already' (3.4.31–2), as Posthumus' letter threatens to perform, in the shock of its unpalatable news, the murder Pisanio has been commanded to commit. Elsewhere in the plays, it is a misdelivered text, disguised by a false print, which condemns Rosencrantz and Guildenstern to death, while Wolsey, in *Henry VIII*, is forced to read the papers which lead to his execution, concluding, as he does so, 'this paper has undone me' (3.2.210).

The associations of text with death are enacted in a profoundly moving manner in Richard Brathwait's *Anniversaries upon his Panarete*, which anticipates Laurence Sterne's paratextual games in a mournful dedication to the memory of his wife, Frances. 'Look not upon me, for I am black', the apocryphal text commands, and the ink-soaked, blacked-out page stands as a textual tombstone and memorial to Brathwait's loss.[38] On a less personal level, the genres of elegy, epitaph, funeral sermon and *ars moriendi* were staples of the Elizabethan and Jacobean trade in printed books, and John Taylor, the water poet, claimed to be wrapping all of England in an inky cloak when he prefaced his 1612 elegy, *Great Britaine, all in blacke. For the incomparable losse of Henry, our late worthy prince*, with a similarly heavily inked title-page. So too, there is a profound sense of posthumousness about many early modern texts which only made the transition from manuscript to print upon or after the death of their author. Perhaps Shakespeare's recognition that ink may at once reveal and stain, reproduce and destroy, may suggest a foreshadowing of his own engraved entombment in the pages of the First Folio. Certainly his

continued reference to the technologies of print and manuscript production, and to the dangers and promises of the written word, suggest
a profound sensitivity to early modern textual culture.
Pondering this sensitivy, Jonas Barish identifies

> [A] paradox in the fact that Shakespeare, so notoriously indifferent to
> the printing of his plays, and apparently so unconcerned about writing
> letters . . . should nevertheless in his plays be so endlessly and inven-
> tively preoccupied with written communication of all kinds, have
> worked it so profoundly into the blood and bone of his plots.[39]

If, however, we take into account Lukas Erne's insistence that
Shakespeare was concerned with the appearance of his plays in both
manuscript and print, the prevalence of textual matters and materials in his plays and poems ceases to seem a paradox, and serves
instead to proclaim the plays' interest in the modes of publication
and circulation in which they were destined to participate. It also
proclaims their author's interest in texts as material objects, circulating between people, and being used for numerous purposes, purposes which included, but were not limited, to reading. Shakespeare,
it seems, is not only a bard of the boards, exploring the limits of 'this
stage-play world', but a playwright of the page, well aware that his
plays, like the indictment of 'the good Lord Hastings' in *King
Richard III*, are set to circulate as texts, texts that 'may be today read
o'er in Paul's' (3.6.3), and may tomorrow be collected in a folio
edition addressing itself 'to the great Variety of Readers'. In his
attention to textual matters, and to the detailed etymological her-
itage of the terms of the press, Shakespeare reveals himself to be a
precise man, a neat man, an exact man: not necessarily a printed
man, but certainly '*a man in print*'.

Notes

All references to the works of Shakespeare are to *The Arden Shakespeare
Complete Works*, edited by Richard Proudfoot, Ann Thompson and David
Scott Kastan, rev. edn (London: Thomson Learning, 2001) unless otherwise
indicated.

1 Francis Bacon, *The New Organon and Related Writings*, ed.
  F. Anderson (New York: Liberal Arts Press, 1960), p. 118.
2 See particularly Elizabeth L. Eisenstein, *The Printing Press as an Agent
  of Change*, 2 vols (Cambridge: Cambridge University Press, 1979);
  Marshall McLuhan, *The Gutenberg Galaxy: The Making of*

Typographic Man (Toronto: University of Toronto Press, 1962); Walter J. Ong, *Orality and Literacy: The Technologizing of the Word*, 2nd edn (London: Routledge, 2002).

3 Cecile Jagodzinski, *Privacy and Print: Reading and Writing in Seventeenth-Century England* (Charlottesville and London: University Press of Virginia, 1999), p. 18.

4 See, for example, Peter Beal, *In Praise of Scribes: Manuscripts and their Makers in Seventeenth-Century England* (Oxford: Clarendon Press, 1998); Adam Fox, *Oral and Literate Culture in England, 1500–1700* (Oxford: Oxford University Press, 2000); Harold Love, *Scribal Publication in Seventeenth-Century England* (Oxford: Clarendon Press, 1993), rpt. as *The Culture and Commerce of Texts: Scribal Publication in Seventeenth-Century England* (Amherst: University of Massachusetts Press, 1998); David McKitterick, *Print, Manuscript and the Search for Order* (Cambridge: Cambridge University Press, 2003); Henry R. Woudhuysen, *Sir Philip Sidney and the Circulation of Manuscripts* (Oxford: Clarendon Press, 1996).

5 See Peter Blayney, 'The Publication of Playbooks', in John D. Cox and David Scott Kastan (eds), *A New History of Early English Drama* (New York: Columbia University Press, 1997), pp. 383–423; Richard Dutton, 'The Birth of the Author', in Cedric C. Brown and Arthur F. Marotti (eds), *Texts and Cultural Change in Early Modern England* (New York: St Martin's Press, Inc., 1997), pp. 153–78; Lukas Erne, *Shakespeare as Literary Dramatist* (Cambridge: Cambridge University Press, 2003); Laurie E. Maguire, *Shakespearean Suspect Texts: The 'Bad' Quartos and Their Contexts* (Cambridge: Cambridge University Press, 1996); Paul Werstine, 'Narratives About Printed Shakespeare Texts: "Foul Papers" and "Bad" Quartos', *Shakespeare Quarterly*, 41 (1990), 65–86.

6 Nicholas Robins, 'The Script's the Thing', review of *Shakespeare as Literary Dramatist*, *Times Literary Supplement*, 7 November 2003, p. 10.

7 See, for example Lionel Abel, *Metatheatre: A New View of Dramatic Form* (New York: Hill and Wang, 1963), and *Tragedy and Metatheatre*, ed. Martin Puchner (New York: Holmes and Meier, 2003); James L. Calderwood, *Shakespeare's Metadrama* (Minneapolis: University of Minnesota Press, 1971), and *Metadrama in Shakespeare's Henriad: 'Richard II' to 'Henry V'* (Berkeley: University of California Press, 1979); Hubert D. Judd, *Metatheater: The Example of Shakespeare* (Lincoln: University of Nebraska Press, 1991); R. J. Nelson, *Play Within the Play: The Dramatist's Conception of his Art, Shakespeare to Anouilh* (New Haven: Yale University Press, 1958); Anne Righter, *Shakespeare and the Idea of the Play* (London: Chatto and Windus, 1962); J. L. Styan, *Shakespeare's Stagecraft* (Cambridge: Cambridge University Press, 1975).

8 Righter, *Shakespeare and the Idea of the Play*, p. 81.

9 Faced with the news of Antony's death, for example, Caesar's response, indicative of the increasingly textual legalism of the Elizabethan period, is to invite his companions: 'Go with me to my Tent, where you shall see / How hardly I was drawne into this Warre, / How calme and gentle I proceeded still / In all my Writings. Go with me, and see / What I can shew in this' (5.1.73–6).

10 Hamlet is also drawing upon the early modern understanding of 'print' as 'an image or character stamped upon the mind or soul' (*OED*, 'print', *n.*, 2a), and this relates his 'book and volume' to the 'books of conscience' discussed by both ancient and Renaissance writers. For a further discussion of the textuality of *Hamlet* see P. K. Ayers, 'Reading, Writing, and Hamlet', *Shakespeare Quarterly*, 44 (1993), 423–39; for books of conscience see Frederick Kiefer, '"Written Troubles of the Brain": Lady Macbeth's Conscience', in David M. Bergeron (ed.), *Reading and Writing in Shakespeare* (Newark: University of Delaware Press, 1996), pp. 64–81.

11 See Jonas Barish, '"Soft, here follows prose": Shakespeare's Stage Documents', in Murray Biggs et al. (eds), *The Arts of Performance in Elizabethan and Early Stuart Drama: Essays for G. K. Hunter* (Edinburgh: Edinburgh University Press, 1991), pp. 32–48; Bergeron (ed.), *Reading and Writing in Shakespeare*; Ernst Robert Curtius, *European Literature in the Latin Middle Ages*, tr. Willard P. Trask (New York: Pantheon, 1953), esp. pp. 332–40; Jerome Mazzaro, 'Shakespeare's "Books of Memory": *1* and *2 Henry VI*', *Comparative Drama*, 35 (2001–2), 393–414; Ian Munro, 'Shakespeare's Jestbook: Wit, Print, Performance', *ELH*, 71 (2004), 89–113; Frederick Kiefer, *Writing on the Renaissance Stage: Written Words, Printed Pages, Metaphoric Books* (Newark: University of Delaware Press, 1996); Robert S. Knapp, *Shakespeare: The Theater and the Book* (Princeton: Princeton University Press, 1989).

12 John Pitcher, 'Literature, the Playhouse and the Public', in John Barnard and D. F. McKenzie (eds), and Maureen Bell (assistant ed.), *The Cambridge History of the Book in Britain, Vol. IV, 1557–1695* (Cambridge: Cambridge University Press, 2002), p. 352.

13 *The Two Gentlemen of Verona*, 1.1.21–2; *Twelfth Night*, 4.2.12–16; *Much Ado About Nothing*, 2.1.121–3.

14 Barbara A. Mowat, 'Prospero's Book', *Shakespeare Quarterly*, 52 (2001), 1–33.

15 As Stephen Booth points out, the word 'books' may, for Shakespeare, mean as little as 'a single sheet of paper with writing on it' (*Shakespeare's Sonnets* (New Haven: Yale University Press, 1977), p. 172). It may also, of course, mean as much as the 'whole volumes in folio' invoked by Armado in *Love's Labour's Lost* (1.2.180).

16 Cf. Geraldo U. de Sousa, who suggests that 'Margaret understands the power and permanence of writing. She wants to print her kisses on the body of Suffolk' ('The Peasant's Revolt and the Writing of History', in Bergeron [ed.], *Reading and Writing*, p. 182).

17 Cf. Wendy Wall, who argues: 'In Sonnet 11, the speaker suggests that . . . economic metaphors have a correlative in tropes of printing. Arguing generally for an amplification that stands for both reproduction and circulation, he advises, "Thou shouldst print more, not let that coppy die"' (*The Imprint of Gender: Authorship and Publication in the English Renaissance* (Ithaca: Cornell University Press, 1993), p. 196). For a detailed exploration of the trope of wax and seal, and its semantic connections to issues of sexual, as well as textual, reproduction, see Margreta de Grazia, 'Imprints: Shakespeare, Gutenberg, and Descartes', in Douglas A. Brooks (ed.), *Printing and Parenting in Early Modern England* (Aldershot: Ashgate, 2005), 29–58.

18 See Thomas Laqueur, *Making Sex: Body and Gender from the Greeks to Freud* (Cambridge, MA: Harvard University Press, 1992), esp. pp. 45–52. Laqueur also points out that during pregnancy a mother was believed to have the ability to stamp the features of her child, particularly if she felt strong desires or experienced a sudden shock.

19 Wall, *Imprint*, pp. 1–2.

20 Thomas Middleton, *Blurt Master Constable, or the Spaniards Night-Walke* (London: Printed [by Edward Allde] for Henry Rockytt, 1602), sig. E4v.

21 Henry Peacham, *The garden of eloquence conteining the most excellent ornaments, exornations, lightes, flowers, and formes of speech, commonly called the figures of rhetorike* (London: Printed by R[ichard] F[ield] for H. Iackson, 1593), sigs I3r; I4v.

22 See Adrian Johns, *The Nature of the Book: Print and Knowledge in the Making* (Chicago and London: University of Chicago Press, 1998).

23 Patricia Parker, *Literary Fat Ladies: Rhetoric, Gender, Property* (London and New York: Methuen, 1987), p. 74.

24 Elizabeth Pittenger, 'Dispatch Quickly: The Mechanical Reproduction of Pages', *Shakespeare Quarterly*, 42 (1991), p. 394. For Pittenger, this concern with textual reproduction structures the play in its entirety: 'What is striking about *MWW* is that it contains a representation of attitudes toward mechanical reproduction (in the scene in which the wives read Falstaff's letters); and because it figures the mechanical and material conditions similar to those that enable its own production as a literary object, the text calls attention to its materiality as a written, produced, and printed play; this feature makes the textual questions of *MWW* especially complex and makes the materiality of the text (e.g., in its typographic and orthographic specificity) especially legible. In this

play about a family of Pages and about the circulation of pages – both letters and boys – the emphasis on material pages takes on a thematic and reflexive density' (pp. 407–8).

25 Pittenger, 'Dispatch Quickly', p. 394.

26 Baley's practice is to some degree unusual in that he makes no attempt to conceal the generic nature of his epistle. Other writers were less transparent. A well-known example is Lambeth Palace Library's holding of six copies of Abraham Darcie's *The honour of ladies* which contain blank spaces at the head of the epistles, waiting for the printed addition of dedicatees who later included Anna Sophia Dormer, Susan Herbert, Bridget Norris and Elizabeth Stanley. On a more seemingly personal note, Margaret Maurer records that 'six years ago, readers of Samuel Daniel's verse epistles had to acknowledge an embarrassing discovery. Arthur Freeman published evidence in *Library* that the epistle to Margaret, Countess of Cumberland, was at one time, and with very few changes, intended for another noblewoman, Lady Elizabeth Hatton of Purbeck. What had seemed an improbable possibility was a demonstrable fact. Daniel's epistles, elevated and apparently so heartfelt, were capable of, if not designed for, dedication to whatever person suited the poet's needs' (Margaret Maurer, 'Samuel Daniel's Poetical Epistles, Especially Those to Sir Thomas Egerton and Lucy, Countess of Bedford', *Studies in Philology*, 74 (1977), p. 418).

27 Wall, *Imprint*, esp. pp. 219–20.

28 W. W. Greg (ed.), *Merry Wives of Windsor* (Oxford: Clarendon, 1910).

29 William Shakespeare, *The tragicall historie of Hamlet Prince of Denmarke* (London: Printed [by Valentine Simmes] for N[icholas] L[ing] and Iohn Trundell, 1603), sig. C3r.

30 De Sousa, 'The Peasant's Revolt', p. 185.

31 For a discussion of contemporary concerns about the loss of traditional rights as a result of a growing dependence on written and printed evidence, rather than the evidence of memory, see Fox, *Oral and Literate Culture*, esp. pp. 259–98.

32 For details of the Marprelate controversy, as read within a revisionist study of Elizabethan press censorship, see Cyndia Susan Clegg, *Press Censorship in Elizabethan England* (Cambridge: Cambridge University Press, 1997), pp. 170–97.

33 See Leigh Ann Craig, 'Royalty, Virtue, and Adversity: The Cult of King Henry VI', *Albion*, 35 (2003), 187–209.

34 Geoffrey Bullough (ed.), *Narrative and Dramatic Sources of Shakespeare*, vol. 3 (London: Routledge and Kegan Paul, 1960), p. 114.

35 The linguistic uncertainty and multiple connotations of 'print' suggest that Brooks is rather overstating his case when he insists what seems 'new and significant about Shakespeare and his contemporaries . . . is

that they rely chiefly on the lexicon of the printing press and the early modern book trade to express these widespread and long-standing pre-occupations [with questions of legitimacy and paternity]' (Brooks, 'Introduction', in Brooks (ed.), *Printing and Parenting*, p. 10).

36 Thomas Middleton, *Wisdom of Solomon Paraphrased*, cited in Wendy Wall, 'Reading for the Blot: Textual Desire in Early Modern English Literature', in Bergeron (ed.), *Reading and Writing*, pp. 131–59. Wall goes on to unpick the multiple connotations of gender, social status and race that Shakespeare packs in to the figure of 'ink'.

37 Margreta de Grazia and Peter Stallybrass, 'The Materiality of the Shakespearean Text', *Shakespeare Quarterly*, 44 (1993), pp. 281–2.

38 Richard Brathwaite, *Anniversaries upon his Panarete* (London, 1634), sig. A1v.

39 Barish, '"Soft, here follows prose"', p. 34.

3

'Penn'd speech': seeing and not seeing in *King Lear*

Richard Meek

In the final scene of *Love's Labour's Lost*, one of Shakespeare's earliest and most self-consciously 'literary' plays, the Princess of France announces that she will refuse to dance with the men, and will treat their play-within-a-play with disdain: 'No, to the death we will not move a foot, / Nor to their penn'd speech render we no grace, / But while 'tis spoke each turn away her face' (5.2.146–8).[1] This fascinating description of dramatic utterances as 'penn'd speech' hints at Shakespeare's awareness of the paradoxical nature of words spoken in dramatic works: that they are always *penned* ('Written (with a pen); set down in writing' (*OED*, ppl.a.[2])) as well as spoken. These words are, after all, spoken by the Princess of France, herself a character in a play; and while the Princess's phrase ostensibly describes the language of the pageant that concludes *Love's Labour's Lost*, it also refers to the entire linguistic fabric of *Love's Labour's Lost* itself – including, of course, the Princess's own utterance. This passage thus raises a wider question concerning the way in which we – as readers and audiences – conceive of dramatic works: are we, like the Princess, always aware of the writtenness of Shakespeare's plays, even when we experience them in performance? Often when we read a play, we try to imagine a performance of it, but perhaps the reverse of this is also true: when we see a play at the theatre, are we always conscious that somewhere offstage there is a script that we could be reading? In this chapter I explore the textuality of Shakespearean drama via a reading of *King Lear*, a play that – like *Love's Labour's Lost* – contains an unusually large number of epistles and other stage documents.[2] The chapter argues that *King Lear* is preoccupied with the relationship between seeing, hearing and reading, and that these different modes of experience comment upon our experience of the play. In other words, *King Lear* raises the intriguing possibility that Shakespeare was himself interested in the larger questions that the present volume is addressing: do his plays work as well on the page as they do on the stage? Did he write with readers in mind? What might *King Lear*'s concern with the relationship between seeing, hearing and reading tell us about the relationship between text and performance?

Harry Berger Jr, a critic whose work has been much concerned with the relationship between text and performance, has argued that 'textuality is deeply woven into Shakespeare's language and its dramatic practice. It preexisted quarto and folio; perhaps it generated them out of the transtheatrical necessities of its practice.'[3] Certainly the First Folio of 1623 was conceived of as a reading text: in their address 'To the great Variety of Readers', Heminge and Condell enjoin us to 'Reade him, therefore; and againe and againe'.[4] As David M. Bergeron has commented, 'This ringing plea for a reader response also underlines a crucial matter of interpretation: the continuous, ongoing process of reading. This extraordinary argument from two actors puts into healthy perspective the legitimate activity of reading and interpreting Shakespeare without insisting that he can only be known from performance.'[5] Heminge and Condell's address thus serves as a powerful rejoinder to those critics who argue that 'the *real* play is the performance, not the text',[6] and reminds us that Shakespeare's plays were being read – and, indeed, reread – by the same people who might have seen and heard the plays' earliest performances. Yet Harry Berger is right to insist that the textuality of the plays *pre-existed* quarto and folio. Most dramatic works originate with a text which a dramatist writes and which actors read, but the fact that Shakespeare's plays themselves contain many figured and explicit acts of reading, and many long narrative passages that are often cut in performance, suggests that Shakespeare was fascinated by the textuality of his plays, and by the possibility of their being read in the manner of his published narrative poems *Venus and Adonis* (1593) and *The Rape of Lucrece* (1594).[7]

Lukas Erne has convincingly argued that Shakespeare 'could not help knowing that his plays were being read and reread, printed and reprinted, excerpted and anthologized as he was writing more plays'.[8] Yet, as Patrick Cheney and Helen Smith have suggested in their chapters in the present volume, we might extend Erne's notion of Shakespeare as 'literary' dramatist by considering the numerous acts of reading that Shakespeare depicts *within* his plays.[9] This fascination with reading and writing suggests that Shakespeare was continually reflecting upon the relationship of the texts that he wrote – the literal inscription of characters upon a page – to their eventual execution in performance. It is particularly suggestive, for example, that one of Shakespeare's characters describes himself as 'a scribbled form, drawn with a pen / Upon a parchment' (King John, 5.7.32–3). Not only, then, are the words of Shakespeare's plays 'penn'd', but also some of the fictional men and women who inhabit his plays seem to display an uncanny awareness that they, too, are written, or merely 'characters'. In this way, a play like King Lear – in its preoccupation with texts and reading – is perhaps typical of Shakespeare's dramatic works inasmuch as it repeatedly 'returns to its origins in the script'.[10] Moreover, while the play often seems to demonstrate the persuasiveness of what we see, implying a pro-theatrical bias, it also points to the problems and limitations of visual representation, and the capacity of narrative descriptions to make us 'see' what drama cannot. Throughout King Lear, different modes of representation – visual, verbal and written – are rendered duplicitous and problematic, as if the play is implicitly questioning any fixed hierarchy between text and performance, or even suggesting that the two are not as different as they at first appear to be.

As many critics have noted, there is a continual emphasis upon 'seeing' in King Lear, and there are many references to both literal and metaphorical blindness, including Kent's 'See better, Lear' (1.1.159) and Gloucester's 'I stumbled when I saw' (4.1.21).[11] In the play's opening scene, Goneril implies that seeing is the most valuable of the senses when she claims that she loves her father 'Dearer than eyesight . . . Beyond what can be valued' (1.1.56–7).[12] Yet the play often asks whether seeing something is genuinely more valuable than having others tell us about it, or perhaps by extension, reading about it. Several of the play's most distinguished critics have argued that the play is better if we don't see it performed. Charles Lamb, for example, preferred to internalise the play, believing that we can experience the tragedy more 'directly' through the solitary experience of reading: 'On the stage we see nothing but corporeal infirmities and weaknesses, the impotence of rage; while we read it, we see not Lear, but we are Lear, we are in his mind.' Lamb concludes that 'Lear is essentially impossible to be represented on a stage'.[13] In his account of the play in Shakespearean Tragedy (1904), A. C. Bradley also argued that the play should be read rather than seen, writing that '*King Lear* is too huge for the stage'.[14] For Bradley, the play is unperformable: the blinding of Gloucester on stage is 'revolting and shocking', he writes, but 'it is otherwise in reading' (p. 251). By reading the play we experience what Bradley calls 'the wider or universal significance of the spectacle presented to the inward eye' (p. 269). *King Lear* is, we learn, 'one of the world's greatest poems' (p. 277). Bradley, then, wishes to experience the play as a 'spectacle', but one that is presented to his 'inward eye'. But what is so interesting about *King Lear* is that one of its characters finds himself in an analogous position to the one that Bradley describes – blinded, Gloucester can only experience the world in what Hamlet refers to as the 'mind's eye' (1.2.185). Bradley would prefer to experience the scene of Gloucester's blinding without actually seeing it, almost as if he would rather be blinded himself.[15] The blinding of Gloucester in 3.7 is an immensely visual scene, a spectacle of violence that almost demands to be seen; but it is also a scene about blinding, about preventing someone from seeing. One might argue that there is something self-reflexive about a scene in which a theatre audience watches someone having their eyes removed, as if the play is committing an act of violence upon our eyes as well. Yet even before he is blinded, the question of what Gloucester can and cannot see is a central concern of the play, as Shakespeare reveals the potential duplicitousness of written texts, spoken narratives and visual signs. This is explored in Edmund's various attempts to hoodwink Gloucester and Edgar, which, as we shall see below, anticipate Edgar's later deception of his father and his extended narrative description of Dover cliff.

In the second scene of the play, Edmund uses a forged letter to dupe his father into believing that Edgar means to assassinate him. By telling his father that the text he holds is 'nothing', Edmund manages to convince his father of its importance: 'The quality of nothing hath not such need to hide itself. Let's see. – Come, if it be nothing, I shall not need spectacles' (1.2.34–6). In this way, Edmund manages to give the letter the quality of something, and Gloucester assumes that this text – which Edmund hides from his sight – is worth reading, failing to entertain the possibility that it might be counterfeit. Gloucester repeatedly demands to see the letter – 'Let's see, let's see' (1.2.43) – with what Sigurd Burckhardt has called 'an ignoble greediness for "the real thing"'.[16] Burckhardt continues:

'Determined as he is to distrust the direct word, [Gloucester] is at the mercy of report, of hearsay, of signs. With this scene, the letter becomes the emblem of the illicit and dangerously mediate' (p. 242). On the one hand, we are reminded that texts do not always offer a faithful account of the reality they purport to represent; but, on the other hand, Edmund's forged letter brilliantly generates the illusion of a real, absent author; as the letter states, 'Come to me, that of this I may speak more' (1.2.51–2). This phrase creates the sense both that the fictional Edgar has more to say, but also that this letter is somehow 'spoken'; that there is an authentic, speaking author behind the letter's forged handwriting. Edmund goes on to suggest that he will allow his father to overhear his conversation with Edgar, so that Gloucester will 'by an auricular assurance have [his] satisfaction' (1.2.91–2): the letter will be backed up by the immediacy of spoken and overheard words.

However, it becomes clear that spoken words are not to be trusted either, as Edmund is equally adept at creating persuasive oral fictions. Edmund informs Edgar that he has offended their father, and that he should stay out of his sight. But Edmund convinces Edgar of the veracity of his tale by stating that he has not been able to convey the authenticity of the event; that there is more to be said: 'Brother, I advise you to the best, ^Qgo armed.^Q I am no honest man if there be any good meaning toward you. I have told you what I have seen and heard – but faintly; nothing like the image and horror of it. Pray you, away!' (1.2.170–4). Edmund has attempted to convey his experience of the event – 'what I have seen and heard' – but he has only done so 'faintly'; it is merely a retelling of the 'actual' events. Edmund apologises for his inability to represent the thing itself: but, by admitting the insubstantiality of his account, he distracts Edgar from the fact that there were no actual events in the first place. Edmund's report is a lie, but it succeeds in tricking Edgar into making something out of nothing by making him complicit in this imaginative enterprise. Edmund admits that his brief description does not have the visual immediacy – or the aural distinctiveness – of the thing itself; it is 'nothing like the image and horror of it'. Here, Edmund uses the figure of hendiadys to describe this 'horrifying picture',[17] but the effect of his rhetorical flourish is to separate the words 'image' and 'horror' in such a way that the phrase anticipates the exchange between Kent and Edgar in the play's final scene: 'Is this the promised end? . . . Or image of that horror?' (5.3.261–2).

Edgar's description, then, not only prefigures the final scene's tragic 'tableau' but also relates to the play's attempts to create a 'horrifying picture' through language. And yet, the horrifying picture that Edmund describes never existed in the first place. If we draw a parallel between Edmund's artistry and that of the playwright, as this verbal echo invites us to, the implication is that Shakespeare's dramatic art is also a lie; an illusion. We might, then, suggest that Edmund and Edgar – both of whom construct morally questionable narratives – can be seen as figures for the playwright, and that Shakespeare uses these two characters to explore and interrogate his own artistry.[18]

Edmund's trickery suggests that a text and a verbal report are no substitute for the thing itself; and yet, for Gloucester and Edgar, this adds a greater plausibility to the two 'original' events that have never existed: Edgar's writing of the letter and 'the heat of [Gloucester's] displeasure' (1.2.160). In a later scene, Edmund offers Gloucester a false report of Edgar: 'Here he stood in the dark, his sharp sword out, / Mumbling of wicked charms, conjuring the moon / To stand^{Q}'s^{Q} auspicious mistress' (2.1.38–40). Edmund then uses his own blood as visual 'evidence' of this encounter: 'Look, sir, I bleed' (2.1.41). Here, Edmund's own body becomes a sign of Edgar's reported evil. But this use of 'seen' evidence suggests that even visual signs can be false, and that their meaning is dependent upon the way in which they are contextualised verbally. The act that caused Edmund to bleed remains merely reported; and Edmund's reportage here substitutes for Gloucester's direct observation of the event. In this way, seeing, hearing and reading are all revealed to be immensely persuasive, but also problematic and potentially deceptive. These problems of representation are heightened when Gloucester is blinded, and we find that the supposedly 'truer' of Gloucester's sons, Edgar, does not construct reliable representations of the world either.

We might have expected Edgar's narratives to be more truthful than those of his brother, but when Edgar says that he will take Gloucester to Dover in 4.6, he subjects his father to an act of deception even more elaborate than Edmund's verbal falsehoods. Edgar's narrative has caused much debate amongst critics: it is designed to deceive the blinded Gloucester in order to prevent his attempting suicide, but how is the audience supposed to react to it? What, precisely, is being described here?

Come on, sir, here's the place. Stand still: how fearful
And dizzy 'tis to cast one's eyes so low.
The crows and choughs that wing the midway air
Show scarce so gross as beetles. Half-way down
Hangs one that gathers samphire, dreadful trade;
Methinks he seems no bigger than his head.
The fishermen that walk upon the beach
Appear like mice, and yon tall anchoring barque
Diminished to her cock, her cock a buoy
Almost too small for sight. The murmuring surge
That on th'unnumbered idle pebble chafes,
Cannot be heard so high. I'll look no more,
Lest my brain turn and the deficient sight
Topple down headlong.

                                              (4.6.11–24)

At first hearing, or at first reading, this passage appears to be a fine
example of Shakespeare's narrative art, conveying to us the absent
Dover cliff.[19] However, this piece of narrative is a rhetorical trick;
Edgar is creating a fiction that is designed to seduce his blinded father.
And indeed, critics who have attempted to describe our response to
this passage have come up with a variety of different readings.
William H. Matchett has written that 'modern critics continue to call
this the Dover cliff scene, though (in spite of the fact that Lear and
Gloucester must be near Dover when they meet) the logic of the scene
turns out to indicate that the cliff is precisely where Edgar has *not*
taken his father. The poetic description is so convincing that, in
naming the cliff, we continue to be taken in by the trick.'[20] For
Matchett, then, Edgar's description is so seductive and 'convincing'
that it is difficult not to be taken in by it. On the other hand, some
critics remain adamant that we are *not* taken in by Edgar's narrative.
Richard Fly has written that 'the entire episode, despite its fine evo-
cation of graphic particularity, demonstrates a general inadequacy of
apprehension . . . We never forget that the entirety of Edgar's speech
is finally an artful structuring of nothing because a felt absence per-
meates the whole elaborate deception.'[21] Similarly, Robert Egan comments that 'We are never allowed to forget that the entire project rests
on the deception and manipulation of a blindman and the substitution of illusory falsehood for experiential truth'.[22] But perhaps these
critics are too certain about what we do or do not forget, and our
response to Edgar's narrative is more complex and ambivalent than

they suggest.[23] We know that his description is an illusion, and yet in order to conceptualise the scene that Edgar describes – and to consider the impact of this description upon Gloucester – readers or audience members must allow themselves to be seduced by the verbal surface of Edgar's narrative.[24] The play seems to be explicitly calling attention to the way in which Edgar is creating an illusion – Shakespeare exposes Edgar's narrative art as a kind of 'nothing'. Yet Edgar's description reminds us that the narrative passages in Shakespeare's dramatic works have *always* been an illusion. Here we are asked to think about the illusion itself and *not* the thing that it represents. But what, then, do we actually 'see' here?

Edgar's description appears to be characterised by absence, as every attempt at describing something is immediately complicated or undermined. Indeed, this description employs some of the 'intangling' effects described by Stanley Fish in his classic account of Milton's *Paradise Lost*, in which the reader is ensnared, or confused, by Milton's complex metaphors that often seem designed to complicate the reader's original interpretation.[25] This suggests that this passage of the play is, to use Harry Berger's term, 'overwritten' from a performance point of view, and that it demands reading and *re*reading.[26] For example, as soon as we have imagined choughs and crows, we are told that they 'Show scarce so gross as beetles' (4.6.14).[27] Presumably we are being asked to imagine jackdaws and crows that are *as small as* beetles, but do we also imagine beetles themselves? The man gathering samphire is 'no bigger than his head' (4.6.16). Edgar could be suggesting that, seen from above, all that can be seen of the man is his head, but on a more literal level this description sounds somewhat peculiar. We are then asked to imagine fishermen walking on the beach, only to be told that they 'Appear like mice' (4.6.18). Once again, this simile further complicates what we 'see': in other words, do we see mice or men? Edgar's description, then, threatens to expose the mechanics of its own similes and metaphors. We are being asked to imagine what Gloucester will imagine as a result of Edgar's narrative, but at the same time its metaphorical descriptions obscure – or, at the very least, complicate – any picture of the scene that we might have in our minds.

Furthermore, it is worth noting that everything Edgar describes is either obscured, or should not be looked at, or 'suffers a diminution in scale', as if to reflect or represent Gloucester's blindness.[28] Edgar says that it makes him feel 'fearful' and 'dizzy' looking down so low

(4.6.11–12), but the following description certainly seems intended to dizzy the mind: 'yon tall anchoring barque / Diminished to her cock, her cock a buoy / Almost too small for sight' (4.6.18–20). We are asked to imagine a tall barque (a small sailing vessel), which is 'diminished to her cock' (4.6.19). Cock here refers to 'A small ship's-boat, *esp.* the small boat which is often towed behind a coasting vessel or ship going up or down river' (*OED*, 'cock-boat'). Does this mean that, according to Edgar, this ship appears to be as small as its cock-boat, or that we can only see this cock-boat? Either way, the boat that we imagine is then renamed as a 'buoy', which, we finally discover, is 'Almost too small for sight' (4.6.20). It transpires, then, that, even if we *were* present at this unseen location, the things that Edgar describes would be hard to see, or even invisible. Similarly, the *sounds* of the scene are described, but then taken away from us: 'The murmuring surge / That on th'unnumbered idle pebble chafes, / Cannot be heard so high' (4.6.20–2). Here, as soon as we have imagined the sound of the sea 'murmuring' against the shore, we are told that it is silent. Edgar's description thus takes us through the process of imagining something outside the text, and demonstrates the ability of language to make us see and hear, but simultaneously reminds us that the things being described do not exist except as an effect of language.[29]

Edgar breaks off his description: 'I'll look no more, / Lest my brain turn and the deficient sight / Topple down headlong' (4.6.22–4). But what has he been looking at? This line suggests that Edgar fears he will become dizzy and fall over the cliff, anticipating Gloucester's impending 'fall', but it also implies that his description of this 'deficient sight' – deficient because it does not exist – will undo itself and collapse if he describes any more. Gloucester appears to have been entirely seduced by Edgar's verbal artistry, but this is perhaps understandable, given his blindness.[30] As Jonathan Goldberg has written, 'Gloucester embraces this illusion and plunges into it. He has been convinced by the *trompe l'oeil* of representation and his fall shows that he is the perfect audience for it.'[31] We might, then, see Gloucester as a figure for a blind, naive audience, and Edgar a figure for the playwright. And yet, the only reason that Gloucester is taken in by Edgar's illusion is that he is blind: Gloucester is perhaps *right* to rely upon Edgar's verbal description, in the sense that he is no longer able to test this description against what he sees. But once again, this corresponds to our experience of this scene. In his stage-centred account of the play, Philip McGuire suggests that Edgar's description 'was written to be spoken by an actor standing on a flat stage at the theatre', and that, by revealing Edgar's description to be false, the play 'completes an extremely risky dramaturgical manoeuvre that involves turning the primary means by which place was signified at the Globe against itself'.[32] Yet the implications of this scene go beyond its immediate theatrical context; to state that Edgar's description was written 'to be spoken by an actor' is on one level undeniable, but this underestimates the extent to which the scene offers a more far-reaching meditation on the relationship between hearing, seeing and reading. Shakespeare demonstrates the power of language alone to act upon our imaginary forces, and suggests that – like Gloucester perhaps – we don't need to *see* his plays for this to happen.

An alternative perspective on this issue is offered by Ben Jonson's play *The Staple of News* (1631), in which the Prologue states that its author wants its audience to listen rather than watch, and that it will be for the audience's own benefit:

> For your own sakes, not his, he bade me say,
> Would you were come to hear, not to see a play.
> Though we his actors must provide for those
> Who are our guests, here, in the way of shows,
> The maker hath not so; he'd have you wise,
> Much rather by your ears than by your eyes.[33]

This Prologue wishes that a play could be something heard and not seen, but acknowledges – albeit unwillingly – that it will be experienced in both ways. This suggests that Ben Jonson's attitude towards the relationship between the visual and the verbal elements of drama was less ambivalent than that of Shakespeare.[34] Michael O'Connell, in his study of idolatry and iconoclasm *The Idolatrous Eye*, writes that this Prologue 'not only distinguishes between the poet and those who perform his words on stage, but seems indeed to yearn for a blind audience . . . This comes but as an extreme version of what Jonson in one way or another seems always to have wanted: near exclusive attention to the verbal element of the mixed art that theater is.'[35] O'Connell is right to suggest that Jonson seems to yearn for a 'blind audience', but it is worth pointing out that Shakespeare creates such an audience in Gloucester. The relationship between the visual and the verbal elements of drama that caused Jonson such anxiety appears to have prompted Shakespeare to further experimentation. Rather than *yearning for* a blind audience, Shakespeare investigates the implications of *including* a blind audience in one of his plays. Derek Peat has commented that, 'As Edgar has trifled with Gloucester, so Shakespeare has trifled with his audience. What he presents is so ambiguous that, to an extent, they are placed in Gloucester's situation: they too must trust the eyes and word of another, because they can't see for themselves.'[36] Peat notes that Shakespeare has trifled with his *audience*, but perhaps we might go further, and suggest that Shakespeare was also reflecting upon the impact that this scene would have upon his readers. For even when we watch this scene unfold before our eyes in a performance, we are asked to imagine a *different* scene to the one that we are literally seeing. Like Gloucester, whether we experience the play on the page or on the stage, we can only 'see' the things that Edgar describes in our mind's eye.

This scene thus offers a suggestive comment on the relationship between text and performance, as well as the relationship between seeing and hearing. Christy Desmet has suggested that here 'the testimony of our own eyes and ears parts company, as *King Lear* challenges our methods for listening to, watching, and even reading Shakespearean drama'.[37] However, Desmet does not fully explore the implications of this suggestion. The fact that Gloucester is blind – he cannot see anything, and is totally dependent upon language – suggests that his position is analogous to that of a reader of the play. To engage with this scene, we have to imagine what it would be like to be in Gloucester's position, and to experience the play *without seeing it*, as if the act of reading is being figured in the text. Moreover, Edgar's description highlights the fact that plays are often reliant upon narrative descriptions such as this, and thus serves to remind us of the textuality of dramatic representations. This scene suggests, then, that the difference between text and performance is not as clear-cut as we might think: both are constructed by language, and dependent upon our ability to imagine things outside the text of the play, whether we see, hear, or read it.

The analogy between Gloucester and a reader of the play is, however, complicated by the fact that to read something you have to be able to see it; and this is highlighted by Lear's encounter with Gloucester on the heath. Gloucester states that he remembers Lear's voice: 'The trick of that voice I do well remember' (4.6.105), but Lear responds rather by stating that he recognises Gloucester by his eyes: 'I remember thine eyes well enough' (4.6.132). Like Edgar, Lear seems to have forgotten, or not seen, that Gloucester is blind. And yet, Lear's statement is ambiguous: does he mean that he recognises Gloucester by his eyes – mistakenly believing that they are still there – or does he mean that he sees that Gloucester's eyes are lost, but remembers what they were like? With a similar lack of propriety, Lear then offers Gloucester something to read, another of the play's stage documents: 'Read thou this challenge, mark ᶠbutᶠ the penning of it' (4.6.135). Lear commands Gloucester to look only at the 'penning' of the letter: he is being instructed to look at the surface of the composition, rather than the 'matter'. Gloucester had, we remember, mistaken Edmund's forged letter for Edgar's handwriting earlier in the play, and had been seduced by the matter of Edmund's false text too readily. Now he is being given a second chance, but after he has been blinded. Gloucester's 'Were all thy letters suns, I could not see ᵠoneᵠ' (4.6.136) could also refer to his *sons*, whom he has misread. But it is interesting that it is at this point in the play – a moment about the inability to read a text; about blindness and misinterpretation – that Edgar says that he would have to *see* this event to believe in it, or experience it properly: 'I would not take this from report: it is, / And my heart breaks at it' (4.6.137–8).

Here, Edgar recognises not only the limits of language but also the inability of a spoken 'report' to convey or represent the tragic 'reality' he sees before him. Edgar admits that he will be unable to construct a coherent, pithy moral out of what he sees; and yet, what he says here *is* a coherent, pithy moral. This paradox would appear to be central to the play: here, when Shakespeare's artistry apparently admits defeat, we have what some commentators have seen as Shakespeare's greatest stroke of genius. Inga-Stina Ewbank goes so far as to say that 'In many ways, this "it is" is the greatest line of Shakespeare, the theatre poet'.³⁸ Ewbank does not specify the way or ways in which this line is great; but Edgar's 'it is' is perhaps striking inasmuch as it is Shakespeare's *least* 'poetic' line. It represents the ultimate paring down of description; so pared down, in fact, that nothing is, or is capable of being, described. The scene Edgar is witnessing is not capable of being turned into narrative form, or described at all. If retold, its immediacy would be lost. Yet Edgar's pointing to the inadequacy of 'report' seems to bring about a far more compelling sense of immediacy than any extended narrative description could provide. Here, despite – or perhaps *because* of – the way in which the phrase professes its inadequacy, the thing that it describes comes to appear more 'real'. James L. Calderwood finds this phrase useful for his argument about mediated and unmediated experience in the play:

> Edgar's term 'report' is convenient to my purpose here since as a secondary verbal account it may be contrasted with the primary 'it is' of direct experience. These two modes might be regarded as dividing up *King Lear* itself, or any play – the mediated *re*-presentation of past affairs, the 'then and there' we call narrative, and the immediate *present*-ation of the 'here and now' we think of as dramatic.[39]

Calderwood suggests that Edgar's comment comments upon the difference between narrative and drama, but we might also see it as an oblique comment on the question of text versus performance. For the line that immediately follows Edgar's contrasting of seen and heard experience is Lear's injunction to *read*:

> *Edgar.* I would not take this from report: it is,
> And my heart breaks at it.
> *Lear.* Read
> *Gloucester.* What? With the case of eyes?
>
> (4.6.137–40)

Edgar's attempt to divide up, categorise or value the two modes of narrative and drama – contrasting experience and 'report' – is framed, perhaps even prompted by, this failed act of reading. Lear commands Gloucester to 'Read', and Gloucester points out that he cannot: 'What? With the case of eyes?' (4.6.139–40). Once again, Shakespeare invites us to reflect upon the difference between seeing, hearing and reading. Shakespeare implies, perhaps, that *reading* this poignant scene might be an alternative to seeing or hearing about it.

This notion also emerges in an earlier scene in Act 4, in which a Gentleman describes Cordelia's reactions to Kent's letter informing her of the events that have befallen Lear. Kent asks 'Did your letters pierce the queen to any demonstration of grief?' (4.3.9–10), and the Gentleman replies:

> Ay sir. She took them, and read them in my presence,
> And now and then an ample tear trilled down
> Her delicate cheek. It seemed she was a queen
> Over her passion, who, most rebel-like,
> Sought to be king o'er her.
>
> (4.3.11–15)

Here the play demonstrates the ability of a piece of text – a letter – to have an emotional impact upon its addressee: Shakespeare suggests that it is not always necessary to see the thing itself in order to be affected by it. This passage is also intriguingly self-reflexive inasmuch as we do not see Cordelia reading this letter – this act of reading is itself absent, and is merely reported to us. Shakespeare places his audience in a situation comparable to that of Cordelia: she does not see her father's suffering, but we do not see Cordelia reading this letter, even in performance. Even though Cordelia was, as the Gentleman says, 'in my presence' (4.3.11), we experience this absent scene of reading through the Gentleman's verbal 'report'.

Lear makes it clear to Gloucester that there are alternative methods of experiencing the world without literally 'seeing': 'Your eyes are in a heavy case, your purse in a light, yet you see how this world goes' (4.6.143–4). Gloucester states, suggestively, that he 'see[s] it feelingly' (4.6.145). Lear continues: 'What, art mad? A man may see how this world goes with no eyes. Look with thine ears. See how yon justice rails upon yon simple thief' (4.6.146–8). Gloucester now must 'look with [his] ears', and experience the world through what he hears. Shakespeare uses an analogous formulation in Sonnet 23, a text that was seen (or rather read), but not heard: 'O, learn to read what silent love hath writ: / *To hear with eyes* belongs to love's fine wit' (13–14).[40] In this sonnet, Shakespeare suggests that one can 'hear' with one's eyes when one reads, while *King Lear* displays a similar interest in synaesthesia with the suggestion that one can 'see' by hearing a description. Lear tells Gloucester to 'Get thee glass eyes, / And like a scurvy politician seem / To see the things thou dost not' (4.6.166–8). In 1.2, Gloucester claimed that he would not need spectacles to see 'nothing' (1.2.35–6): now that he literally sees nothing, Gloucester is being told to wear spectacles, or 'glass eyes', in order to *pretend* that he can see. But perhaps when reading *King Lear*, we, too, 'seem / To see . . . things'. Gloucester states that he has 'ingenious feeling / Of [his] huge sorrows' (4.6.275–6). Again, the play demonstrates that we do not necessarily need to *see* sad sights to have 'ingenious feeling' of them.

The scene ends with Edgar's discovery of a letter in Oswald's pocket. But, interestingly, Edgar's 'Let's see these pockets' (4.6.251) and 'Let us see' (4.6.253) echo his father's demand to see Edmund's pocketed forged letter in 1.2. Now, Edgar seems to think that writing *can* possess immediacy and truth, and, breaking open the letter's seal, states that it will be a reliable way of finding out people's inner thoughts: 'To know our enemies' minds we rip their hearts' (4.6.255). He assumes that Goneril's heart is in the contents of the letter. Edgar reads the letter out loud – perhaps reminding us that his speech is always 'penn'd' – and states that he will show the letter to Albany. He also suggests that the letter will have a powerful *visual* impact: Edgar will 'With this ungracious paper strike the sight / Of the death-practised duke' (4.6.271–2). Here, 'strike the sight' suggests a successful showing, and Edgar's use of the word 'strike' even suggests that the letter will have a performative function. Edgar seems to think that this written 'report' – a letter – *will* have the force of the thing itself. When Albany finally confronts Goneril with the letter, and finds himself unable to find words to describe her, he uses the letter as a more expressive alternative: 'Thou worse than any name, read thine own evil' (5.3.154). Throughout the course of the play, Edgar finds himself reliant upon narratives and texts, despite his claims that he would prefer to experience the world directly. And perhaps this explains the presence of Edgar's long – and problematic – narrative account of Gloucester's death.

In the play's final scene, Albany invites Edgar to give a narrative account of what has taken place – 'Where have you hid yourself? / How have you known the miseries of your father?' (5.3.178–9) – and Edgar is all too happy to oblige. He provides a highly self-conscious, rhetorical, and – arguably – overlong, account: 'By nursing them, my lord. List a brief tale; / And when 'tis told, O, that my heart would burst!' (5.3.180–1). Edgar's narration appears to be intended to elicit such an emotional response, and designed to justify his role in the play, as he evades all of the difficult questions that critics have asked about him. As Harry Berger comments, Edgar's tale 'drastically foreshortens his performance on the heath, edits out all his darker moments, and stresses his devoted dependence'.[41] Edgar attempts to explain how and why his father died, in a redemptive reading that could be read as a gloss on Lear's forthcoming demise:

I asked his blessing and from first to last
Told him our pilgrimage. But his flawed heart,
Alack, too weak the conflict to support,
'Twixt two extremes of passion, joy and grief,
Burst smilingly.

(5.3.194–8)

Edgar interprets Gloucester's death in a (relatively) positive light, stating that he was suspended between joy and grief; but do we believe this interpretation? After all, we know that Edgar has constructed artful but deceptive narratives before. Yet while Gloucester's death occurs offstage and is reported to us by Edgar, the death of Lear happens before our eyes; or at least, it does when we see the play performed. Shakespeare seems to be asking us to compare Edgar's narrative account of Gloucester's death with the unexplained and uninterpreted sight of Lear and the dead Cordelia. We are being asked to compare narrative and dramatic modes of representation: which offers the more authentic or affecting experience?

Certainly the power of the play's ending owes much to our inability to understand what is going on, and there are several references in these final moments to 'uninterpreted seeing'.[42] It is not always clear what we are supposed to be looking at: 'This is a dull sight' (5.3.280); 'I'll see that straight' (5.3.285); 'O, see, see!' (5.3.303), and 'Do you see this?' (5.3.309). The experience of reading this final scene is clearly very different to seeing it performed. In reading, we miss the visual immediacy of performance; and yet, performance, too, fails to reveal the 'meanings' of this scene. Perhaps, then, in the play's representation of Lear's death we also miss the mediacy of report. For if we interpret the play's final moments in the context of Edgar's narrative, then we might wonder how Lear's death could be rendered in narrative form. And yet, this scene is so preoccupied with the question of seeing and not seeing, and the difficulty of interpreting visual signs, that it comes to highlight the limitations of both text *and* performance. Albany attempts to offer a moralising summary of the play's events, but he finds it to be contradicted by what he sees before him, suggesting that the characters' attempts to turn the play's ending into a satisfactory, conventional one are contradicted in the face of experience. Here, Albany's 'report' of the play is contradicted by what he sees:

>   All friends shall taste
> The wages of their virtue and all foes
> The cup of their deservings. O, see, see!

> (5.3.301–3)

Whatever it is that Albany has seen, it seems to have dismantled his facile moralising summary: here the play resists both narrative and interpretative closure. Towards the close of the Folio text of the play,

Lear tells the onlookers to 'look', but we are unable to 'see' or understand, because we are not told what we are supposed to be looking
for. Indeed, it is not clear whether Lear thinks Cordelia to be dead
or alive. One moment he states that 'she's gone forever. / I know
when one is dead and when one lives; / She's dead as earth' (5.3.257–
9), but then asks for a looking glass: 'If that her breath will mist or
stain the stone, / Why then she lives' (5.3.260–1). Lear even admits
that his vision is blurred – 'Mine eyes are not o' the best' (5.3.277) –
further complicating our sense of what he is seeing. Consequently
it is extremely difficult to know how to interpret Lear's dying
moments, even more so given the disparity between the two texts of
the play:

> [*to Edgar?*] Pray you undo this button. Thank you, sir.
> QO, o, o, o.Q
> FDo you see this? Look on her: look, her lips,
> Look there, look there!   *He dies.*F
>
> (5.3.308–10)

What is Lear looking at? And what is the meaning of what he sees?
A. C. Bradley writes that 'any actor is false to the text who does not
attempt to express, in Lear's last accents and gestures, an unbearable
joy'.[43] But it is not clear which text Bradley is attempting to be true
to. In the quarto text, Lear remains alive long enough to deliver the
line 'Break, heart, I prithee break' (5.3.311), suggesting that he dies
in a state of grief.[44] However, in the Folio, this line is spoken by Kent,
and Lear's last line before the stage direction '*He dies*' is 'Look there,
look there!' (5.3.310). Thus Lear's death in the Folio is more ambiguous, and it is even possible that Lear dies in the same manner as
Gloucester, ''Twixt two extremes of passion, joy and grief' (5.3.197).
In the Folio the two lines before Lear's death might be of despair and
not joy, and they could be read as conforming to the previous pattern
of Lear's veering from certainty to possibility, and not knowing when
one is dead and when one lives. Alternatively, the Folio text could
suggest that Lear *does* now know the difference between life and
death, with the additional 'no' in 'No, no, FnoF life' (5.3.304) and
the additional two nevers in 'Never, never, never, Fnever, neverF'
(5.3.307), suggesting the certainty of death. Either way, the very
ambiguity of Lear's death retrospectively implies that Edgar's narrative account of Gloucester's death might be suspect. For if
Gloucester's death was anything like that of Lear, then for Edgar to

say that he died betwixt 'joy and grief' comes to sound like a rather dubious interpretation, and not an accurate account of the event.

In his Arden edition, R. A. Foakes includes the stage direction '[*to Edgar?*]', speculating that it might be Edgar who undoes the button Lear refers to, while the Oxford editors suggest that Lear's request is addressed '*To Kent*' (*The Tragedy of King Lear*, 5.3.285) – but we cannot even be certain whether it is Lear's or Cordelia's button.[45] We are confronted with a variety of interpretative possibilities; we are told to interpret, but any single interpretation remains a reduction of Lear's death. In his study of Shakespeare's 'open silences', Philip McGuire explores the different possibilities of Lear's request: does Edgar or Kent undo Lear's button? Or does Albany undo Cordelia's button? Or does Edgar undo Cordelia's button? Or is Lear's request ignored?[46] The point is, perhaps, that we do not know, and that the text of the play refuses to tell us. When we read this scene, we almost strain our eyes as we read to try to see what is happening, wishing that we could see it performed; and yet performances of this scene will not necessarily reveal to us the meaning of the scene either, and might even restrict some of its ambiguities.

At the end of his deconstructionist account of *King Lear*, Jonathan Goldberg offers the following reflection on the play's textual and representational multiplicity:

> Perhaps in the fact that there is not a *King Lear*, not one text but two, we can have a final perspective on the multiplicities of representation. A perspective on *original* re-presentation apt for a playwright who never published any of his plays and who nonetheless allows the Chorus of *Henry V* to imagine performance embodied in printing – the printing that Shakespeare never in fact sought for his texts.[47]

Goldberg suggests that the play's textual multiplicity – its lack of a single, 'original' text for us to consider – mirrors its multiple perspectives on the issues of representation that it raises. And yet, Goldberg's assertion that this multiplicity is 'apt for a playwright who never published any of his plays', and that the notion of performance embodied as printing is 'nonetheless' figured in *Henry V*, needs qualifying in two important respects. Firstly, Erne's *Shakespeare as Literary Dramatist* has effectively demonstrated the ways in which Shakespeare's apparent indifference to print – and the claim that he 'never in fact sought [printing] for his texts' – has been overstated. Secondly, as I have attempted to show in this chapter,

Shakespeare's fascination with the textuality of his plays suggests that the allusion to 'Printing' in the first Chorus in *Henry V* ('Think, when we talk of horses, that you see them, / Printing their proud hoofs i'th' receiving earth' (26–7)) is hardly the anomaly that Goldberg describes, but is rather part of an extended – and ultimately open – Shakespearean meditation on the interrelationship between seeing, hearing and reading. Perhaps, then, rather trying to determine whether Shakespeare is pro- or antitheatrical in any simple sense, we should think more about the ways in which his works themselves explore the relationship between text and performance, and even dismantle the distinction between the two. As we saw with Edgar's description of Dover cliff, Shakespeare suggests that there is a kind of absence in both reading *and* performance; that both are constructed through language – through Shakespeare's 'penn'd speech' – and that both require an imaginative leap of faith.

Notes

1 Unless otherwise stated, all quotations from Shakespeare's works are be taken from *The Riverside Shakespeare*, 2nd edn, ed. G. Blakemore Evans (Boston: Houghton Mifflin, 1997). Patrick Cheney has commented that 'Perhaps more than any play in Shakespeare's corpus, *Love's Labour's Lost* takes as its topic the relation between lyric poetry and staged theatre', in *Shakespeare, National Poet-Playwright* (Cambridge: Cambridge University Press, 2004), p. 37.

2 In his Arden edition of *Love's Labour's Lost*, H. R. Woudhuysen notes the play's emphasis on letters – not only epistles but also the letters of the alphabet – and makes a suggestive link with *King Lear*: '*King Lear* likewise places a heavy reliance on letters whose postal histories are confused and slightly confusing; but in the tragedy the letters are a means to an end, whereas in the comedy they are an end in themselves. Shakespeare wants to keep what is written and the business of writing itself to the fore' (*Love's Labour's Lost*, ed. Woudhuysen (Walton-on-Thames: Thomas Nelson, 1998), p. 20). I would argue that *throughout* his works Shakespeare keeps the business of writing to the fore. For an attempt to read the letters in *King Lear* in the context of the work of Erasmus see Lisa Jardine, 'Reading and the Technology of Textual Affect: Erasmus's Familiar Letters and Shakespeare's *King Lear*', in *Reading Shakespeare Historically* (London: Routledge, 1996), pp. 78–97.

3 Harry Berger Jr, 'Text Against Performance: The Example of *Macbeth*', in *Making Trifles of Terrors: Redistributing Complicities in Shakespeare* (Stanford: Stanford University Press, 1997), p. 102. See also his earlier

study, *Imaginary Audition: Shakespeare on Stage and Page* (Berkeley: University of California Press, 1989). For a valuable essay that explores the critical disagreement over 'whether Shakespeare wrote incidentally actable poems or incidentally poetic scripts' see Michael Dobson, 'Shakespeare on the Page and Stage', in Margreta de Grazia and Stanley Wells (eds), *The Cambridge Companion to Shakespeare* (Cambridge: Cambridge University Press, 2001), pp. 235–49 (p. 235).

4 The address is reproduced in *The Riverside Shakespeare*, p. 95. Heminge and Condell go on to bemoan the fact that Shakespeare himself did not live to see his plays into print: 'It had bene a thing, we confesse, worthie to haue bene wished, that the Author himselfe had liu'd to haue set forth, and ouerseen his owne writings' (p. 95). Heminge and Condell describe a playwright who would not only have been *capable* of 'set[ting] forth' his writings in print, but also, perhaps, who would have *wanted* to 'ouerse[e]' the publication himself.

5 David M. Bergeron, 'Introduction' to Bergeron (ed.), *Reading and Writing in Shakespeare* (Newark: University of Delaware Press, 1996), p. 15.

6 Stephen Orgel, 'Shakespeare Imagines a Theater', in Kenneth Muir, Jay L. Halio and D. J. Palmer (eds), *Shakespeare, Man of the Theater* (Newark: University of Delaware Press, 1983), pp. 34–46 (p. 43).

7 Patrick Cheney observes that critics are beginning to describe a Shakespeare who was 'not simply the writer of plays who assiduously avoids print and bookish immortality, but rather the author of both plays and poems whose works as a whole show a fascination with – sometimes also a fear and distrust of – print publication' (*Poet-Playwright*, p. 209). See also Cheney, *Shakespeare's Literary Authorship* (Cambridge: Cambridge University Press, 2008).

8 Lukas Erne, *Shakespeare as Literary Dramatist* (Cambridge: Cambridge University Press, 2003), p. 25.

9 Jonas Barish notes that, among Shakespeare's dramatic works, only *The Two Noble Kinsmen* does not allude to a single 'stage document', and he writes that 'The action of [Shakespeare's] plays swarms with writings, and especially with epistles'. See '"Soft, here follows prose": Shakespeare's Stage Documents', in Murray Biggs et al. (eds), *The Arts of Performance in Elizabethan and Early Stuart Drama: Essays for G. K. Hunter* (Edinburgh: Edinburgh University Press, 1991), pp. 32–49 (p. 33). See also Barish's classic study of *The Antitheatrical Prejudice* (Berkeley: University of California Press, 1981).

10 Stephen Orgel, '"Counterfeit Presentments": Shakespeare's Ekphrasis', in Edward Chaney and Peter Mack (eds), *England and the Continental Renaissance: Essays in Honour of J. B. Trapp* (Rochester NY: Boydell Press, 1990), pp. 177–84 (p. 179).

11 All quotations from the play are taken from R. A. Foakes's Arden edition (Walton-on-Thames: Thomas Nelson and Sons, 1997). Foakes identifies words and passages unique to Quarto and Folio by framing them with superscript ^{Q}s and ^{F}s respectively, which I have retained. For a valuable review of Foakes's edition that offers a incisive account of the play's textual controversies see John Lyon, 'What Need Two?', *English Language Notes*, 36 (1998), 58–70. See also Foakes, 'Plays and Texts', in *Hamlet versus Lear: Cultural Politics and Shakespeare's Art* (Cambridge: Cambridge University Press, 1993), ch. 4, and Kiernan Ryan, '*King Lear*: A Retrospect, 1980–2000', *Shakespeare Survey*, 55 (2002), 1–11.

12 On the trope of seeing in the play from the perspective of performance see Philip C. McGuire, '*King Lear*: "O! See, See"', in *Shakespeare: The Jacobean Plays* (London: Macmillan, 1994), pp. 85–107.

13 Charles Lamb, 'On the Tragedies of Shakespeare, considered with reference to their fitness for stage representation' (1811), reprinted in Jonathan Bate (ed.), *The Romantics on Shakespeare* (Harmondsworth: Penguin, 1992), pp. 123–24. More recently, Harold Bloom has concurred: 'Our directors and actors are defeated by this play, and I begin to agree with Charles Lamb that we ought to keep rereading *King Lear* and avoid its staged travesties' (*Shakespeare: The Invention of the Human* (London: Fourth Estate, 1999), p. 476).

14 A. C. Bradley, *Shakespearean Tragedy*, 2nd edn (London: Macmillan & Co., 1905), p. 247.

15 For a complex account of Bradley's reading of *Othello* that addresses some of the concerns of the present chapter see Mark Gauntlett, 'The Perishable Body of the Unpoetic: A. C. Bradley Performs *Othello*', *Shakespeare Survey*, 47 (1994), 71–80.

16 Sigurd Burckhardt, '*King Lear*: The Quality of Nothing', in *Shakespearean Meanings* (Princeton: Princeton University Press, 1968), p. 242.

17 Foakes's gloss; see his note to 1.2.173.

18 *King Lear* thus anticipates Shakespeare's late plays, and in particular the figure of Autolycus in *The Winter's Tale*. I discuss the figure of Autolycus and the reliability of narrative in more detail in 'Ekphrasis in *The Rape of Lucrece* and *The Winter's Tale*', *SEL*, 45 (2006), 389–414.

19 On this speech as an example of ekphrasis, or vivid narration, see David Rosand, ' "Troyes Painted Woes": Shakespeare and the Pictorial Imagination', *Hebrew University Studies in Literature*, 8 (1980), 77–97 (p. 81), and B. J. Sokol, *Art and Illusion in 'The Winter's Tale'* (Manchester: Manchester University Press, 1994), p. 19.

20 William H. Matchett, 'Some Dramatic Techniques in *King Lear*', in Philip C. McGuire and David A. Samuelson (eds), *Shakespeare: The Theatrical Dimension* (New York: AMS Press, 1979), p. 206, note 6.

21 Richard Fly, *Shakespeare's Mediated World* (Amherst: University of Massachusetts Press, 1976), p. 95.

22 Robert Egan, *Drama Within Drama: Shakespeare's Sense of His Art in 'King Lear', 'The Winter's Tale', and 'The Tempest'* (New York and London: Columbia University Press, 1975), p. 26.

23 Stephen Orgel comments that this is 'a scene in which Shakespeare's conception of his audience is particularly problematical', and that 'It is a scene bewildering in its confusion of false and true, in which the real and the imaginary are indistinguishable' ('Shakespeare Imagines a Theater', p. 40).

24 As Jay L. Halio has commented, 'The trick Edgar plays on his father's imagination is also the trick Shakespeare plays on ours – except that here he means us to be conscious of everything that is happening, including the way in which our imagination is being made to work' (Halio (ed.), *The Tragedy of King Lear* (Cambridge: Cambridge University Press, 1992), p. 22).

25 See Stanley Fish, *Surprised by Sin: The Reader in Paradise Lost* (London: Macmillan, 1967), esp. ch. 1.

26 See Berger, *Imaginary Audition*, pp. 29–30, and Erne, *Shakespeare as Literary Dramatist*, p. 25.

27 Foakes glosses *chough* as 'jackdaws', but the OED favours 'the Red-legged crow, which frequents the sea-cliffs in many part of Britain, being particularly abundant in Cornwall; whence distinguished as the *Cornish chough*' (*OED*, 2).

28 Harry Levin, 'The Heights and the Depths: A Scene from *King Lear*', in *Shakespeare and the Revolution of the Times* (New York: Oxford University Press, 1976), p. 177. More recently, Christopher Pye has commented that 'The scene of Gloucester's blinding – the horrific extrusion of his eyes – is picked up in the description of the threat posed by the vertiginous view', in *The Vanishing: Shakespeare, the Subject, and Early Modern Culture* (Durham NC: Duke University Press, 2000), p. 91.

29 For a deconstructionist account of Edgar's speech see Jonathan Goldberg, 'Perspectives: Dover Cliff and the Conditions of Representation', in David M. Bergeron and G. Douglas Atkins (eds), *Shakespeare and Deconstruction* (New York: Peter Lang, 1988), pp. 245–66. Goldberg makes a suggestive analogy with the Chorus in *Henry V*, and suggests that the words of the Chorus's vivid descriptions 'stamp themselves on the mind so that what is seen as a picture is something like words as they come to be on a page . . . But unlike Edgar's vision, the emphasis [in *Henry V*] is verbal, on the power of words to work on the imagination' (p. 251). Yet the distinction that Goldberg sets up here does not hold: the emphasis in Edgar's description is also

verbal, and is *precisely* concerned to explore the power of words to work on the imagination, whether on the page or on the stage.

30 Burckhardt comments that 'always in the dark, [Gloucester] is now enclosed in darkness and made to feel the mediacy of report' ('The Quality of Nothing', p. 244).

31 Goldberg, 'Perspectives: Dover Cliff', p. 252.

32 McGuire, '*King Lear*: "O! See, See"', p. 90.

33 Ben Jonson, 'The Prologue for the Stage' in *The Staple of News* (1626; pub. 1631), in *The Complete Plays of Ben Jonson*, ed. G. A. Wilkes, 4 vols (Oxford: Clarendon Press, 1981–82), vol. 4, p. 250.

34 For a fascinating account of Jonson's antitheatricality see Barish, 'Jonson and the Loathèd Stage' in *The Antitheatrical Prejudice*, ch. 4. See also D. J. Gordon, 'Poet and Architect: The Intellectual Setting of the Quarrel between Ben Jonson and Inigo Jones', in *The Renaissance Imagination: Essays and Lectures by D. J. Gordon*, ed. Stephen Orgel (Berkeley: University of California Press, 1975), pp. 77–101; and Stephen Orgel, 'The Poetics of Spectacle', in *The Authentic Shakespeare and Other Problems of the Early Modern Stage* (New York and London: Routledge, 2002), pp. 49–69.

35 Michael O'Connell, *The Idolatrous Eye: Iconoclasm and Theater in Early Modern England* (New York: Oxford University Press, 2000), p. 121.

36 Derek Peat, '"And that's true too": *King Lear* and the Tension of Uncertainty' *Shakespeare Survey*, 33 (1980), 43–53 (p. 48).

37 Christy Desmet, *Reading Shakespeare's Characters: Rhetoric, Ethics and Identity* (Amherst: University of Massachusetts Press, 1992), p. 129.

38 Inga-Stina Ewbank, '"More Pregnantly than Words": Some Uses and Limitations of Visual Symbolism', *Shakespeare Survey*, 24 (1971), 13–18 (p. 18). Anne Barton has also written about the significance of this line in her essay 'Shakespeare and the Limits of Language', reprinted in *Essays, Mainly Shakespearean* (Cambridge: Cambridge University Press, 1994), pp. 51–69: 'to those two words, the barest possible indication of existence, much of what happens in *King Lear* must be reduced' (p. 62). Burckhardt writes that '*It is* – it no longer means. Report and interpretation try to make sense, to clothe the nakedness of being in the orderly garments of discourse. They either falsify *Lear* at this point or break at it. It is – the worst' ('The Quality of Nothing', p. 254).

39 James L. Calderwood, 'Creative Uncreation in *King Lear*', *Shakespeare Quarterly*, 37 (1986), 5–19 (p. 8).

40 For further discussion of this sonnet see Lukas Erne, 'Revisiting Shakespearean Authorship', *Shakespeare Studies*, 61 (forthcoming,

2008). See also Garrett Stewart, '"To hear with eyes": Shakespeare as Proof Text', in *Reading Voices: Literature and the Phonotext* (Berkeley: University of California Press, 1990), pp. 37–65; and Mark Robson, *The Sense of Early Modern Writing: Rhetoric, Politics, Aesthetics* (Manchester: Manchester University Press, 2006), pp. 155–6.

41 Harry Berger Jr, 'Text Against Performance: The Gloucester Family Romance', in *Making Trifles of Terrors*, p. 64.

42 See Calderwood, 'Creative Uncreation', p. 16.

43 Bradley, *Shakespearean Tragedy*, p. 291.

44 In his Arden 2 edition of the play (London: Methuen, 1972), Kenneth Muir explains Lear's use of the word 'Look' by asserting that 'Lear dies of joy, believing Cordelia to be alive (Bradley)', failing to acknowledge both the textual and interpretative difficulties in coming to this conclusion (see his note to 5.3.309). Indeed, it is perhaps worth noting that there is no stage direction to indicate Lear's death in the Quarto, so it is far from clear *when* Lear dies in the earlier text.

45 See Stanley Wells and Gary Taylor et al. (eds), *The Oxford Shakespeare: The Complete Works* (Oxford: Clarendon Press, 1988), p. 973.

46 See Philip C. McGuire, *Speechless Dialect: Shakespeare's Open Silences* (Berkeley: University of California Press, 1985), pp. 101–5.

47 Goldberg, 'Perspectives: Dover Cliff', p. 263.

'A stringless instrument': *Richard II* and the defeat of poetry

Richard Wilson

Northumberland. My liege, old Gaunt commends him to your majesty.
King Richard. What says he?
Northumberland. Nay, nothing: all is said.
His tongue is now a stringless instrument.
Words, life, and all, old Lancaster hath spent.
(*Richard II*, 2.1.148–51)[1]

'All is said' in *Richard II* with that sweet sadness the dying John of Gaunt attributes to 'music at the close, / As the last taste of sweets, is sweetest last, / Writ in remembrance more than things long past' (12–14). But this 'remembrance more' or *memento mori* attaches to more here than just those 'sad stories of the death of kings' (3.2.151) that earn Shakespeare's Histories, 'sad, high, and . . . full of woe', the final fatalistic subtitle, 'All is True' (*Henry VIII*, Prologue, 3). For if this text had a subtitle it would have to be '*Richard II, or All Is Said*', because its 'sadness' seems to be about what has itself been 'said'. And the 'sadness' that 'all is said' in vain is given an institutional context when Gaunt deludes himself that, although the King would never listen to his past counsel, 'My death's sad tale may yet undeaf his ear'. So, the specific *saidness* of *Richard II* is of a culture where the saddest stories, such as the swansongs from 'tongues of dying men' that are supposed to 'Enforce attention, like deep harmony', fall on the deaf ears of an audience 'stopped with other, flattering sounds . . . Lascivious metres to whose venom sound / The open ears of youth doth always listen' (2.1.15–20). For 'Death's sad tale' as told by Gaunt is only one of the many 'sad stories' drowned out by more popular sounds in this drama, which is constructed as a set of variations on the scene reported by the Welsh Captain, when 'lean-looked prophets whisper fearful change' whilst 'ruffians dance and leap' (2.4.11–13). From Gaunt's 'sad aspect', which plucks four years off his son's exile (1.3.202–8); to Isabella's sigh she 'cannot but be sad: so heavy-sad', after she is told she is 'too much sad' (2.2.1–30); and the Queen's 'sad look' at 'the triumph of great Bolingbroke' (3.4.99–100); or 'That sad stop', as 'misgoverned hands from window tops / Threw dust and rubbish' on Richard's head, when weeping made York 'break the story off' (5.2.1–6); to the King's final service from 'that sad dog' who brings him prison food (5.5.70); and his rival's order, in the last lines, to 'March sadly after . . . In weeping after this untimely bier' (5.6.51–2), the sadness of *Richard II* is at the futility of all that is said, despite the old courtier's hope that 'Where words are scarce, they are seldom spent in vain; / For they breathe true that breathe their words in pain, / He that no more must say is listen'd more / Than they whom youth and ease hath taught to glose' (2.1.7–10). When 'all is said' in this play, its sadness is not just that of a story of the death of kings, but of an arena where 'the antic' actor usurps the royal poet, and a player defeats the sovereign story-teller himself: 'Scoffing his state and grinning at his pomp, / Allowing him a breath, a little scene, / To monarchize' (3.2.158–9). As Mowbray images it, in the metaphor of a broken lute later given Gaunt, the sadness of *Richard II* is the melancholy of the exile alienated from the kingdom of language itself:

> The language I have learnt these forty years,
> My native English, now I must forgo,
> And now my tongue's use is to me no more
> Than an unstringed viol or a harp,
> Or like a cunning instrument cased up,
> Or, being open, put into his hands
> That knows no touch to tune the harmony.
>
> (1.3.153–9)

'All is sad' in *Richard II* because language is finally the 'Nothing' that is all that can be said between a servant and a king; a nullity to which Richard's word is also reduced, when Bolingbroke mocks it by returning home. So, the *vanitas* of the unstrung violin belongs with other Renaissance icons – like that broken string on the lute in Holbein's *The Ambassadors*, which shows this useless instrument will not be played – that silently announce the 'nothing' of an art commissioned where Death 'Keeps . . . court' (3.2.158).[2] Such a 'nothing', Richard learns, is truly 'the breath of kings' (1.3.208). Gaunt warned him that 'Thy word is current . . . for my death, / But dead, thy kingdom cannot buy my breath' (224–5); and, indeed, the King then threatened that these words would get the 'lunatic, lean-witted fool' beheaded on his own deathbed: 'This tongue that runs so roundly in thy head / Should run thy head from off thy shoulders' (2.1.123–4). But the reason Gaunt's 'Nothing' echoes through the plays – until Cordelia hurls it at King Lear – is that what this bought breath expresses is Shakespeare's primal scene, repeated in every play, in which a tyrannical ruler or lover sets up a drama of allegiance or desire, and coerced performers react as Ross now does to Richard: 'My heart is great, but it must break with silence / Ere't be disburdened with a liberal tongue' (229–30). As Francis Barker remarked, the paradigm of Shakespearean history is played out in that great hall 'aptly named the *presence* chamber', where knots of courtiers gather beneath the throne, and as servants ply 'the throng with sweet wine and honey cakes', the sovereign dares his subjects to 'unfold' themselves in a pantomime of loyalty or love.[3] In *Secret Shakespeare* I argue that this truth game, and the players' defiance that they 'have that within which passes show' (*Hamlet*, 1.2.86), relates to those oaths of allegiance, tortures and executions ordered by Elizabeth's regime in its anti-Catholic war on terror.[4] But the play-within-the-play at the opening of *Richard II* also puts the truth test into a theatrical context, when the King rigs a show trial-by-combat to suppress the facts about his incrimination in the murder of his uncle, the regent Gloucester, for which Bolingbroke has indicted Mowbray: 'Then call them to our presence. Face to face / And frowning brow to brow, ourselves will hear / The accuser and the accused freely speak' (1.1.15–17). Like Claudius, Richard will stage-manage this duel to death to silence his incriminators. And his duplicity in assuring his accomplice of free speech – 'Free speech and fearless I to thee allow' (123) – puts him with other Shakespearean despots, such as Theseus, Caesar and Macbeth, who host festive charades to obliterate the violence of their own succession. Critics call Richard a poet; but the travesty of 'free speech' he acts out with Mowbray to conceal his crime shows he is a poet after the fashion of Nero:

> Mowbray. However God or fortune cast my lot,
> There lives or dies, true to King Richard's throne,
> A loyal, just, and upright gentleman.
> Never did captive with a freer heart
> Cast off his chains of bondage, and embrace
> His golden uncontroll'd enfranchisement,

More than my dancing soul doth celebrate
This feast of battle with mine adversary.
Most mighty liege, and my companion peers,
Take from my mouth the wish of happy years;
As gentle and as jocund as to jest
Go I to fight: truth hath a quiet breast.
Richard.   Farewell, my lord, securely I espy
Virtue with valour couched in thine eye.
Order the trial, Marshal, and begin.

$$(1.3.85\text{–}99)$$

Editors note how Shakespeare altered his sources, Holinshed's *Chronicles* and the play *Woodstock*, to reveal Mowbray's bad faith, with an 'embarrassed and ambiguous speech' hinting at disobeying Richard by not killing the regent with his own hands; and to highlight Gaunt's dilemma, as a law-abiding subject silenced by the contradiction that legal 'correction' for his brother's murder lies 'in those hands / Which made the fault that we cannot correct' (1.1.132–3; 1.2.4–5).[5] Gaunt's politic decision that, since 'God's is the quarrel; for God's substitute, / His deputy anointed in his sight, / Hath caused his death', he must 'Let heaven revenge, for I may never lift / An angry arm against his minister' (37–41), puts him into the same position as loyal Catholics under Elizabeth; and places the play itself among texts that address the problem posed by Montaigne, Pascal, the Nazi jurist Carl Schmitt, and most recently Derrida, of the legitimacy of a regime where laws are maintained 'not because they are just, but because they are laws. It is the mystical foundation of their authority; they have none other', for 'Whosoever obeyeth them because they are just, obeys them not justly the way as he ought'.[6] Montaigne was not printed in London until 1603; but in the mid-1590s, when *Richard II* was written, his translator, John Florio, was tutor to the Earl of Southampton, Shakespeare's Catholic patron. So, it seems likely that the dramatist was already aware of the thesis of the *Essays*: that the 'mystical foundation of authority', to which Gaunt defers, was a mere necessary fiction, like false teeth. For though the King insists that 'The breath of worldly men cannot depose / The deputy elected by the Lord', conflict in this History arises precisely from the tragic impasse when a criminal state demands that 'the breath of worldly men' pays lip-service to those 'lawful fictions on which it groundeth the truth of [its] justice' (3.2.52–3).[7] The first 1597 quarto in fact titles the text *The Tragedy* of *Richard II*; and its opening words, where Richard disingenuously asks Gaunt whether he has 'sounded' the bottom of the murder accusation (1.1.1–15), shows that tragedy originates here in the 'Montaigne experience' discussed by Derrida, when 'Discourse meets its limit – in itself, in its very performative power', because 'There is here a silence walled-up' in the violence of law's founding act: 'walled up, walled in because this silence is not exterior to language'.[8] As Richard's accomplice, Mowbray admits, when the King halts the trial and seals their guilty secret by 'breathing' on to his henchman the 'hopeless word of "never to return"' (1.3.146), the silence he likewise sees as an immurement is the self-suppression of a language which can now never speak the truth:

> Within my mouth you have enjailed my tongue,
> Doubly portcullised with my teeth and lips,
> And dull unfeeling barren ignorance
> Is made my jailer to attend on me.
> I am too old to fawn upon a nurse,
> Too far in years to be a pupil now.
> What is thy sentence then but speechless death,
> Which robs my tongue from breathing native breath?
>
> (1.3.160–7)

Richard terminates the trial by banishing both accusers, walling up his crime with an iteration of his mystical authorisation that 'Not all the water in the rough rude sea / Can wash the balm from an anointed king' (3.2.50–1), which exactly fits Derrida's account of how in the founding of the criminal state 'the same problem of justice will have been posed and violently resolved, that is to say buried, dissimulated, repressed'.[9] And as if to highlight the violence of this repression, Shakespeare has the King end his charade over-turning his order to the exiles to 'Forget, forgive, conclude, and be agreed', by forcing them to swear on oath never to 'write, regreet, nor reconcile' their 'hate, / Nor never by advised purpose meet / To plot, contrive, or complot any ill / 'Gainst us, our state, our subjects, or our land' (1.1.156; 3.180–4). So, tragedy begins for Shakespeare, we see, in a problem of truth-telling strikingly like the one consid-ered by Foucault, in his last lectures, *Fearless Speech*, to be the birth of tragedy in ancient Greece. There, Foucault suggested, the stand-off between power and the messenger it itches to silence was repre-sented, in dramas like *The Bacchae*, as a breach of *parrhesia*: the pact to speak and hear the truth spoken which was struck between the ruler 'who has power but lacks truth, and the one who has truth but lacks the power'. Thus, what ancient tragedy dramatised, again and again, Foucault argued, was the deadlock when the powerful revoke the contract to permit the truth to be spoken that is essential in a culture where 'the king's messenger is still vulnerable, and takes a risk in speaking'.[10] Greek tragedy, in Foucault's analysis, was a fight to the death between sovereign and servant over 'free speech' and the sound of silence. So, it might not be chance that in *Richard II* the template for Shakespearean tragedy is also laid out as just such a legitimacy crisis, in the predicament of Bolingbroke as the unwelcome messenger determined on fearless speech: 'Look what I speak, my life shall prove . . . Besides I say, and will in battle prove . . . Further I say, and further will maintain' (1.1.87; 92; 98). Gloucester's nephew casts himself in a revenge play where blood of the murder victim 'cries / Even from the tongueless caverns of the earth . . . for justice and rough chastisement' (104–6). He is sure, then, to disrupt the murder mystery the murderer himself 'attempts to stage, by royal command', in which he will 'play the controlling part of *deus ex machina*' himself.[11] In fact, history pointedly unfolds here as a clash between the opposed genres of comedy and tragedy, which is also, it emerges, a contest for mastery between the London street where Bolingbroke is applauded for playing the revenger, and that private theatre where Richard acts in his own mind the part of the sun-god Apollo, in the apotheosis of some masque. For though he designs a similar *mise-en-scène* of caves and curtains as his rival, this royal poet has an illusion of power that exactly follows the tragic-comic happy ends of those entertainments composed by Shakespeare's competitors for Queen Elizabeth's court:

> . . . when the searching eye of heaven is hid
> Behind the globe, that lights the lower world
> Then thieves and robbers range abroad unseen
> In murders and in outrage bloody here;
> But when from under this terrestrial ball
> He fires the proud tops of the eastern pines,
> And darts his light through every guilty hole,
> Then murders, treasons, and detested sins,
> The cloak of night being plucked from off their backs,
> Stand bare and naked, trembling at themselves.
> So, when this thief, this traitor, Bolingbroke,

Who all this while hath revelled in the night
Whilst we were wand'ring with the Antipodes,
Shall see us rising in our throne, the east,
His treasons will sit blushing in his face,
Not able to endure the sight of day,
But, self-affrighted, tremble at his sin.

(3.2.33–49)

In portraiture and pageantry Elizabeth was habitually flattered as 'Like Heaven's eye, which from his sphere / Into all things prieth; / Sees through all things everywhere, / And all their nature's trieth'.[12] Not for nothing was this Queen's motto *Tutto vendo*: 'I see all'. But when Shakespeare staged the panoptic scenario Richard proposes, in his Jacobean 'disguised duke' plays, *Measure for Measure* and *The Tempest*, he problematised the royal form of tragi-comedy as sabotaged by resistance. Stephen Greenblatt follows Foucault in assuming that the reason why Shakespeare cannot dream of a surveillance in which the most intimate secrets are 'open to the view of an invisible authority' is that the machinery of policing had not yet been developed in England.[13] But Richard's hypocrisy about just such a detective story implies that the author understood the absolutist dramaturgy emerging in his time, and dissociated from royal mystifications of crime. He has Bolingbroke depart the King's lying masquerade, in any case, with the fatalism of 'a journeyman' player on 'a long apprenticehood' touring the provinces in a season when, as his father says, 'Devouring pestilence hangs in the air / And thou art flying to a fresher clime'. Gaunt fancies his son's exile from the plague-infected city to be a sojourn in some palace, with 'singing birds musicians, / The grass whereon thou tread'st the presence strewed, / The flowers fair ladies, and thy steps no more / Than a delightful measure or a dance'. But 'Having freedom', for this 'apprentice' means liberation from 'flattering sounds' of court theatricals, where 'Lascivious metres . . . Report of fashions in proud Italy, / Whose manners still our tardy-apish nation / Limps after in base imitation' (1.3.256.17–24; 2.1.17–23). That will be Mowbray's destination, when he takes the truth about Gloucester's murder to his grave, having retired 'To Italy, and there at Venice' given up 'his body to that pleasant country's earth' (4.1.87–9). When we next meet Bolingbroke, however, it is not in an Italian palazzo but in the murder-victim's Cotswolds, leading a band of his 'good friends' down the lanes of Gloucestershire. Bolingbroke's grief that foes have

'Disparked my parks and felled the forest . . . torn my household coat . . . leaving me no sign, / Save men's opinions . . . To show the world I am a gentleman' (3.2.23–7), brings these Midland scenes very close to the author's Forest of Arden, and Shakespeare's own fears about disinheritance. And when he pleads not to be 'condemned / A wandering vagabond', the fugitive's need to sue for his Lancaster livery is precisely that of the Stratford actor who arrived in London, around 1590, in the Lancastrian costume of Lord Strange's players. 'Frighting pale-faced villages with war / And ostentation', this wandering minstrel's 'sweetened' travel from castle to castle has been uncannily like that of the young entertainer, we notice, known for his 'honey-tongue' as 'Sweet William' himself (2.3.92–3;118–29):

> Believe me, my noble lord,
> I am a stranger here in Gloucestershire.
> These wild hills and rough uneven ways
> Draws out our miles and makes them wearisome;
> And yet your fair discourse hath been as sugar,
> Making the hard way sweet and delectable.
>
> (2.3.2–7)

Shakespeare's implied authorisation of Bolingbroke's 'sweet and delectable' discourse suggests that what this text projects is indeed the Stratford poet's dream of creative autonomy, the 'golden uncontrolled enfranchisement' from royal 'chains of bondage' of which Mowbray vainly boasted at the start. So, in contrast to Richard's court, the rebel leads a mêlée of 'White beards . . . boys with women's voices', veterans, and spinning-women, whose carnival mixture of 'both young and old' (3.2.112–19) resembles nothing so much as the audience for *Richard II* itself, when it was acted on tour or at The Theatre in Shoreditch. Bolingbroke's charisma, as Richard enviously reports, is therefore precisely that of a star of the London stage: 'Ourself and Bushy, Bagot here, and Green / Observed his courtship to the common people, / How he did dive into their hearts / With humble and familiar courtesy' (1.4.22–5). Thus, the disappointment built into this drama – when Richard frustrates the audience both on stage and in the auditorium by interrupting the trial, and so resigns the prime privilege of a Renaissance prince, to put power on display in spectacular rites of violence[14] – enacts the attention drift the plot confirms, from princely to public stage, and patronage to playhouse. The part of Richard was, in fact, the role of the lead actor, Richard Burbage. So, there is a complex metadramatic irony when the stage 'Richard' describes how his rival becomes the idol of the groundlings: 'What reverence he did throw away on slaves, / Wooing poor craftsmen with the craft of smiles . . . Off goes his bonnet to an oysterwench, / A brace of draymen bid God speed him well, / And had the tribute of his supple knee / With "Thanks, my countrymen, my loving friends"' (1.3.26–33). Later, as king, Bolingbroke lectures his son Hal that Richard's fatal mistake had, in fact, been to vacate the stage to become a spectator instead of a performer: 'The skipping King, he ambled up and down / With shallow jesters and rash bavin wits . . . Mingled his royalty with cap'ring fools . . . To laugh at gibing boys, and stand the push / Of every beardless vain comparative.' The former ruler was upstaged by sinking into the crowd, becoming 'stale and cheap to vulgar company', and being 'swallowed' when he 'Grew a companion to the common streets'. So, the secret of Bolingbroke's rise, he admits, was not 'popularity' but box-office manipulation: 'By being seldom seen, I could not stir but, like a comet, I was wondered at' (*1 Henry IV*, 3.2.40–70). Throughout the Histories Shakespeare traces this transfer of symbolic value from palace to playhouse, as the showman succeeds by winning 'The hearts of all that he did angle for' (4.3.86), and the empowered audience slowly comes to realise that, in the words of the Chorus to *Henry V*, ''tis your thoughts that now must deck our kings' (Prologue, 28). Traditionalists still piously like to believe that 'A substitute shines brightly as a king / Until a king comes by' (*Merchant of Venice*, 5.1.94–5). But what *Richard II* proves is that this revolutionary exchange of value between the prince and the pretender is now commercially irreversible:

As in a theatre the eyes of men,
After a well-graced actor leaves the stage,
Are idly bent on him that enters next,
Thinking his prattle to be tedious,
Even so, or with much more contempt, men's eyes
Did scowl at Richard.

(5.2.23–8)

As the impostor is applauded by Londoners until 'You would have thought the very windows spake, / So many greedy looks of young and old / Through casements darted their desiring eyes' (12–14), Shakespeare seems to be proclaiming victory for his own professional theatre over the 'tedious prattle' patronised at court. Now it is a player-king who controls the stage, as he scripts Richard's abdication, stages his own coronation and triumphal procession, and then produces the pardon of Aumerle, with repeat challenges, as a rebuke to the injustice of the original trial. Tellingly, the new king clinches his accession by announcing a change of genre and 'recasting his authority in comedic form' as he mocks his own mercy: 'Our scene is altered from a serious thing, / And now changed to "The Beggar and the King"' (5.3.77–8).[15] For by citing the bawdy story of 'King Cophetua and the Beggar Maid' King Henry promises to become a merry monarch and the people's choice. And a key defection in this shift comes when we hear that the Lord Chamberlain, the Earl of Worcester, 'hath forsook the court, / Broken his staff of office, and dispersed / The household of the king' (2.3.26–8). Whether or not it refers to the actual Earl of Worcester who was a chief protector of Catholic artists such as the composer William Byrd, this news reverberates with implications for Shakespeare's dealings with the great. Like Gaunt's unstrung lute, Worcester's broken staff marks a definitive end to the older system of cultural patronage based on the power of the aristocratic house. It cannot be coincidence, therefore, that *Richard II* was, we think, the first work acted by Shakespeare's company after the most revolutionary, and indeed violent, reorganisation in the history of the Elizabethan stage. In 1595, when the play was put on under Burbage, the actors had just been given unprecedented status as the Lord Chamberlain's Men, after their patron Lord Strange, then Earl of Derby, died in circumstances as shocking but mysterious as those surrounding the murder of Gloucester. He was probably poisoned by Protestants to extinguish Catholic plots for him to succeed his cousin Elizabeth. Immediately, however, the Burbage troupe put on the badge of a new protector, as servants of another of the Queen's relations, Henry Carey, Lord Hunsdon. This elderly courtier ran the Revels Office as Lord Chamberlain with a light touch, and may be portrayed in the play as the bluff old Duke of York. He was the bastard of Henry VIII by a sister of Anne Boleyn, and illegitimacy seems to have characterised his businesses. Theatre historians agree, in any case, that his control of the Chamberlain's Men was another convenient fiction. From this point, for Shakespeare, patronage art like royal portraiture was only ever what the fallen Richard calls his mirror, a sycophantic 'folly' made for lies:

> O flatt'ring glass,
> Like to my followers in prosperity,
> Thou dost beguile me! Was this face
> That every day under his household roof
> Did keep ten thousand men? Was this the face
> That like the sun did make beholders wink?
> Is this the face which faced so many follies,
> That was at last outfaced by Bolingbroke?
> A brittle glory shineth in this face.
> As brittle as the glory is the face,
>   [*He shatters the glass*]
> For there it is, cracked in a hundred shivers.
> Mark, silent King, the moral of this sport:
> How soon my sorrow hath destroyed my face.

(4.1.269–81)

'Like the routes of domination, the routes of autonomy are complex', observed Pierre Bourdieu, for 'struggles at the heart of the political field may best serve the interest of writers most concerned about literary independence'.[16] In the case of *Richard II*, certainly, the 'by-paths and indirect crook'd ways' (*2 Henry IV*, 4.3.312) by which Henry reaches the crown run parallel to those by which Shakespeare approached his artistic sovereignty after the murder of the Earl of Derby. Thus, a few months before the play was staged the author signed a contract to become one of the first shareholders in the joint-stock company that was the real capitalist foundation of the Chamberlain's Men as future owners of the Globe. This document has not survived, but we know from others that it would have assured Shakespeare a life income from receipts and royalties in return for two plays a year and rights to these in perpetuity.[17] It may not be irrelevant, therefore, that in the text written at this time the dethronement of Richard begins as he signs away his kingdom, 'With inky blots and rotten parchment bonds' (2.1.64). For Shakespeare's contract would be the most damaging of all instruments in the downfall of the patronage system that previously underwrote security for English writers, as it opened up the playhouse to the new commercial monarchy of the mass market. No wonder, then, that in a London that prefers a bawdy ballad to poetry, the less poetry Bolingbroke speaks the higher he rises, while the more Richard says the further he falls: 'like a deep well / That owes two buckets filling one another, / The emptier ever dancing in the air, / The other down, unseen, and full of water' (4.1.174–7). With this economy, Richard's abdication, which makes 'Proud majesty a subject' when he resigns 'All pomp and majesty' and is forced to 'ravel out' his 'weaved-up follies' (201–19), acquires the extra-textual significance of Shakespeare's own devil's contract in the summer of 1594. For what the author also surrendered, by exchanging his private patron for a paying public, this play implies, was the gorgeous 'pomp and majesty' and 'weaved-up follies' of his poetry itself. Here, then, is the secret *sadness* of *Richard II*. As events 'undeck the pompous body of a king' (240) what we also watch is another professional abdication, as the dramatist disavows everything he has himself previously said by unpicking the pompous rhetoric of his own 'disordered spring', stripping out the 'superfluous branches' of his art, just as the Gardeners prune their trees, 'That bearing boughs may live' (3.4.49–65). So Richard, critics note, increasingly resembles the bathetic, hyperbolic and fantastic Queen of *Venus and Adonis*; and, like hers, his poetry is comically subverted as (in the verdict of the Gardener) 'a waste of idle hours' (67).[18] We might well infer that it was part of Shakespeare's contract to satisfy the 'Gardeners' in the playhouse audience by curbing the music of his own verse. The crisis of representation in *Richard II* reads, therefore, in the light of such a shrewd commercial deal, like Shakespeare's own sad renunciation of those 'flattering sounds' he had composed for private patrons, as 'an unstringed viol' or a broken harp:

> Music do I hear.
> Ha, ha; keep time! How sour sweet music is
> When time is broke and no proportion kept.
> So is it in the music of men's lives.
> And here have I the daintiness of ear
> To check time broke in a disordered string;
> But for the concord of my state and time
> Had not an ear to hear my true time broke.
> I wasted time, and now doth time waste me.

(5.5.41–9)

'I wasted time': the confession he has Richard make reads like Shakespeare's *mea culpa* when we recognise how different his career had been up to this traumatic turning-point, for until 1595 the author of *Richard II* was celebrated not as a playwright but as the author of the *de luxe* books of poems, *Venus and Adonis* and *The*

Rape of Lucrece. Both were dedicated to Shakespeare's own courtly patron, the Earl of Southampton, who in the preface to *Lucrece* was promised everything the poet wrote in future, since 'What I have to do is yours'. That was printed in the spring of 1594, a few days before Shakespeare signed the contract to write commercially competitive plays. As Shakespeareans explain, 'No one could have known what an extraordinary moment this was' in the history of literature, especially as the writer had also just begun a sequence of luscious 'sugared sonnets' inspired by the boy Southampton, which was already circulating 'among his private friends' in the elite.[19] Legend has it that the young Earl rewarded Shakespeare with a colossal tip of £1000.[20] Yet the Sonnets would sour into the diary of a failed patronage relationship; and, after *Richard II*, the creator of *Venus* and *Lucrece* would never publish a narrative poem again. Patrick Cheney proposes that Shakespeare still persisted, even as a committed commercial playwright, in evading consumer expectations by writing as a 'poet-playwright'; and Lukas Erne argues that soon after *Richard II* he also started to envisage himself as a 'literary dramatist', with playtexts consecrated in the printed form of a folio for the appreciation not of playhouse auditors but of discerning *readers*.[21] Yet from now on his notion of the private patron would be like the monarch in his plays, 'a mockery king of snow' (4.1.250), as the symbolic revolution through which court protection was permitted to survive as a legal fiction – with playhouses owned by entrepreneurs but licensed in the name of their supposed noble sponsors[22] – was registered in his professional metaphor of the flawed Lord of Misrule.[23] Shakespeare would learn to fend off bourgeois demands by appealing to this convenient scarecrow of princely support.[24] But in *Richard II* the tragedy represents a literary art that for the moment seems imprisoned to make 'The Commons . . . satisfied', as the King concedes: 'They shall be satisfied. I'll read enough / When I do see the very book indeed / Where all my sins are writ, and that's myself' (4.1.262–5). Thus, Richard's fantasy of God as the ultimate royal patron – with 'A glorious angel' in 'heavenly pay' for 'every man that Bolingbroke hath pressed' into the amphitheatre – seems an apt prospectus, in 1595, for a moribund literary system, subjected to the 'desiring eyes' of 'So many greedy looks of young and old'. For while 'twelve thousand . . . twenty thousand' and even 'forty thousand' spectators applaud the antics of the player, 'within the hollow crown' of the defunct patronage system, where Death now keeps court, the

solipsistic poet is without an audience as reads alone from the book
of himself:

> Of comfort no man speak.
> Let's talk of graves, of worms and epitaphs,
> Make dust our paper, and with rainy eyes
> Write sorrow on the bosom of the earth.
> Let's choose executors and talk of wills . . .
> For God's sake, let us sit upon the ground
> And tell sad stories of the death of kings . . .
>
>   (3.2.66–152)

'All is said' in *Richard II* with the sadness of a poet whose paper
turned to dust as he wrote 'sorrow on the bosom' of the system that
had nurtured him, and 'cut himself from the hope implicit' in his
dedications to his god-like patron, with 'a cold sense of disappointment and loss'. As Park Honan comments, Shakespeare's biographers underestimate the conflicted emotions of this moment of
opportunity, 'just as they neglect the difficulties now faced by his
troupe'. For 'once committed to the theatre', it was unlikely that any
play-book would equal the prestige of his poems, and 'whatever he
did, he might be less than respectable' from now on. So, though 'his
fidelity to one troupe would be unique among poets, that loyalty is
no sign of contentment', Honan warns, as 'there are underlying com-
plications in his ambiguous writing' to imply that he opposed his
new vocation as much as he accepted it, and 'defied his medium'
even as 'he made use of a compromised way of life'. Shakespeare
'subverted many norms of the theatre', we are reminded, and
'mocked popular assumptions' in his most popular works.[25] And
Richard II suggests that this was because the chance provided by the
murder of their patron released the players from the problem the
play poses – of mouthing lies at court – but at the price of delivering
the writer as a hostage to the modern tyranny of consumer demand.
We can confirm this interpretation since, by chance, we have some
market research on exactly what the public thought of Shakespeare's
'pompous' poetry and 'disordered' words. William Scott was an official of the defence ministry in 1597 when he compiled a guidebook
to good usage where the Bard is faulted for 'stuffing' *Richard II*
with his 'very idle verse' and 'ambiguous' style. 'By the placing of
his words', Scott complains, Shakespeare ensures that no one
understands a thing he says, an obscurity achieved 'by heaping

words and piling one phrase upon another, to double and redouble'. Revealingly, the 'ill phrase' this Polonius thinks most 'vile' (*Hamlet*, 2.2.111) is Richard's self-portrait as a Sun King, which he deplores because it leaves unclear whether power is in the 'searching eye of heaven' or on earth. The bad science belongs to the King; but Shakespeare's first close reader has put his finger on an authorial equivocation over the key metaphor for sovereignty and figure of value in the plays. *Richard II*, the bureaucrat notices, is a schizophrenic text.[26] And no wonder, since what this drama about the defeat of poetry actually represents is Shakespeare's own ambivalent position between crown and crowd, the monarch and the mob. The author would go on to please his paying public with plays which became the world's greatest box-office success, 'wooing poor craftsmen with the craft of smiles'. Yet always, this drama predicts, in sadness at discarding the now 'stringless instrument' of a poet at the court. Prompted by the murder of his patron in that house of lies, *Richard II* leaves Shakespeare neither a king nor a beggar, but the 'nothing' between palace and playhouse, the pricelessness of the poetry and the profits from the prose:

> Thus play I in one person many people,
> And none contented. Sometimes am I king;
> Then treason makes me wish myself a beggar,
> And so I am. Then crushing penury
> Persuades me I was better when a king.
> Then am I kinged again, and by and by
> Think that I am unkinged by Bolingbroke,
> And straight am nothing. But whate'er I be,
> Nor I, nor any man that but man is,
> With nothing shall be pleased till he be eased
> With being nothing.
>   *The music plays*
>
>   (5.5.31–41)

Notes

1 All quotations are from *The Norton Shakespeare*, ed. Stephen Greenblatt et al., based on the Oxford text (New York: Norton, 1997).

2 For the broken string as a symbol of discord in a post-Reformation world see John North, *The Ambassador's Secret: Holbein and the World of the Renaissance* (London: Phoenix, 2004), pp. 290–305; and

Susan Foster, Ashok Roy and Martin Wyld, *Holbein's Ambassadors* (London: National Gallery Publications & Yale University Press, 1997), pp. 30–2.

3 Francis Barker, *The Tremulous Private Body: Essays on Subjection* (London: Routledge, 1984), pp. 25–6, 35.

4 Richard Wilson, *Secret Shakespeare: Studies in Theatre, Religion and Resistance* (Manchester: Manchester University Press, 2004), pp. 19–37.

5 See Peter Ure, *King Richard II*, The Arden Shakespeare (London: Methuen, 1956), pp. 11, 16, 9.

6 Michel de Montaigne, *Essais* 3, ch. 13, 'De l'expérience' (Paris: Bibliothèque de la Pléaide, 1962), p. 1203; *The Essayes of Montaigne*, trans. John Florio (New York: Modern Library, 1933), p. 970.

7 Ibid., *Essais*, 2, ch. 12, p. 601; *Essayes*, p. 482.

8 Jacques Derrida, 'Force of Law: The "Mystical Foundation of Authority"', in *Acts of Religion*, trans. Mary Quaintance, ed. Gil Adair (London: Routledge, 2002), p. 242.

9 Ibid., p. 252.

10 Michel Foucault, *Fearless Speech*, trans. anon., ed. Joseph Pearson (New York: Semiotext(e), 2001), pp. 32–3.

11 M. M. Mahood, *Shakespeare's Wordplay* (London: Methuen, 1968), p. 75.

12 John Davies, 'Hymns to Astraea', xv, quoted in Roy Strong, *The Cult of Elizabeth: Elizabethan Portraiture and Pageantry* (London: Thames and Hudson, 1977), p. 52.

13 Stephen Greenblatt, *Renaissance Self-Fashioning: From More to Shakespeare* (Chicago: University of Chicago Press, 1980), p. 80.

14 See Michel Foucault, *Discipline and Punish: The Birth of the Prison*, trans. Alan Sheridan (Harmondsworth: Penguin, 1979), esp. p. 51.

15 Leonard Tennenhouse, *Power on Display: The Politics of Shakespeare's Genres* (London: Methuen, 1986), p. 81.

16 Pierre Bourdieu, *The Rules of Art: Genesis and Structure of the Literary Field*, trans. Susan Emmanuel (Cambridge: Polity Press, 1996), p. 52.

17 Peter Thomson, *Shakespeare's Professional Career* (Cambridge: Cambridge University Press, 1992), p. 117.

18 See Gary Schmidgall, *Shakespeare and the Poet's Life* (Lexington: University of Kentucky Press, 1990), pp. 139–41.

19 Thomson, *Shakespeare's Professional Career*, p. 111; Francis Meres, *Palladis Tamia: Wit's Treasury Being the Second Part of Wit's Commonwealth* (1598), quoted in Park Honan, *Shakespeare: A Life* (Oxford: Oxford University Press, 1998), p. 180.

20 Thomson, *Shakespeare's Professional Career*, p. 111.

21 Patrick Cheney, *Shakespeare, National Poet-Playwright* (Cambridge: Cambridge University Press, 2004); Lukas Erne, *Shakespeare as Literary Dramatist* (Cambridge: Cambridge University Press, 2003).

22 See Richard Dutton, *Mastering the Revels: The Regulation and Censorship of English Renaissance Drama* (Basingstoke: Macmillan, 1991), pp. 31–2.

23 For the classic account of the illegitimate patronage of the Lord of Misrule see Anne Barton, *Shakespeare and the Idea of the Play* (Harmondsworth: Penguin, 1967), pp. 109–24.

24 See Richard Wilson, 'The Management of Mirth: Shakespeare *via* Bourdieu', in Jean Howard and Scott Shershow (eds), *Marxist Shakespeares* (London: Routledge, 2001), pp. 159–77.

25 Honan, *Shakespeare: A Life*, p. 197.

26 William Scott quoted in Stanley Wells, 'By the Placing of His Words', *Times Literary Supplement*, 26 September 2003, pp. 14–15; see also Chapter 10, below.

Part II
Texts

5

Foucault's epistemic shift and verbatim repetition in Shakespeare

Gabriel Egan

Since the mid-1980s the ideas of Michel Foucault have had a powerful effect upon Shakespeare studies. First appearing in French in
1969, Foucault's essay 'What Is an Author?' was published in
English in 1975,[1] two years before Roland Barthes's 'The Death of
the Author'[2] which, from different premises, argued essentially the
same point: the 'author' is a phenomenon frequently misunderstood
in literary studies. For Foucault, an author was not the simple
concept it might seem: some kinds of writing have authors and
others do not. A contract, for example, is usually not the writing of
any of the persons who sign it. With the rise of empiricism in the
seventeenth and eighteenth centuries, science, which had hitherto
valued the author, became impersonal (relying on verifiable, repro-
ducible, tests) while literary works, which hitherto had been relatively indifferent to authors, became personal.[3] Authors are not so
much intrinsic originators of texts but rather extrinsic products of
the consumption of texts; author are assigned to texts which need
them and not others. It is better, Foucault argued, to think not of
authors but of the author-function, an exegetic principle applicable
not only to written texts but whole fields of study. Above all, the
author-function is 'the principle of thrift in the proliferation of
meaning', used coercively to exclude outlandish interpretations.[4]
Appropriately enough for an argument about textual multiplicity,
this famous summation of Foucault's idea does not appear in all versions of his essay and is absent from the first English translation.
Foucault located the important epistemic break around 1800 when
the needs of private intellectual property generated our modern
sense of an author. In another area of Shakespeare studies,
Foucault's work on sexual identity achieved a wide audience via
Alan Bray, whose *Homosexuality in Renaissance England* argued

that in the early modern period there was no subject-position from which one could identify oneself as a homosexual.[5] For the early modern, sodomy was a matter of doing, not being: sinful, to be sure, but not a matter of self-definition. This claim is more contentious than the matter of the author-function, and Joseph Cady has made a convincing case that in the work of Francis Bacon and Thomas Heywood there is evidence that a homosexual identity was in existence, contrary to Foucault's and Bray's claims.[6] In early modern printing and theatre practice there is evidence to counter the Foucauldian claim that their sense of verbatim repetition was quite unlike ours.

Near the end of a ground-breaking study of the notion of authenticity in relation to the Shakespearian text, Margreta de Grazia observed a textual phenomenon that is disturbing for us, but apparently was not for the early moderns. Edmond Malone's 1790 edition of *The Plays and Poems of William Shakespeare* marked a sudden shift in Shakespeare studies in which a new rigorous objectivity, based on factual records, was required, and by reference to the earliest available printings Malone attempted to reproduce Shakespeare with as little interference as possible, ideally 'verbatim'. But Malone noticed that Shakespeare did not share his concern with verbatim reproduction: in a play a single document can be read aloud by different people using different words. Specifically, De Grazia cited *2 Henry VI* in which the articles of peace are twice read aloud with differences in wording. Malone put this down to carelessness on Shakespeare's part, but De Grazia sought an explanation using Michel Foucault's notion of the author-function:

> For Malone, these deviations within the text were symptomatic not of the medium's instability, but rather of Shakespeare's 'negligence'. Indeed, he found them so characteristic in the contested works that he considered them conclusive proof of Shakespeare's authorship. At this point, we can see how the notion of a single authorial consciousness (with its occasional lapses into unconsciousness) serves a regulatory function, converting what we have called the 'copiousness' of both mechanical and rhetorical 'copy' into personal idiosyncrasy. Verbatim repetition requires a language in standardized stasis, put under the mastery of precisely the historicized, individuated, and entitled subject Malone both presumed and projected in his 1790s Shakespeare.[7]

Although De Grazia does not mention Foucault's notion of the author-function for another two pages, and then only in a footnote concerning the anti-Stratfordian conspiracy theorists, the above paragraph is clearly informed by Foucault's assertion that authors are a thrifty brake upon copious interpretative proliferation. Elsewhere De Grazia had already explicitly invoked Foucault's author-function in relation to twentieth-century editing theory,[8] especially New Bibliography, and in her book-length study she traced the search for authenticity to its source: Malone's Shakespeare edition (revised in 1821), the first to display the concern for rigorous authenticity which was to characterise subsequent work in the field. With the late eighteenth-century 'invention of man', a grand reorganization of knowledge into subject-oriented disciplines according to Foucault, literary scholarship created 'Shakespeare' as 'an exemplary instance of the autonomous self'[9] comprising the biography and the works, and, most enduringly, a set of rules and practices for relating the constructed author to the artistic output.

In support of Foucault's assertion De Grazia claims that around 1800 the use of what we call quotation marks in printed works changed. Previously the symbol marked *sententiae*, sayings which because of their importance were worth remembering and repeating and thus were worth circulating freely (a form of public ownership), but, around the time Foucault identifies as the birth of the modern author-function, quotation marks began to be used to acknowledge borrowing of another's words and thus showed a respect for private intellectual property.[10] At this time novels began to distinguish one character's words from another's by use of quotation marks. We can easily accept that when repeating another's words in a play a character might garble, compress or paraphrase what is heard, but surely a letter read twice should not change its contents. De Grazia comments:

> With predictable indignation, Malone observed that when even a written document – a letter or proclamation, for example – was read at one point in a play and then again at some later point, 'inaccuracies' were introduced: 'When [Shakespeare] had occasion to quote the same paper twice (not from memory, but *verbatim*) from negligence he does not always attend to the words of the paper which he has occasion to quote, but makes one of the persons of the drama recite them with variations, though he holds the very papers before his eyes.' In a scene from *Henry VI Part II*, for example, the same articles of peace between France and England are twice read aloud, first by the Bishop who reads 'dutchy of Anjou and the county of Maine' and then by the Duke who read 'the dutchies of Anjou and of Maine'.[11]

If proven, this claim would take the principle of Shakespearian textual instability to a new level, since indifference to textual variation might then exist not only between authorial versions, as E. A. J. Honigmann showed,[12] but also within a single document, and simply because of a pre-1800 mindset which did not care for logical regularity in the way we do. No longer could such variation be taken as a sign of the imperfect work of memory or unusually careless transcription, but would actually be the normal habit of the time. Fortunately for those who value the Enlightenment, and despite De Grazia's reference to 'a letter or a proclamation' and her apparent choice of 2 *Henry VI* 'for example', there is only the example of F 2 *Henry VI* and it is not as De Grazia describes it.

De Grazia's works are concerned with the presence of non-authorial writing, with the 'wide array of collective and extended contributions and transformations'[13] which find their way into textualisations, and she refuses to demote these in relation to authorial writing. Anyone who misquotes De Grazia has the ready excuse that her own work validates such transformations, whether conscious or unconscious. By the same token, one is entitled to imagine a smirk on Jacques Derrida's face as he corrects printers' errors in the proofs of his published work, entirely putting others' contributions and transformations under erasure. Equally playful is Randall McLeod's deliberately inaccurate quotations from and allusions to Shakespeare criticism, such as calling the love of punning Shakespeare's 'fertile Cleopatra'[14] instead of Samuel Johnson's 'fatal Cleopatra'.[15] Amongst such textual *jouissance* it might appear boorish to insist that one's quotation of De Grazia renders accurately her quotation of Malone, but mine does. However, her quotation does not render accurately her source, the 'Dissertation on the three parts of King Henry VI', in which Malone actually wrote:

> When he ha<u>s</u> occasion to quote the same paper twice, (not from memory, but verbatim,) from negligence he does not always attend to the words of the paper which he has occasion to quote, but makes one of the persons of the drama recite them with variations, though he holds the very paper_ quoted before his eyes.[16]

My underlining marks points where De Grazia's quotation of Malone deleted or inserted material, which error – failure to repeat verbatim – Malone is in the act of lamenting and which troubles the post-Enlightenment sensibility. However, the sense of the passage is not really altered, so why not let this sort of thing pass? Because De Grazia's concern for the materiality of the text will not permit such sloppy idealism: there is, she insists in this book and elsewhere, nothing but the textualization.[17]

So apt for my argument are De Grazia's slips that one is tempted to resort to Freud to explain them: surely something other than inadvertence must be at work. Whatever witty spirit commanded De Grazia's hand, it did not leave for at least another sentence, making her write that the articles of peace are read 'first by the Bishop . . . and then by the Duke'. Rather, in all early versions of the play the order of speaking in the scene (1.1) is the other way around: the Duke reads, breaks off, then the Bishop takes over. De Grazia quoted from the Folio text and modernised the spelling, as the rules of quotation allow, but she added an extra word of her own, which they do not. The second reading is not 'the dutchies of Anjou and of Maine' (as she has it) but 'the dutchies of Anjou and Maine' (a modernisation of F's 'the Dutchesse of Aniou and Maine'). De Grazia invoked Foucault and *2 Henry VI* to claim that the early moderns would not have perceived a significant discrepancy in a document being read aloud twice with different wordings. Whether there was such an epistemic shift is too large a question to address here, but it is demonstrable that the evidence from Shakespeare does not support the argument that there was. To see why, we must attend to the processes of the early modern theatre and the printing-house that, quite impersonally and for no epistemological reason, tended to produce the textual coherence that De Grazia and Foucault claim was not typical until after 1800.

The First Part of the Contention / 2 Henry VI begins with Suffolk's return from France bringing Margaret, King Henry VI's bride-to-be, and the articles of peace which specify a kind of negative dowry of English possessions in France to be given to her father. In the quarto, Humphrey Duke of Gloucester begins to read the articles:

> *Humphrey. Imprimis,* It is agreed betweene the French King *Charles,*
> and *William de la Poule,* Marquesse of *Suffolke,* Embassador for
> *Henry* King of England, that the said *Henry* shal wed and espouse
> the Ladie *Margaret,* daughter to *Raynard* King of *Naples, Cyssels,*
> and *Ierusalem,* and crowne her Queene of England, ere the 30. of
> the next month.
> *Item.* It is further agreed betwene them, that the Dutches of *Anioy*
> and of *Maine,* shalbe released and deliuered ouer to the King her fa.
> Duke *Humphrey* lets it fall.

Gloucester breaks off reading, saying he is overcome by a 'sodain qualme', and Cardinal Beaufort, Bishop of Winchester, takes over:

> *Cardinall. Item*, It is further agreed betweene them, that the Dutches of *Anioy* and of *Mayne*, shal be released and deliuered ouer to the King her father, & she sent ouer of the King of Englands owne proper cost and charges without dowry.[18]

Where the two recitations overlap ('*Item* . . . fa') the words in the quarto version are identical, although the punctuation and spelling vary. The same events in the Folio version are thus:

> *Glo. Reads*. Inprimis, *It is agreed betweene the French K. Charles, and William de la Pole Marquesse of Suffolke, Ambassador for Henry King of England, That the said Henry shal espouse the Lady Margaret, daughter vnto Reignier King of Naples, Sicillia, and Ierusalem, and Crowne her Queene of England, ere the thirtieth of May next ensuing.*
>
> > *Item, That the Dutchy of Aniou, and the County of Main, shall be released and deliuered to the King her father.*
>
> *King*. Vnkle, how now?
> *Glo*. Pardon me gracious Lord,
> Some sodaine qualme hath struck me at the heart

As in the quarto, Cardinal Beaufort, Bishop of Winchester, takes over reading the articles:

> *Win. Item, It is further agreed betweene them, That the Dutchesse of Aniou and Maine, shall be released and deliuered ouer to the King her Father, and shee sent ouer of the King of Englands owne proper Cost and Charges, without hauing any Dowry.*[19]

As De Grazia noted, in the Folio there are substantial differences between the first and second readings of the articles. The second reading inserts '*It is further agreed betweene them*' after the listing tag '*Item*', changes '*Dutchy*' to '*Dutchesse*', cuts '*the County of*' and inserts '*ouer*' before '*to the King her Father*'. If the Folio represents what was performed, the theatre practitioners must have thought the audience would not notice or would not care if two men read the same piece of paper differently, and this suggests habits of mind which we, as modern readers and writers, do not share. Even if the Folio does not represent what was performed, it might well represent what was in the underlying manuscript (whose writer did not notice or noticed and did not care) and in any case it shows that those involved in printing the play were not sufficiently concerned, or not sufficiently attentive, to regularise the two readings.

In the quarto version of this scene, the second reading is identical to the first, as we have seen. More importantly, however, the two quarto readings are almost identical to the Folio's second reading. The New Bibliographical consensus is that the quarto text was probably based on a memorial reconstruction (perhaps made for the purpose of touring the play) and the Folio printing was based on foul papers, perhaps reworked for a revival, supplemented by Q3, itself a Q1 reprint.[20] Without accepting this view, we can make some initial inferences about the performances represented by these texts. Whether or not the papers that were passed to the actors contained a discrepancy between the first and second readings of the articles of peace, one additional copy of those words would have been made as a property document to be used on the stage. In a study of such documents, Tiffany Stern argues that the words to be read on stage would be specially marked in authorial papers: they would be headed 'letter' (or some such) so that the theatrical scribe would know to leave them out of the actor's 'part' and instead to write them on a separate piece of paper to be handed to the actor during the performance.[21] In the play-book used backstage to run the performance, Stern argues, it would be essential that speakers' names were clearly marked but the words themselves could be omitted since these existed on the property itself, so only the tag 'The letter' need be recorded. However, it would be wise for the play-book to repeat the speech prefix after the letter to make absolutely clear that the same person is still speaking, and thus in early printed texts the use of a particular speech prefix after the reading of a letter does not indicate that someone else read the letter, as has often been thought in the case of Antonio's letter to Bassanio in *The Merchant of Venice*.[22] Not all of this is convincing, since it is difficult to believe that a play-book would be licensed if it were manifestly an incomplete record of the words to be spoken on stage, and we have no evidence of the licensing of supplementary textual properties. Stern quotes E. K. Chambers's belief that early modern actors did not memorise their 'letters' since the property documents would be available to them during the performance.[23] Whether or not actors memorised their 'letters', the creation of a property document enforces singularity: it can be only one thing or another. A professional dramatist who in his authorial papers created a discrepancy between two readings of the same letter – a discrepancy of the kind seen in F *2 Henry VI* and pointed out by Malone and De Grazia – could hardly be unaware that the making of the property document would in any case eliminate one of the variants. Strong evidence that during performance actors read aloud the lines in their property documents (rather than memorising them beforehand) is supplied by Edward Alleyn's 'part' for the title role in *Orlando Furioso* lacking the verses he reads aloud, as Stern points out,[24] so any authorial discrepancy between two readings of a document necessarily disappeared in performance.

Whether or not the papers passed to the theatrical scribe were consistent in the two readings of the articles of peace in *2 Henry VI*, the theatre scribe must have chosen one of the readings to form the copy for the property document. A moment's reflection would make him choose Cardinal Beaufort's reading, because it is complete, rather than Duke Humphrey's which is not. If the actors relied on the property document for their lines, both men would speak what was written down for Cardinal Beaufort in the papers passed to the theatrical scribe. This conclusion is consistent with (but does not prove) the New Bibliographical view that the Folio represents the discrepant authorial papers and the quarto represents the non-discrepant performance, since the two quarto readings are virtually identical with Cardinal Beaufort's reading from the Folio. There is a small difference between Cardinal Beaufort's reading in the Folio and the two readings in the quarto, and it too is consistent with F representing the authorial papers and Q representing the performance. If in the authorial manuscript Cardinal Beaufort referred to 'the Dutches of Anioy and Maine' to be 'released and delivered' to Margaret's father, there might be an unwanted suggestion that a person (a duchess of Anjou and Maine) rather than lands were to be freed and handed over. Indeed this is what Beaufort appears to say in the Folio: 'the Dutchesse of Aniou and Maine'. There is no such duchess in the play: only lands are to be handed over. To prevent the potential misunderstanding that the spelling 'Dutches' creates, the theatre scribe making the property document could have repeated the word 'of' before 'Maine' so that the phrasing becomes unambiguous, since no one could be the 'duchess of Anjou and of Maine'. Thus a long 'e' pronunciation (in the phonetic alphabet, 'i:') of 'Dutches', indicating two duchies, would be ensured. This is what Q has, and again this is consistent with that text representing what was performed and, in this case, including an alteration which removed an unwanted ambiguity.

There is an alternative explanation for the differences between Q and F concerning the articles of peace. In the textual introduction to the Oxford *Complete Works*, William Montgomery recorded that in editing the play for his doctoral thesis he decided that F's second recitation derived not from the single manuscript used for most of the play but from a quarto, probably Q3.[25] In the textual note for Cardinal Beaufort's recitation (numbered 1.1.55–9 in the Oxford edition), Montgomery reported that 'F has been contaminated by Q here: the Cardinal's reading should be identical with Gloucester's'.[26] To understand why Montgomery thought this we need to turn to his doctoral thesis in which he considered the long-recognised phenomenon that certain passages in the play show 'extraordinarily close correspondence in Q and F', so close that the memorial reconstruction hypothesis cannot provide the explanation because no one's memory could be so good.[27] Peter Alexander's answer was that the reconstructors had scraps of manuscript to supplement their memories, but R. B. McKerrow's explanation has won out: F was intermittently set up from a copy of Q. Curbing the excesses of Andrew S. Cairncross's Arden edition of the play,[28] Montgomery observed that the only way to demonstrate the dependence of one edition on another is to show that the latter maintains a clear error which is also in the former. It is no good showing that indifferent variants (that is, those which are equally as good as a different word which appears in a third text) agree since these can happen independently of one another, and it is equally pointless to show, as Cairncross frequently did, that good readings agree since these can come from a reliable manuscript source and not the earlier printing. An error which Montgomery thought significant was the spelling 'Dutchesse' in the Cardinal's reading of the articles of peace in the Folio text and in Q3, as against 'Dutches' which appears in Q2 and Q1. Montgomery admitted that a compositor might make such a change in spelling whatever his copy read, and especially if he saw 'Dutches' and thought this meant a person more unambiguously spelt 'Dutchesse'. If a compositor did this, he is responsible for creating in Q3 the absurdity of 'the Dutchesse of *Anioy* and of *Mayne*', which perhaps does not seem wrong until one has to say it aloud. Because the spelling could be compositorial, Montgomery thought this not a strong Q3/F link, but none the less suggestive of some Q/F connection or that 'very similar manuscripts lay behind this part of both Q and F'.[29] Considering all the Q/F agreements in error, Montgomery showed that if a quarto was consulted to make F then it was probably Q3.[30] In all Montgomery found seven moments in the play where F seems dependent on Q, and he decided that because the link is transcriptional – Q3 was consulted to fill gaps in the copy for F – it was now reasonable for him to 'extend these seven points of demonstrable transcriptional contact to include that portion of their immediate context in which Q and F, for the most part, verbally agreed'.[31] Starting from each moment of agreement in error, Montgomery worked outwards until F and Q3 ceased to agree, and, because several of the seven spots of agreement are close to one another, this 'join the dots' procedure makes them merge, producing three substantial chunks of F where Q3 was consulted: F TLN 63–79, 858–904, 2598–639. To these three sections Montgomery added two more where stage directions in F are so like those in Q that a transcriptional link was, he thought, certain: the entrance of the mayor of St Albans (F TLN 795–6) and the entrance of the armourer and his neighbours in 2.3 through to the end of that scene and the opening direction of the next one (F TLN 1115–70). The first section where Montgomery saw a transcriptional link between Q and F is the Cardinal's reading of the articles of peace and continuing on for a dozen lines until the King, Queen and Suffolk exit.

Having noted that the Dutchesse/Dutches spellings were not strong evidence that F was printed directly from Q3, Montgomery admitted that the other evidence pointing to a transcriptional link between F and one of the quartos is even weaker.[32] This other evidence is five cases of mislineation of verse which F shares with all the quartos, and a speech prefix problem in F at TLN 2625–8 where Butcher and Dicke (the same person) get different successive speeches.[33] Cairncross explained the Butcher/Dicke confusion by imagining that an additional speech was added to the Q used to make F and this should have been accompanied by the deletion of a speech prefix, but by error the deletion was not made. This error in F, then, seems to be at a point where F depends on Q, but of course the error could just as easily be an error in the authorial manuscript underlying F, as Montgomery observed.[34] The mislineation evidence Montgomery characterised as 'not conclusive' of Q influencing F, but he did not speculate how else the agreement in error might have come about;[35] coincidence must be one possibility. Montgomery decided that 'The "duches" [*sic*] evidence is perhaps the strongest ... but again, by no means conclusive'.[36] Having declared the evidence for a transcriptional link between F and Q inconclusive, it is surprising that Montgomery chose to merge the seven points of 'demonstrable transcriptional contact' into three larger sections where F can be assumed to have been set from Q3. Montgomery assumed that Q3 was used as copy for F starting from the Cardinal's reading of the articles of peace and continuing on for the next dozen lines as well. But this hypothesis requires that, as Q3 was copied, some of it was left out and invented additions put in, for there are differences. The second 'of' was removed from Q3's 'of Anioy and of Mayne', Q3's 'without dowry' was supplemented by two additional redundant words to make F's 'without hauing any Dowry'. An additional 'the' was added to Q3's 'we heere create thee first Duke of Suffolke' to make F's 'create thee the first Duke of Suffolke', which extra 'the' is semantically redundant but regularises the metre. In what might be a simple correction, a redundant 'and' was removed from Q3's list 'Winchester, Gloster, Yorke, and Buckingham, Somerset, Salisbury, and Warwicke'. In Montgomery's hypothesis, the person who copied this chunk of Q3 to make F (whether scribe or compositor) made these four minor alterations as he went, one of which improved metre and another removed redundancy, and yet he made no attempt to adjust the new material to fit what had already been read out from the same document in Gloucester's broken-off reading of it. It is hard to know how to take the word 'should' in Montgomery's observation that 'the Cardinal's reading should be identical with Gloucester's',[37] since his explanation of the textual situation rests upon the existence of an early modern copyist or compositor even less concerned with coherence and fidelity than the haphazard norm posited by De Grazia.

The New Bibliographical consensus that Q1 represents a necessarily imperfect memorial reconstruction of a play better represented by F was attacked by Steven Urkowitz who saw Q1 as an equally viable dramatic version,[38] but Roger Warren's response convincingly countered with a series of moments for which a conjecture of garbling best explains Q1's relation to F.[39] Warren did not, however, explicitly counter Urkowitz's observation that Q1's stage directions contain verbal parallels with those of F, which ought not to be the case in a report since these elements of the script are not spoken, or memorised other than as actions.[40] How can memorial reconstruction explain actors remembering not only their lines but the exact phrasing of a play's stage directions? Montgomery had spotted these parallels in the phrasing of stage directions but pointed out that there is only a limited number of ways to describe an action.[41] In any case, all but one of the stage directions that Urkowitz thought 'terminally embarrassing' to the theory that the quartos derive from a memorial reconstruction – F TLN 784, 795–6, 902–4, 1115–19, 1169–70 and 2633–4[42] – fall in sections of F which Montgomery had decided were directly copied from Q3, this being Montgomery's explanation of the Q/F likenesses. Urkowitz's one example not covered by Montgomery's transcriptional-link hypothesis is a stage direction that includes dialogue (Q1 C2r: 'Enter one crying, A miracle, a miracle'; F TLN 784: 'Enter one crying a Miracle'), so, even if not discounted by Montgomery's principle that there is only a limited number of ways to describe an action, it can none the less be discounted because verbal memory was needed for it, and hence it is not out of place in an alleged memorial reconstruction.

Montgomery's claim of an F/Q transcriptional relationship for Beaufort's reading of the articles and the following twelve lines is unconvincing because of the small differences listed above. If, however, Montgomery is right, then the discrepancy between Gloucester's reading of the articles and Beaufort's that is seized on by De Grazia exists only in F and arises from the printer switching copy between Gloucester's and Beaufort's readings; such a printer's error does not constitute evidence of an epistemological shift. If Montgomery is wrong, then De Grazia is right inasmuch as the Folio shows that a writer could make a manuscript in which there was a discrepancy between the two readings of a single document in a play. But since it would be known to all that the textual processes of the theatre would eliminate one of the variants before performance we can hardly conclude from this that the early moderns did not share our dislike of inconsistency. Only one other Shakespeare play dramatises the reading and rereading of a single property document, and it shows no discrepancy between the first and second reading. Indeed, it shows such extraordinary agreement in every particular between the first and second readings that it can only be understood in terms of the economics of printing. In *Cymbeline*, 5.4, Posthumus awakes to find a 'tablet' (also called a 'label' and a 'book') on his breast and he reads it aloud:

> *Reades*
> *Whenas a Lyons whelpe, shall to himselfe vnknown, without seeking*
> *finde, and bee embrac'd by a peece of tender Ayre: And when from a*
> *stately Cedar shall be lopt branches, which being dead many yeares,*
> *shall after reuiue, bee ioynted to the old Stocke, and freshly grow, then*
> *shall Posthumus end his miseries, Britaine be fortunate, and flourish in*
> *Peace and Plentie.*[43]

In the next scene Philharmonus the Soothsayer is called upon to read aloud this prophecy and to declare its meaning.[44] Although the dramatist presumably wrote the prophecy twice, the theatre scribe would have made only one property document and if this controlled what was said on the stage there could be no variation between the two readings. But the two Folio readings are identical not only in wording but also in punctuation and spelling; what is more, the line-endings fall in exactly the same places in each reading, and the relative positions of the lines within the measure are also preserved with greater accuracy than can be achieved when type is distributed and recomposed. For example, in both readings the bottom of the stem of the 'f' in '*himselfe*' exactly meets the top of the 'b' in '*by*'. A close examination of irregularities such as the break at the top of the second 'e' in '*tender*' indicates what happened: the same block of type was used in the first (5.4) and second (5.5) readings. After the printing of forme bbb3v:4 (the end of 5.4 and beginning of 5.5), the block of italic type was set aside to be reused for the printing of forme bbb1v:6 (the end of 4.2 and final printed page of the Folio). In a study of the recurrence of individual types, Charlton Hinman's analysis of the printing of these formes did not draw attention to this unusual movement of a whole block of type.[45] Because the Folio was set by formes it is likely that this labour-saving opportunity was noticed during casting off when the content and sequence of formes was determined. If verbal differences existed between the two readings of the 'Labell' in the underlying copy, they must have been sufficiently small for this interference in the text to have been acceptable. Warren Smith noticed that the two printings of the prophecy were identical in the tiniest matters, but like Stern he believed that the words of the prophecy did not occur in the prompt-book and so had to be set by consulting the property document twice.[46] However, being set twice from the same copy would not produce identical letter spacing, nor would the same broken 'e' be likely to occur in the same word twice.

There are no other occasions in a Shakespeare play when a document is read and reread on stage, although in *Contention of York and Lancaster / 2 Henry VI* there is a conjuring scene (1.4) during which the spirit Asnath's words are written down as he speaks them and this incriminating document is later read aloud. The case of Asnath is inconclusive because the onstage transcriber might be supposed to have failed to record exactly what he heard, so there is a perfectly simple explanation for the reading of this document not matching Asnath's prophecies. Thus, in the only two Shakespearian examples of the onstage rereading of documents (neither of which is De Grazia's claimed 'letter or proclamation') the technology of textual reproduction (scribes making properties and printers making books) and the needs of the repertory system (which impelled actors to rely on property documents) worked together to promote coherence. Knowledge of these economies of labour should inform a materialist approach to the subject. The fashionable insistence that there are only the surviving printed texts and that we should have nothing to do with Platonic idealisations of the work ignores the fact that those who spoke and printed the texts did idealise, even if those who wrote and copied the texts had not. Perhaps the underlying manuscript for the printing of *Cymbeline* had the two readings of the prophecy in identical words, spelling and punctuation. This would be untypical, but not impossible and it would make a useful example to counter De Grazia's use of non-verbatim repetition in *2 Henry VI*. If, as is somewhat more likely, the two manuscript versions of the prophecy differed in small details such as spelling or larger ones such as punctuation and choice of words, a printing-house worker none the less felt that the opportunity to save labour was more important than the preservation of these differences, and he effaced them by reusing his first setting of type. The textual materialism advocated by De Grazia treats non-verbatim repetition as symptomatic of an epistemological difference between then and now, but the printing-house worker must have decided that a verbatim, literatim and indeed punctilious reproduction would be perfectly acceptable. It is the same prophecy, after all. Our textual materialism is not materialist enough if it overlooks the regularising effects of performance practices and of textual reproduction in the playhouse and the printing-house, and too materialist if it denies the professionals concerned their reasonable idealisations, such as 'it is the same prophecy, after all'. The economies of labour in playhouse and printing-house operated to reduce the proliferation of variation well before Foucault's claimed epistemic shift of 1800.

Notes

1 Michel Foucault, 'What Is an Author?,' *Partisan Review*, 42 (1975), 603–14.
2 Roland Barthes, *Image-Music-Text*, trans. Stephen Heath (London: Fontana, 1977), pp. 142–8.
3 Michel Foucault, 'What Is an Author?,' in Josue V. Harari (ed.), *Textual Strategies: Perspectives in Post-structuralist Criticism* (Ithaca: Cornell University Press, 1979), pp. 141–60 (pp. 148–9).
4 Foucault, 'What Is an Author?,' p. 159.
5 Alan Bray, *Homosexuality in Renaissance England* (London: Gay Men's Press, 1982).
6 Joseph Cady, '"Masculine Love", Renaissance Writing, and the "New Invention" of Homosexuality', in Claude J. Summers (ed.), *Homosexuality in Renaissance and Enlightenment England: Literary Representations in Historical Context* (New York: Haworth Press, 1992), pp. 9–40.
7 Margreta de Grazia, *Shakespeare Verbatim: The Reproduction of Authenticity and the 1790 Apparatus* (Oxford: Clarendon Press, 1991), p. 223.
8 Margreta de Grazia, 'The Essential Shakespeare and the Material Book', *Textual Practice*, 2 (1988), 69–86, 80–2.
9 De Grazia, *Shakespeare Verbatim*, p. 10.
10 De Grazia, *Shakespeare Verbatim*, pp. 214–19. Edmund G. C. King ('"Small-Scale Copyrights?"': Quotation Marks in Theory and Practice', *Papers of the Bibliographical Society of America*, 98 (2004), 39–53) challenges De Grazia on this point, showing that the practices she considers typical of the Enlightenment are found in books from much earlier.
11 Ibid., pp. 222–3, citing Malone, *PPWS*, vi. 416.
12 E. A. J. Honigmann, *The Stability of Shakespeare's Text* (London: Edward Arnold, 1965).
13 De Grazia, 'The Essential Shakespeare and the Material Book', p. 82.
14 Random Cloud (Randall McLeod), 'What's the Bastard's Name?', in George Walton Williams (ed.), *Shakespeare's Speech-headings: Speaking the Speech in Shakespeare's Plays: The Papers of the Seminar in Textual Studies, Shakespeare Association of America, March 29, 1986, Montreal* (Newark: University of Delaware Press, 1997), pp. 133–209 (p. 136).
15 William Shakespeare, *The Plays*, ed. Samuel Johnson, 8 vols (London: J. and R. Tonson [etc.], 1765), vol. 1, Preliminary Matter; *The Tempest*;

A Midsummer-Night's Dream; *The Two Gentlemen of Verona*; *Measure for Measure*; *The Merchant of Venice*, xxiii.

16 William Shakespeare, *The Plays and Poems*, ed. Edmond Malone, 10 vols (London: Rivington, 1790), vol. 6, *1 Henry VI*; *2 Henry VI*; *3 Henry VI*; Dissertation on the Three Parts of King Henry VI; *Richard III*, 416.

17 Margreta de Grazia and Peter Stallybrass, 'The Materiality of Shakespeare's Text', *Shakespeare Quarterly*, 44 (1993), 255–83.

18 William Shakespeare, *[2 Henry VI] The First Part of the Contention Betwixt the Two Famous Houses of Yorke and Lancaster*, STC 26099 (Q1) (London: Thomas Creede for Thomas Millington, 1594), sigs A2v–A3r.

19 William Shakespeare, *Mr. William Shakespeares Comedies, Histories, & Tragedies. Published According to the True Originall Copies*, STC 22273 (F1) (London: Isaac Jaggard and Edward Blount, 1623), sig. m2v.

20 Stanley Wells et al., *William Shakespeare: A Textual Companion* (Oxford: Oxford University Press, 1987), pp. 175–8; William Montgomery, 'The Original Staging of *The First Part of the Contention* (1594)', *Shakespeare Survey*, 41 (1989), 13–22 (p. 22).

21 Tiffany Stern, 'Letters, Verses and Double Speech-prefixes in *The Merchant of Venice*', *Notes and Queries*, 244 (1999), 231–3.

22 Ibid., p. 232.

23 My informal poll of actors working at Shakespeare's Globe in London found them equally divided between learners and non-learners of their 'letters', but they are only ersatz early moderns.

24 Stern, 'Letters, Verses and Double Speech-prefixes in *The Merchant of Venice*', p. 231.

25 Wells et al., *William Shakespeare: A Textual Companion*, p. 176.

26 Ibid., p. 179.

27 William Montgomery, *The Contention of York and Lancaster: A Critical Edition*, Unpublished D.Phil. thesis, University of Oxford, 1985, 2, xxxvii.

28 William Shakespeare, *The Second Part of King Henry VI*, ed. Andrew S. Cairncross, The Arden Shakespeare (London: Methuen, 1957).

29 Montgomery, *The Contention of York and Lancaster: A Critical Edition*, 2, xlii.

30 Ibid., 2, xlvii.

31 Ibid., 2, xlvi.

32 Ibid., 2, xlvii.

33 Ibid., 2, xliii–xliv.

34 Ibid., 2, xliv.

35 Ibid., 2, xlvii.

36 Ibid., 2, xlvii.
37 Wells et al., *William Shakespeare: A Textual Companion*, p. 179.
38 Steven Urkowitz, '"If I Mistake in Those Foundations Which I Build Upon": Peter Alexander's Textual Analysis of *Henry VI Parts 2 and 3*', *English Literary Renaissance*, 18 (1988), 230–56.
39 Roger Warren, 'The Quarto and Folio Texts of *2 Henry VI*: A Reconsideration', *Review of English Studies*, 51 (2000), 193–207 (pp. 195–201).
40 Urkowitz, '"If I Mistake in Those Foundations Which I Build Upon"', pp. 252–3.
41 Montgomery, *The Contention of York and Lancaster: A Critical Edition*, 2, xliv–xlv.
42 Urkowitz, '"If I Mistake in Those Foundations Which I Build Upon"', p. 253.
43 Shakespeare, *Mr. William Shakespeares Comedies, Histories, & Tragedies*, sig. bbb3v.
44 Ibid., sig. bbb6r.
45 Charlton Hinman, *The Printing and the Proof-reading of the First Folio of Shakespeare*, 2 vols (Oxford: Clarendon, 1963), vol. 2, pp. 322–4. Martin Butler ('Running-titles in *Cymbeline*', *The Library*, 7th series, 1 (2000), 439–41) has established that a single skeleton forme was used for quire bbb and confirmed that Hinman's order of printing, the usual order working from the middle of the quire (3v:4) to the outside (1:6v), was employed.
46 Warren D. Smith, 'New Light on Stage Directions in Shakespeare', *Studies in Philology*, 47 (1950), 173–81 (p. 180).

6

'As sharp as a pen': *Henry V* and its texts

Duncan Salkeld

Much twentieth-century thinking about the origins of Shakespeare's texts drew upon theories of 'good' and 'bad' quartos, piracy and memorial reconstruction. Yet these categories are currently meeting with increasing scepticism.[1] When, in 1986, the Oxford editors sought to recover 'the play as it appeared when performed', they set a new objective for Shakespeare scholarship, building on prior editorial practice. But even this ideal now faces criticism as a futile attempt to freeze the variegated conditions of early modern performances.[2] The cumulative effect of this scepticism is beginning to make its mark, but assessing the merits of its dissent is no straightforward task. So diverse is the field of Shakespearean textual studies that such assessment can be undertaken only in relation to specific texts. Consequently, I shall restrict my discussion to consideration of editorial theory and practice regarding the two versions of *Henry V* – the 1600 quarto and the longer version printed in the First Folio of 1623. The purposes of doing so are to gauge the early reception of the play both in performance and in print; to evaluate claims recently made about the play's textual history; and to respond to some of the questions raised by those claims. Taking *Henry V* as an index to wider debate about the provenance of Shakespearean texts, my position will be essentially a holding argument to the effect that, in a number of respects, recent scepticism regarding issues such as memorial reconstruction, piracy and the 'badness' of some of the early imprints has yet to prove persuasive. This argument is advanced in four sections. The first outlines a divide in interpretative attitudes that has, at least since the early nineteenth century, highlighted the play's ambivalent politics and argues that these interpretative controversies are rooted in fundamental instabilities identified by textual criticism. The second considers recent editorial approaches to the play, focusing in particular on Andrew Gurr's editions of the Folio and quarto texts. The third gives some assessment of claims made for the 1600 quarto by Lukas Erne in his deservedly acclaimed book, *Shakespeare as Literary Dramatist* (2003). Finally, I argue that evidence of memorial error, misreading and mishearing suggest that the quarto was produced via a combination of memorial reconstruction and dictation, probably in that order.

Since the Romantic era, *Henry V* has presented audiences, readers and critics with a variety of interpretative puzzles. William Hazlitt observed in 1817 that 'Henry v. is a very favourite monarch with the English nation', and yet Shakespeare depicted him as an 'amiable monster'. 'We feel', Hazlitt wrote, 'little love or admiration for him'.[3] Criticism after Hazlitt has increasingly recognised this ambivalence. A. C. Bradley found the king less than the 'ideal man of action', and Harley Granville-Barker complained that 'all the while Shakespeare is apologizing – and directly apologizing – for not being able to make the action effective'.[4] Even the recently much assailed E. M. W. Tillyard wrote – in the same year as Olivier's famously heroic film depiction – that Shakespeare's attempt at depicting 'the great hero king' produced 'the very reverse of what [he] was growing truly interested in'.[5] While one recent critic finds the play 'works splendidly . . . at a speed which prevents awkward questions, and it is charged with a rich and compelling emotion', others regard its 'obsessive preoccupation' as 'insurrection'. This interpretative ambiguity – the play as both nationalistic and anti-heroic – found its most precise expression in Norman Rabkin's Wittgensteinian argument that the play simply gives us two perspectives at the same time, a view subsequently given new historicist spin by Stephen Greenblatt who has seen the play's 'subversive doubts' as serving 'paradoxically to intensify the power of the king and his war'.[6]

Textual criticism of *Henry V* has brought these interpretative dilemmas into yet sharper relief, since the status of the manuscripts on which these readings depend is itself in dispute. The play's early printings occurred in two forms: three quartos Q1 (1600), Q2 (1602) and Q3 (1619, its title-page deliberately misdated 1608) under the title of *The Chronicle History of Henry the Fift*; and a much the longer version in the First Folio, with a slightly altered title (as stated in the catalogue), *The Life of King Henry the Fift* (1623).

Of these, Q2 and Q3 are essentially reprints of Q1, with some corrections. The two substantive early imprints of the play are thus the 1600 quarto (hereafter 'Q') and the 1623 Folio (hereafter 'F'), versions which differ radically from each other in many important respects, most obviously in length, F running to almost double the number of lines in Q. In 1979, Gary Taylor's *Three Studies in the Text of Henry V* proffered a careful analysis of the relationship between Q and F, and advanced (in forbidding detail) three key arguments: first (against Andrew Cairncross), that F's editors did not draw upon either Q2 or Q3 in establishing their text; second, that Q constituted an abridged text, reconstructed from memory, for a cast of eleven players, probably playing in the provinces; and third, that, though many of Q's interpolations and transpositions were memorial corruptions, Q should be followed where it has the more plausible or appropriate reading.

These claims were consolidated in Taylor's 1982 Oxford edition, and again in the 1986 Oxford *Complete Works*, though with an increasing concession to Cairncross over the question of imports from Q3 into F. Taylor's single edition put these arguments, first outlined in *Three Studies*, squarely on the map. In a far-reaching editorial manoeuvre, Taylor replaced the Dauphin with the Duke of Bourbon for the scenes set at Agincourt. As explained in *Three Studies*, among Q's many alterations, substitutions and departures from F, the Dauphin is replaced by the Duke of Bourbon in scenes that correspond to F's 3.7, 4.2 and 4.5.[7] This substitution, Taylor argued, accords with other elements in the play, including Bourbon's mute appearance in Q's equivalents for F's 2.4, and 3.5, and the French King's clear instruction in 3.5.64–6 that the Dauphin should remain at Rouen. Taylor regarded this structural alteration, found only in Q, as authorial. As he put it, 'The simplest explanation . . . is that Shakespeare, who in his own draft wavered about whether to include the Dauphin at Agincourt, eventually decided not to, reverted to his original intention (as spelled out in 3.5.64–6), put the Duke of Bourbon in the Dauphin's place and altered 2.4 and 3.5 to accommodate this change'.[8] Adopting the substitution, Taylor's edition recognised an important feature of Q: that, amid its extensive abridgements, the quarto yet retains something of Shakespeare's revising hand. Indeed, far from disparaging the quarto, Taylor preferred Q's readings to those in F in at least eighteen additional instances.[9]

Taylor's edition renewed critical attention to the relationship between the two versions. Combining historicist and textual approaches, Annabel Patterson argued that the play's political ambivalences are especially apparent in the divergences between them. In brief, Patterson maintained that Q is 'tonally different' from F. It tells, she claimed, a far more straightforward, even jingoistic, story of English nationalism than F. It was entered on to the Stationers' Register during a crisis precipitated by Sir John Hayward's dedication of his *History of Henry IV* to the Earl of Essex, a crisis worsened by Essex's doomed insurrection of 1601. Given this political background, Q presents 'an *almost* unproblematic view of a highly popular monarch whose most obvious modern analogy was Elizabeth herself'. Perhaps this suggestion – that Henry is to be identified with Elizabeth – may seem a little strained, but the parallel is apt at least in the fact that Elizabeth's full official title at the time was 'Elizabeth Dei gratia Anglie Francie et Hibernie Regine fidei defensoris'. Henry's line 'No king of England, if not king of France' (2.2.190) would have reminded a contemporary audience that English claims to the throne of France lay unresolved even in 1599.[10] For Patterson, then, F tells a far more ambiguous and unstable tale of national unity than Q. The phrasing of the Chorus for Act 5 (occurring only in F), where Shakespeare directly anticipates the triumphant return of Essex from Ireland, remains, she argues, subtly cautious:

As, by a lower but high-loving likelihood,
Were now the General of our gracious Empress
– As in good time he may – from Ireland coming,
Bringing rebellion broached on his Sword,
How many would the peaceful city quit
To welcome him!

(5.0.29–34)

Essex had left England on his fateful venture on 27 March 1599. He would return in failure in September the same year. According to Taylor, 'The hero returned defeated and disgraced on 28 September; but it had been clear since midsummer that he would not be "Bringing rebellion broached on his sword". If this allusion is accepted, completion of Shakespeare's play can be firmly dated from January to June 1599'.[11] Patterson detects in the clamorous 'how many would the peaceful city quit' a hint of the unruly 'popular voice' to which Essex hoped to appeal in his ill-fated attempted coup nearly two years later. The publication history of *Henry V* is thus entangled, she claims, with 'major critical disagreements over the play's meaning and cultural function'.[12] Q's many cuts to F bring about a change in critical perspective, Patterson argues, in response to contemporary historical events and pressures.

Most of what we know of Q, apart from its date, is uncertain. On 4 August 1600, 'Henry the ffift: a booke' was entered into the Stationers' Register as a work 'to be staied', along with three other Chamberlain's plays, *Much Ado*, *As You Like It* and Jonson's *Every Man In His Humour*. That the 'staied' work was Q is apparent from the fact that ten days later the publishing rights to a copy 'formerlye printed' were transferred for sixpence from Millington and Busby, who had paid Thomas Creede to print it, to Thomas Pavier. Q was reprinted, with some corrections, in 1602 (Q2, by Creede for Pavier) and 1619 (Q3, one of the surreptitiously produced 'Pavier quartos'). The Folio version subsequently printed in 1623 is a much more coherent piece of work, and thought to derive from a transcript of Shakespeare's own draft (his 'foul papers'). It provides the basis for most modern editions. Given F's probable allusion to Essex's return in the fifth Chorus, it is almost certainly the earlier of the two versions. Q is an unusually short text, having only 1622 lines to F's 3381 lines.[13] With its many inconsistencies and errors, Q has been regarded as one of the so-called 'bad quartos', a term applied in 1909 by the textual scholar A. W. Pollard to the first imprints of *Romeo and Juliet*, *Henry V*, *The Merry Wives of Windsor* and *Hamlet*. To these four, *2 Henry VI*, *3 Henry VI*, *Pericles* and, tentatively, *The Troublesome Reign of King John* and *The Taming of a Shrew* have been added.[14] The term 'bad quarto' has in recent years come in for a good deal of criticism, and it is true that each imprint so designated displays weaknesses of a different kind and extent. But it is also true that all these early imprints were substantially rejected (though occasionally consulted) by Shakespeare's first editors, his co-actors John Heminge and Henry Condell, as unreliable. Not without cause have these early quartos been taken to be what Heminge and Condell refer to as 'stolne, and surreptitious copies, maimed, and deformed by the frauds and stealthes of iniurious imposters, that exposed them'.[15]

As with other so-called 'bad quartos', Q has been regarded as a relatively poor reconstruction from memory by two or three of the actors who had at some time played a longer version similar or identical to F. Players in the roles of Gower and Exeter have been thought to be responsible for producing Q, since (it is claimed) where they speak, or when they are on stage, the text more accurately conforms to F. All the evidence suggests that Q is an abridgement of the earlier F (or similar version).[16] Q excises all the Choruses, the opening speeches between the archbishops, sections from longer speeches by Henry, Canterbury, the French King and the Dauphin, entire speeches by Ely, Exeter, Westmorland, Canterbury and Henry including the whole of 'Once more into the breach . . .' at 3.1, the debate between Gower, Fluellen, Macmorris and Jamy in 3.2, substantial sections of the petty quarrelling among the French nobility, Henry's conversation with Erpingham and much of his debate with Bates, Court and Williams (in Q merely designated 'three souldiers'), his soliloquy on 'ceremony' and re-encounter with Erpingham, dissension in the French camp and sections from the 'Saint Crispian' speech. Q reverses F's 4.3 and 4.4, reduces exchanges between Pistol and the prisoner Le Fer, and simplifies dialogue between Gower, Fluellen and the King. Discrepancies of timing and wording become increasingly marked in their versions of 4.8 and 5.1. Finally, Q dispenses with 'Queen Isabel', and cuts long sections from concluding terms with the French and sealing the marriage with Katherine.

In addition to these omissions, Q's stage directions are at times remarkably inconsistent. Directly following the King's dialogue with the three soldiers, Q has, '*Enter the King, Gloster, Epingam, and Attendants*'. Following the King's prayer, Q indicates, '*Enter Gloster*'. The King has a brief exchange with Gloster, and then a stage direction ensues, '*Enter* Clarence, Gloster, Exeter, and Salisburie'. These apparent flaws arise simply from substantial cutting where stage directions belonging to separate scenes are brought together as a result of excision. Q also omits some stage directions. Where F has an entry for '*Captaines, English and Welch, Gower and Fluellen*' at 3.6.0, Q has simply, '*Enter Gower*', even though Fluellen must enter with him. When Warwick is first required on stage he is given no entrance. Exits are missing for the departure of the Hostess at Q's equivalent of 2.1.88–9, for the Governor at its version of 3.3.50, and for the King, Herald and Gloucester before the entrance of 'Burbon, Constable, Orleance, Gebon' at 3.7. Later, Q requires the immediate re-entry of Pistol after he has led away Le

Fer, but only for a single phrase, 'Couple gorge', at the end of the scene. A similar immediate re-entry for Fluellen is required after he and the king agree that God 'did us great good' in the battle. What these inconsistencies highlight is that the manuscript for Q was evidently not checked for stagecraft before it went to press. Yet Q also provides some stage directions missing from F. It adds, for example, '*They drawe*' at Q's equivalent of F's 2.1.59, and '*Enter* Flewellen *and beates them in*' at the equivalent of 3.2.18, and also marks some exits not in F (cf. 2.1.122; 2.2.190). What these inconsistencies and discrepancies suggest is that an acting version incorporating elements of authorial revision does indeed lie behind Q, but that, after severe abridgement, its manuscript was not checked for stagecraft or intended for use in performance. It seems unlikely that experienced actors would have regarded Q, in the form we have it, as anything like a finished product for performances in the provinces or elsewhere, and, by the same token, one might find it difficult to imagine that such a text would have been authorised by Shakespeare's company for printing. Yet that is precisely the claim most recently made for Q.

Andrew Gurr's 1992 edition for the New Cambridge Shakespeare (hereafter NCS) followed Taylor's in retaining the Dauphin/Bourbon substitution but argued that Q 'was not primarily designed for acting'. In Gurr's view, the manuscript of Q was transcribed mostly from dictation, helped out here and there by the players' memories of their parts. His primary evidence for this claim is that Q repeatedly breaks the Elizabethan rule of continuous staging. On three occasions in Q, actors leave the stage and re-enter immediately for the next scene, something that Gurr asserted 'Shakespeare's plays never require'.[17] Observing that such conventions will hardly matter to a reader, Gurr argued that, by April 1597, the Lord Chamberlain's Men had lost The Theatre and needed to fund the new Globe. For this reason, they sold eleven 'good' texts of their major successes for publication in quarto form, including a text of *Henry V*, the 1600 quarto. Consequently, Gurr maintained, Q cannot be assumed to shed light on how the play might have been performed on the stage in 1600.[18] Gurr subsequently fine-tuned these views for his edition of Q (published in 2000) in the New Cambridge Shakespeare 'Early Quartos' series (hereafter NCSQ). Again, he argued that Q was probably prepared for sale to a printing-house in order to fund the

Globe. But whereas he had earlier held both that copy for Q was probably unauthorised and that Q remained unreliable as a guide to early performance,[19] Gurr's preface to NCSQ argued the reverse: that Q was set up from 'Shakespeare's company's own performance script of the play, a text made for or from its first performances in 1599' and that the so-called 'reporters' were in fact 'revisers' working from 'a transcription which was fully authorised'.[20] For Gurr, then, Q is in fact far closer than F to what was actually performed on stage by Shakespeare's company, but was assembled for the printing-house, not for performance either in London or elsewhere. This distinctive claim has proved influential. Editing the play for the third Arden series, T. W. Craik declined Taylor's option of the Bourbon/Dauphin switch, yet observed in relation to Q that '[p]robably it was compiled simply to provide a reading text of the play'.[21]

Gurr regarded Q as deriving from 'the play as first staged in Shakespeare's presence', but prepared for the printer not for a theatre audience. His account of F (in NCS) took a similar interpretative line to Hazlitt, Rabkin and Patterson (though Patterson is nowhere mentioned in the edition). In a long section devoted to 'The coercive Chorus', Gurr outlined the many ways in which 'the events of each act belie the claims made by the Chorus that introduces it'.[22] Each magniloquent Chorus seems to be followed by bathetic scenes involving relatively petty squabbles among either the English or the French camps. In a follow-up essay published just prior to NCSQ, Gurr argued that 'The absence of the six famous choruses from the 1600 quarto of *Henry V*, a text much nearer the play as performed than the author's first manuscript on which the Folio text is based, probably indicates that the original players never actually did ask their audiences to piece out the play's imperfections with their thoughts'.[23] This bold statement supplied Gurr's opening shot in NCSQ where, in a Preface, he remarked that F 'with its famous Choruses and speeches . . . was unlikely to have been heard at the Globe at any time before 1623, and probably not until . . . the eighteenth century' (p. ix). So remarkable a statement clearly stands in need of assessment.

This last claim seems contrary to just about every intuition generated when reading the play. Together with Henry's rousing speeches, 'Once more into the breach, dear friends, once more, . . .' (3.1.1ff) and 'What's he that wishes so . . .' (4.3.18–67), the Choruses are the play's most distinctive feature. Their various allusions to 'this unworthy scaffold', 'this cockpit', 'this wooden O', 'the girdle of these walls', 'there is the playhouse now', 'our performance', 'vile and ragged foils', 'things . . . here presented', and 'which oft our stage hath shown' all seem to speak of the immediacy of live performance. When Shakespeare penned the Choruses, he undoubtedly did so both to convey an impression of actual performance and to render them in such a way that they *could* indeed be acted. The fourth Chorus asks the audience to 'sit and see' the events unfold (4.0.52). The idea that the Choruses would never have been spoken on the Elizabethan stage may be radical, even eye-catching, but does it stand up to scrutiny? Gurr's is essentially an argument from silence (or absence) and it is in the nature of such arguments that they are often difficult to refute. Yet there are reasons to believe that the Choruses were indeed performed in 1599. Without the last Chorus, as Craik points out, 5.1 would result in the immediate re-entry of Fluellen who had departed at the end of 4.8 – a flaw that duly occurs in Q. Craik, with characteristic acuity, suggests that Q's equivalent phrasing for 2.2.67–8, 'Sir Thomas Gray knight of Northumberland', transposes the exact word order from F's Chorus at the start of Act 2, indicating that Q's reporting actor must have remembered the Choric line from an earlier performance. To these considerations we may add that Shakespeare drew upon his principal source, Raphael Holinshed's *Chronicles*, when writing the Choruses (e.g. 2.0.20–30; 4.0.4–9, 17–19; 5.0.17–22), a sign that he probably wrote them very nearly contemporaneously with the rest of the play. He had begun his previous work, *2 Henry IV*, with the choric 'Rumour painted full of tongues', and closed it with an Epilogue similar in function if not in tone. The performance of these speeches has never been in doubt and it seems entirely plausible that Shakespeare might have wished to develop this practice in *Henry V*.

It is worth considering the case of *2 Henry IV* a little further. Its Epilogue stands out very distinctly in F, printed in italic on a separate page (recto), after both the 'FINIS' and the printer's ornament on the preceding verso. Consisting of three paragraphs, it promises that 'our humble Author will continue the story (with Sir Iohn in it) and make you merry, with faire Katherine of France: where (for any thing I know) Falstaff shall dye of a sweat', and it disavows Falstaff's identification with Sir John Oldcastle, a significant controversy at the time. As A. R. Humphreys has argued, the Epilogue's three paragraphs show signs of having been adopted for different occasions: the first (perhaps spoken by Shakespeare) refers to a recent performance ('I was lately here in the end of a displeasing play') which would quickly date. The second and third paragraphs require a dancer.[24] F's version of the Epilogue ends with a bid to pray for the Queen which the 1600 quarto places at the end of the first paragraph: at either point, the line plausibly would have served to invite applause. It seems probable, then, that, soon after having completed the play, Shakespeare submitted epilogues to *2 Henry IV* on separate sheets, which were then printed independently from the play in F. Ernst Honigmann explains:

> Since Elizabethan-Jacobean plays were written on loose sheets of paper a fluent dramatist wishing to start a new scene before its turn has come could easily make up a new sheet, make a 'foul' draft – and later insert this material in its proper place.

Among other examples of insertion, Honigmann cites the speech by 'Time, the Chorus' in *The Winter's Tale* which speaks of 'sixteen' years passing, as against the 'fifteen' mentioned in the following scene.[25] If Shakespeare similarly wrote the Choruses of *Henry V* on detached sheets, their absence from Q is more easily explained. In the Folio version of *Henry V*, the 'Prologue' is printed in italic and clearly lined off from the body of text that follows, indicating insertion. The sonnet that closes the play is similarly a single item, reminding the audience of stage performances of the story of Henry VI. But there are still further reasons for thinking that London performances did not omit the Choruses.

Towards the end of his introduction to NCSQ, Gurr cites a poem by Christopher Middleton, *The Legend of Humphrey Duke of Glocester* (1600), which repeats the exact wording of the seventh line of *Henry V*'s Prologue: 'And in their steeds brought *famine, sword, and fire*'.[26] As Gurr acknowledges, 'Conceivably, therefore, Middleton had recently seen the play and heard the Prologue'. Notwithstanding the greater accuracy of its parallel with *Henry V*, Gurr postulates that both Middleton and Shakespeare were echoing a line in *1 Henry VI* which runs, 'Lean Famine, quartering Steele, and climbing Fire' (TLN 1960–1). But by 1600, *1 Henry VI* was an old play and Middleton had written his poem very shortly after Shakespeare's *Henry V*. Furthermore, as Gurr is well aware, since he mentions it in NCS, Jonson's Prologue to *Every Man In His Humour* (added c. 1605 to the play by Chamberlain's Men in 1598) refers to performances of Shakespeare's first tetralogy, and satirises the Chorus that 'wafts you ore the seas'.[27] A similar complaint is made in *Every Man Out of His Humour* where Mitis remarks, 'How comes it then, that in some one play we see so many seas, countries and kingdoms, passed over with such admirable dexterity?' Cordatus replies, 'O, that but shews how well the authors can travel in their vocation, and outrun the apprehension of their auditory'. *Every Man Out* was performed by Chamberlain's Men both at the Globe and at court in late 1599, and takes a hit at *Histriomastix*, a play revived by Marston that autumn. Given that Jonson's knock at 'some one play' probably refers, editors agree, to *Henry V*, and that the allusion in *Every Man In* almost certainly does, the onus remains very much upon the sceptic to produce evidence that the Choruses were not performed in Shakespeare's time.[28]

Gurr's scepticism regarding F as a performance text underlies Lukas Erne's view of *Henry V* in *Shakespeare as Literary Dramatist* (2003). In this important and original work, Erne argues that F, being among Shakespeare's longest works, would probably have been cut for performance, and that its longer speeches, including the Choruses, were written for readers, not for audiences. Erne argues that 'short, theatrical texts . . . record in admittedly problematic fashion the plays as they were orally delivered on stage to spectators', while 'the long, literary texts correspond to what an emergent dramatic author wrote for readers'.[29] This distinction marks a significant departure from prior accounts of the relationships between the early quartos and F. The Oxford editors, in 1986, had regarded both shorter and longer versions of the plays equally as performance texts in different states of revision. The crucial distinction, for them, lay between texts having the better authority, and those assembled by process of 'memorial reconstruction'. Drawing upon work by Laurie Maguire, Scott McMillin and, in particular, Peter Blayney, Erne repeatedly challenges the assumptions behind the theory of 'memorial reconstruction' – that one or two actors pirated dramatic scripts from memory, perhaps for performance in the provinces by a reduced cast. In a much cited essay, Blayney argued that Humphrey Moseley's preface to the 1647 Beaumont and Fletcher *Folio* gives a better account of how shorter texts like Q emerged. Moseley had remarked: 'When these *Comedies* and *Tragedies* were presented on the Stage, the *Actours* omitted some scenes and Passages (with the *Author's* consent) as occasion led them; and when private friends desir'd a Copy, they then (and justly too) transcribed what they Acted.' In Blayney's view, 'The quality of such texts would vary greatly . . . depending on the infinitely variable circumstances of their origins'.[30]

Erne favours Blayney's case that the 'bad quartos' probably derived from private transcripts in the manner described by Moseley. For Erne, F, like Shakespeare's other longer plays, was written for readers, not for the stage. The Choruses appeal, he suggests, not to a theatre audience but to the 'imaginary audition' of the reader's mind.[31] Following Gurr, he avers that the early quartos, including Q, 'are in some ways the best witnesses we have of what would actually have been performed on London's stages'. In particular, he adds, the first quartos of *Romeo and Juliet*, *Henry V* and *Hamlet* 'are the closest we can get to what Shakespeare and his fellows performed'. Yet Erne shortly declares (just over the page) that, 'It would . . . be simplistic to affirm without further qualifications that the "bad" quartos reflect the plays as they were performed in Shakespeare's time'.[32] Following Maguire, McMillin and Blayney, Erne holds that, though the 'bad' quartos of *Henry V*, *Romeo and Juliet* and *Hamlet* may indeed have indeterminate origins, they involved actors dictating or reporting their parts to a scribe for the purpose of making private copies. It is not entirely clear in this account how a private copy with elementary flaws in stagecraft and destined for the printer's shop can constitute a theatrical version of the play. Erne's fundamental position, then, appears to be that no single explanation – for example, 'memorial reconstruction' – is sufficient to account for all the difficulties presented by the 'bad quartos'.

Such a position is relatively uncontroversial, yet, in repeatedly foregrounding Moseley's *Preface*, other prefaces are omitted from the account. In particular, Thomas Heywood, in an address 'To the reader' before *The Fair Maid of the West*, expressed the hope that his plays will prove 'as gracious in thy private reading as they were plausible in the public acting'. Heywood gives no hint that the play to be read is any different from the play as it was performed. He adds that the work has been printed 'without any deviations or winding indents', that is without alteration or addition. Heywood, in other words, claims to have seen his work printed without specifically *literary*, non-performative material included. His epistle 'To the

Reader' appended to *The English Traveller* explains that some of his
plays were withheld because the actors believed it was 'against their
peculiar profit to have them into print'. Some players apparently felt
that a dramatic manuscript was of more value to a company
unprinted; fears that once a play was sold to a publisher it might be
further traded to others' profit are understandable. Heywood's
address 'To the reader' of his drama *The Rape of Lucrece* com-
pounds these uncertainties:

> Yet since some of my plays have (unknown to me, and without any of
> my direction) accidentally come into the printer's hands, and therefore
> so corrupt and mangled (copied only by the ear) that I have been as
> unable to know them as ashamed to challenge them, this therefore I
> was the willinger to furnish out in his native habit: first being by
> consent; next because the rest have been so wronged in being published
> in such savage and ragged ornaments.[33]

Heywood diplomatically complains that some of his plays arrived at
the printers 'accidentally', without either his knowledge or instruction, and, 'copied only by the ear', were published in 'corrupt and
mangled' form. Heywood was not Shakespeare, of course, and so
inferences from one to the other remain speculative, but his language
is strikingly reminiscent of Heminge and Condell's complaint
about 'stolne, and surreptitious copies, maimed, and deformed' by
imposters. A play 'copied only by the ear' would be one produced
by means of recollection and/or dictation, and there is a good deal
of evidence, as we shall see, that Q was produced by a combination
of memorial reconstruction and dictation. Before getting to the
detail of that evidence, it is worth considering some of the specific
claims Erne makes for the 1600 quarto of *Henry V*. When Erne compares parallel sections from Q and F, he draws fascinating but puzzling conclusions from them. Arguing that Q and F sometimes
resemble each other too perfectly for memory to have produced Q,
he cites an example from the dialogue between Pistol and the disguised King (4.1.36–50 in F).[34]

F

Pist. Che vous la?
King. A friend.
Pist. Discusse vnto me, art thou Officer, or art thou base, common, and
  popular?
King. I am a Gentleman of a Company.

Pist. Trayl'st thou the puissant Pyke?
King. Euen so: what are you?
Pist. As good a Gentleman as the Emperor.
King. Then you are a better then the King.
Pist. The King's a Bawcock, and a Heart of Gold, a Lad of Life, an Impe
of Fame, of Parents good, of Fist most valiant: I kisse his durtie shooe,
and from heart-string I loue the louely Bully. What is thy Name?
King. Harry le Roy.

Q
Pist. Ke <u>ve</u> la?
King. A friend.
Pist. Discus vnto me, art thou <u>Gentleman</u>?
Or art thou <u>common</u>, base, and popeler?
King. <u>No sir,</u> I am a Gentleman of a Company.
Pist. Trailes thou the puissant pike?
King. Euen so sir. What are you?
Pist. As good a gentleman as the Emperour.
King. <u>O</u> then <u>thou art better</u> then the King?
Pist. The kings a <u>bago</u>, and a hart of gold.
Pist. A lad of life, an impe of fame:
Of parents good, of fist most valiant:
I kis his durtie shoe: and from <u>my</u> hart strings
I love the louely bully. What is thy name?
King. Harry le Roy.

In this example, Erne concludes that Q 'seems simply too accurate'
to be a recollection of F by other actors. But though there is broad
accuracy here, there are – even disregarding orthographical and
print-house differences – significant variants (underlined above)
between them, including the mistake of 'bago' for 'Bawcock' which
seems to be a memorial confusion with 'figo', mentioned a few lines
later. When Q has Pistol ask, 'art thou Gentleman' instead of F's
'Officer', the actor seems to be relying upon memory of the word
'Gentleman' used by the King in the next line, and by himself in his
later line, 'As good a gentleman as the Emperor'. Moreover, as this
conversation between the King and Pistol continues (if it is followed
to line 64), the accuracy breaks down, with Q adding lines for the
King ('I sir he is my kinsman') and for Pistol ('Pistoll is my name').
The possibility that Q's version was reconstructed from memory by
actors who had not played either role cannot be ruled out.
Erne's second parallel quotation is designed to make the point that

Texts

since the alleged memorial reporters (Exeter and Gower) sometimes fail to recall their *own* lines as successfully as those of other characters, one cannot assume that they were indeed reporters from memory in the first place. Erne quotes the Q and F versions of Fluellen's exchange with Gower (in F, 4.7.1–10):

F

Flu. Kill the poyes and the luggage, 'Tis expressely against the Law of Armes, tis as arrant a peece of knauery marke you now, as can bee offert in your Conscience now, is it not?

Gow. Tis certaine, there's not a boy left aliue, and the Cowardly Rascalls that ranne from the battaile ha' done this slaughter: besides they haue burned and carried away all that was in the Kings Tent, wherefore the King most worthily hath caus'd euery soldiour to cut his prisoners throat. O 'tis a gallant King

Q

Flew. Godes plud kil the boyes and the lugyge,
Tis the arrants peece of knauery as can be desired,
In the worell now, in your conscience now.

Gour. Tis certaine, there is not a Boy left aliue,
And the cowerdly rascals that ran from the battell,
Themselues haue done this slaughter:
Beside, they haue carried away and *burnt*,
All that was in the kings Tent:
Whervpon the king caused euery prisoners
Throat to be cut. O he is a worthy king.

Erne comments that 'the most cursory reading' will demonstrate that 'the differences are far more numerous and important than in the Pistol/King encounter quoted above'.[35] But the variants in Gower's speech (underlined above) number no more than those in the earlier passages. Oddly, Erne later observes that these Fluellen/Gower exchanges are only 'slightly differing'.[36] Erne's conclusion, following Paul Werstine, that scholars' 'inability to agree on the identity of the memorial reporters also militates against memorial reconstruction' is open to question.[37] Uncertainty as to the identity of the reporters is no argument against the hypothesis that some process of memory lies behind Q, for which, as Gurr and Craik repeatedly demonstrate, the evidence is so compelling.

In a third parallel quotation, Erne cites Henry's speech in 4.7 (F: 'I was not angry since I came to France / Vntill this instant.') together with lines immediately following by Exeter and Gloucester announcing the entrance of the Herald, Montjoy.[38] In Q, Exeter and Gloucester's lines are cut. Erne's point is that Exeter and Gloucester's words are omitted in Q because 'they can be *acted* and therefore do not need to be spoken'.[39] Erne maintains that, being a theatrical text, the quarto may dispense with deictic cue-lines like these because they are unnecessary for a performance, though helpful in a printed text. But if this were so, we would expect to find deictic lines cut elsewhere in the quarto. We find the opposite: repeatedly in Q characters are announced as they come onstage:

1
Enter Pistoll *and Hostes Quickly, his wife.*
Bar. Godmorrow ancient Pistoll.
   Here comes ancient *Pistoll*, I prithee *Nim* be quiet.

2
Exe. O the Lord of *Massham.*
Enter the King and three Lords.

3
Enter Gloster.
Glost. My Lord.
King. My brother *Glosters* voyce.
Glost. My Lord, the Army stayes vpon your presence.

4
Enter Gower, Flewellen, and the Souldier.
Flew. Captain *Gower*, in the name of Iesu,
   Come to his Maiestie, there is more good toward you,
   Then you can dreame off.

These examples show that the cutting of deictic lines in Q cannot be taken as a general principle in distinguishing the text's literary from its performance features. Cuts to such lines in the 'readerly' longer text (F) are not routinely made in the 'theatrical' shorter text (Q) to reduce the time-length and pace of performance. Erne does not explicitly make this claim (indeed he backs away from it at times) but it is essentially the point of the single example he cites. Yet it is not even clear that the distinction between longer play texts for readers, and shorter scripts for performance, even survives in Erne's own discussion. Erne makes the following, rather puzzling, comment:

> The manuscripts from which the 'bad' quartos were set up do not seem to have been the result of attempts to create a theatrical text that radically departs from what was performed in London – a kind of text for

which there is no good evidence. Rather, they are likely to have been set up from manuscripts that were put together according to what Moseley suggests became a common practice among the King's Men. Accordingly, their purpose is likely to have been *literary* rather than theatrical.[40]

Erne's final comment – that copy for the 'bad' quartos was literary in purpose – seems out of kilter with his repeated conjecture that the shorter quartos emerge from the pressures of performance. Erne's book is so rich with argument that perhaps it should not surprise if occasionally a point is obscured by complexity. Erne holds out little prospect of ever 'recovering what specific effect various agencies had upon the differences between the "bad" and "good" texts', yet that prospect is presumably the point of citing Moseley's reference to copies made by private transcript, and indeed, the point of the theatrical/readerly distinction so arrestingly made in his book.[41]

Finally, Erne's ingenious solution to the 'stolne, and surreptitious copies, maimed and deformed by the frauds and stealthes of iniurious imposters' merits consideration. Erne proposes that Heminge and Condell allude in their complaint not to the early ('bad') imprints but to the Pavier quartos, printed with false dates in 1619 as part of a larger project to bring Shakespeare's works together for the first time. Erne's position is not that the Pavier quartos were pirated but that Heminge and Condell thought they were.[42] He writes, 'The passage on which our understanding of the so-called "bad" quartos was long based may thus well have more to do with the Pavier collection than with the textual quality of a group of Shakespearean quartos'.[43] This hypothesis, like much of Erne's work, is intriguing and strikingly original. Yet, for the argument to succeed, clear distinction has to be drawn between the 1619 texts and the earlier 'bad' quartos, so clearing the charge of piracy entirely from the early imprints, and relocating it as a suspicion in the minds of Shakespeare's first editors. The principal obstacle to this argument is that the 1600 quarto of *Henry V* was one of the quartos Pavier published in 1619 (Q3). That Heminge and Condell did have in mind at least one of the 'bad quartos' is simply confirmed by Erne's hypothesis. The problem is resituated rather than resolved.

Recognition and respect are generated by critique, and Erne's work may justifiably take great credit for stimulating new enthusiasm in considering old problems. Throughout this chapter, I have cautioned against too ready an acceptance of what promises – but in the end I suspect cannot deliver – a substantially new perspective on Shakespeare's texts. But critique alone is not enough. What kind of text is Q? Can we identify some or all of the processes that lie behind its production? Almost all editors agree that F, as we have it, is a trimmed version of Shakespeare's early draft, probably his 'foul papers'.[44] Imprecision in F's speech headings suggests a text unregularised and unimproved by a copyist or bookkeeper, and so points to 'foul papers'. Taylor's edition supplies perhaps the fullest evidence for this view.[45] Having completed a draft of F, Shakespeare seems subsequently to have made a number of minor revisions. Q has 'at the brute thereof' for F's 'at th'ill neighbourhood',[46] 'the lazy caning Drone' for F's 'lazy yawning drone',[47] 'one selfe sea' for F's 'one salt sea', 'secrets of my heart' for 'bottom of my soul', 'And for that cause according to his youth' (cf. *1 Henry VI*, 2.3.34) for F's 'To that end as matching to his youth and vanity'; Q also gives two impressive lines, 'I have a steed like the Palfrey of the sun' and 'we weare out the day' (cf. *King John*, 3.1.36), neither of which is in F, and it has the elevated phrase 'like a bace leno' for F's 'Like a base pander'.[48] All of these variants point to possible authorial revision, and to 'foul papers' as the ultimate source for Q.[49]

Gurr, as we have seen, held that, although Q was prepared for the printing-house, it also gives an idea of how the play would have been performed. That Q may indeed derive from performance copy is signalled from moments where actors' improvisation seems to have been recorded. Pistol's warning that his 'flashing firy cock is up', his counsel to Hostess Quickly, 'Keepe fast thy buggle boe [vagina]' and the Boy's question, 'whats French for fer, ferret and fearkt [fucked]' all seem to be examples of crowd-pleasing bawdy. Q's mistake of 'cophetua' (cf. *Love's Labour's Lost*, 4.1.65; *2 Henry IV*, 5.3.103) for F's 'caveto' seems also to have been an actor's error, though not necessarily as a consequence of performance. Overall, it seems that Q retains players' cues in F. On the relatively few occasions where the cue phrase is missed, it is attempted, unless, that is, the sequence is disrupted by improvisation (for example, Bardolph, Nim and Pistol in Q's equivalent of 2.1). Q adds in a cue line for Masham that F does not have: 'O the Lord of Massham', a feature explicable from rehearsal.

From Q, we know that F was substantially abridged, probably for performance. This much reduced text remained in the possession of actors who made a copy of it, certainly by remembering parts – if not the majority – of it, and perhaps by dictating it to a scribe. Gurr's view is that Q was produced by actors dictating an abridged, performance version, 'helped in places by the players' memories' to provide a text passable in the printing-house.[50] While this view is certainly not implausible, it is also not the only possibility. That Q was dictated at some point in its development is evident from a number of evident misreadings and mishearings preserved within its text. Misreadings include Q's 'defect' for F's 'defeat', 'fate' for 'state', 'concuaveties' for 'concavities' (though this could be a mishearing) and 'Gwigzard' for 'Guichard'. Perhaps the most obvious and absurd mishearing occurs when F's 'defunction of King Pharamond' is rendered in Q as 'the function'. Other examples include Q's 'Shure' for F's 'sure', 'Faramount' for 'Pharamond', 'Elme' for 'Elbe', 'Inger' for 'Lingare, 'Pippin' for 'Pepin', 'short nooke Ile' for 'nook shotten isle', 'said eyde' for 'sad-ey'd', 'approach' for 'reproach', 'partition' for 'perdition', 'cocks-come' for 'coxcomb', 'crasing' for 'grazing', 'twise' for 'thrice', 'turne' for 'turn'd'. All of these misreadings and mishearings point to a text dictated to a copyist, but, as Taylor points out, they 'could have occurred in the printing house, or during any of the scribal stages which intervened between Shakespeare's foul papers and the written parts of the actors in the abridgement'.[51] It remains possible, then, that Q was initially written up from memory alone and that errors of recollection were later compounded by scribal mistakes.

Q shows clear signs of having been constructed either in part or in whole from memory. The clearest indication that a memorial error has occurred is the misplacement of a word that we know belongs elsewhere (usually later) in the text. When Q opens with the King's line about 'serious matters touching vs and France', the word 'touching' is transposed forward from 1.1.79. Similarly, Q's 'the coursing sneakers onely' brings forward (and so misplaces) the word 'sneaking' in F by some 28 lines (see 1.2.171). Q's replacement of F's 'purpose' (1.2.212) with 'moment' mistakenly renders F's phrasing as 'End in one moment', in all likelihood carrying over from Q's wording just six lines earlier, '20 actions once a foote, may all end in one moment'. Q's clumsy attempt at F's 'our grave, / Like Turkish mute, shall have a tongueless mouth / Not worshipp'd with a waxen epitaph' is best explained as an effort of recollection.[52] The Hostess's line on Falstaff in F, 'he is so shak'd of a burning quotidian tertian' becomes in Q, 'he is so troubled with a burning tashan contigian fever'.[53] The Boy's soliloquy in F 3.2.28–53 is severely foreshortened, probably from memory. When Burbon in Q renders F's 'a slobb'ry and dirty farm' as a 'foggy farme', he brings 'foggy' forward from the Constable's line about the climate (3.5.16). In the same scene, Q mistakenly reverses F's 'sodden water . . . barley broth' (ll. 18–19), and in the following scene transposes the word 'furious' to the preceding line (3.6.26). When Montjoy in Q says 'England shall repent her folly, see her rashnesse', the reporter seems to be relying upon memory of F's line, 'advantage is a better soldier than rashness' (3.6.121–2). As Gurr observed, poor memory produces a long line in Q for its equivalent of F's 3.6.158–9.[54] In the account of the deaths of Suffolk and York, Q anticipates the word 'ore' from F's 'all haggled ouer' (4.6.11). Similarly, the word 'worthy' is misplaced from F's 'The King most worthily hath . . .' (at 4.7.9) to Q's 'O he is a worthy king'. All these instances are examples of what Harold Jenkins has described as 'phrases at a distance from where they belong'.[55] The distance may vary but the readiest explanation for them is misty recollection. Gurr picks out the King's line in Q, 'Now sirs, the windes faire, and we will Aboord' as one that cannot be explained but as a lapse of memory. F's equivalent for this line runs, 'Now sits the wind fair, and we will aboard' (2.2.12). As Gurr points out, Q's reporters – or, as he prefers, transcribers – mistook the word 'sits' for 'sirs' and duly altered 'wind' to 'windes' (i.e. 'wind is') to make the line intelligible. They would have made this alteration, Gurr observes, only if they had forgotten the original line.[56]

Whereas Gurr initially took Q to be a text prepared for printing on the basis that stagecraft invariably ruled out immediate re-entry, he reversed this view in NCSQ, arguing that these re-entries could in fact have been staged: 'For a character to exit and then quickly cross back-stage and re-enter was possible.'[57] Leaving aside this inconsistency, Gurr's view of Q hangs crucially upon the following inference regarding the process of its composition: 'Most of the manuscript was recorded by dictation, chiefly from the rough playscript, helped in places by the players' memories of their parts.'[58] We can be certain that some of the manuscript was dictated, but, if 'most' had been, one would anticipate fewer variants and memorial errors than in fact appear in Q. Memory would have served only where it was needed – where the text was lacking – and it seems unlikely that a predominantly dictated text would throw up so many flaws. It is worth observing that Q's version of the Boy's lines at 3.2.27–51 offers tell tale signs of a single speech entirely reconstructed (and drastically reduced from 25 lines to five) from remembered fragments of F. Q invents its opening phrase 'Well, I would I were once from them'. It then transposes F's 3.2.45–6, and follows it with snippets from F (lines 40–9): 'They will steal anything', 'Bardolph stole a lute case', 'carried it three mile' (an attempt at F's 'bore it twelve leagues', 'and sold it for three ha'pence', 'stole a fire shovel', 'I knew by that', 'carry coals', 'leave them'. The transposition rules out simple abridgement as the process behind Q's lines in this instance, and renders dictation seriously improbable.

To sum up, the sheer variety of errors in Q points to a complex sequence of mediations behind its textual transmission, a sequence difficult to ascertain precisely. Just about everyone agrees that Shakespeare wrote a draft of what would become F, that the actors learned their lines for performances, that an abridgement was made, and that this (or a similar) shorter version provided the copy for Q.[59] But there is disagreement over how exactly that happened. For Gurr, two actors dictated the abridgement, relying upon memory to fill in gaps. For Taylor and Craik, two actors reconstituted the abridgement mainly from memory. Inaccuracies of memory, reporting, reading, hearing, transcription and composition point to a filtered, multi-stage process by which Q was formed. Shakespeare's hand in Q can only remotely be traced where revision is suspected. It is, of course, a truism that *any* printed text is prepared for a readership and this includes the early quarto. It is also a truism that a play-text originates with the possibility of its performance, and this includes F. So a neat distinction between shorter and longer texts as theatrical and literary can never quite hold. Additional stage directions, apparent improvisation and the mostly successful retention of actors' cue lines across both versions suggests that a performance script does indeed lie somewhere behind Q. But when Craik echoes Gurr in concluding, '[p]robably it was compiled simply to provide a reading text of the play', we may feel that statement to be at once both obviously true and reductive of what seems from the evidence a far more tangled process.[60] Q has survived as an unusually short and unstable text and its many imperfections and difficulties yet pose a variety of challenges to criticism. If, in the end, they permit no tidy solution to their puzzles, we are indebted to those imperfections for what more may be learnt of early drama and its texts.

Notes

1 See for example, Leah S. Marcus, *Unediting the Renaissance: Shakespeare, Marlowe, Milton* (London and New York: Routledge, 1996); Randall McLeod, 'Fiat Flux', in McLeod (ed.), *Crisis in Editing: Texts of the English Renaissance* (New York: AMS, 1994); Laurie E. Maguire, *Shakespearean Suspect Texts* (Cambridge: Cambridge University Press, 1996); Paul Werstine, 'Post-Theory Problems in Shakespeare Editing', *Yearbook of English Studies*, 29 (1999), 103–17; and Lukas Erne and M. J. Kidnie (eds), *Textual Performances: The Modern Reproduction of Shakespeare's Drama* (Cambridge and New York: Cambridge University Press, 2004).

2 Andrew Gurr, 'Maximal and Minimal Texts: Shakespeare v. the Globe', *Shakespeare Survey*, 52 (1999), 68–87.

3 Jonathan Bate (ed.), *The Romantics on Shakespeare* (Harmondsworth: Penguin, 1992), pp. 361, 363–5.

4 Bradley cited in T. W. Craik (ed.), *Henry V* (London and New York: Routledge, 1995), pp. 71–2, 79. For Granville-Barker see Michael Quinn (ed.), *Shakespeare: 'Henry V', A Casebook* (London: Macmillan, 1969), pp. 62–4.

5 E. M. W. Tillyard, *Shakespeare's History Plays* (1944; rpt. Harmondsworth: Penguin, 1986), pp. 309, 311.

6 A. R. Humphreys (ed.), *Henry V* (Harmondsworth: Penguin, 1968), pp. 22–3; Jonathan Dollimore and Alan Sinfield, 'History and Ideology: The Instance of *Henry V*', in John Drakakis (ed.), *Alternative Shakespeares* (London and New York: Methuen, 1985), p. 216; Norman Rabkin, 'Rabbits, Ducks and *Henry V*', *Shakespeare Quarterly*, 28 (1977), 279–96, reprinted as 'Either/Or: Responding to *Henry V*', in *Shakespeare and the Problem of Meaning* (Chicago and London: The University of Chicago Press, 1981), pp. 33–64; Stephen Greenblatt, 'Invisible Bullets: Renaissance Authority and Its Subversion, *Henry IV* and *Henry V*', in Jonathan Dollimore and Alan Sinfield (eds), *Political Shakespeare: New Essays in Cultural Materialism* (Manchester: Manchester University Press, 1984), pp. 18–47 (p. 43).

7 Gary Taylor, *Three Studies in the Text of 'Henry V'* (Oxford: Clarendon Press, 1979), pp. 101–3.

8 Gary Taylor (ed.), *Henry V* (Oxford: Clarendon Press, 1982), p. 25.

9 Ibid., p. 24, note 2.

10 Annabel Patterson, *Shakespeare and the Popular Voice* (Oxford: Blackwell, 1989), pp. 73, 81. I quote Elizabeth's official title from a bond of sureties of 1582 concerning Shakespeare's licence to marry, reprinted in E. K. Chambers, *William Shakespeare: A Study of Facts and Problems*, 2 vols. (Oxford: Clarendon, 1930), vol. 2, p. 41.

11 Taylor (ed.), *Henry V*, p. 5. Half a century ago, W. D. Smith unconvincingly argued that the passage 'beautifully' fits Charles Blount, Lord Mountjoy, in 'The *Henry V* Choruses in the First Folio', *Journal of English and Germanic Philology*, 53 (1954), 38–57 (p. 40); see R. A. Law, 'The Chorus in *Henry the Fifth*', *University of Texas Studies in English*, 35 (1956), 11–21. The play's date allows that the 'wooden O' may well have been the Curtain, the temporary residence of the Chamberlain's, since the Globe at this time was still under construction. Gurr takes a relative imprecision regarding staging to indicate uncertainty as to which venue might host the work; see Andrew Gurr (ed.), *King Henry V* (Cambridge: Cambridge University Press, 1992), p. 43.

12 Patterson, *Shakespeare and the Popular Voice*, p. 73.

13 Craik, (ed.), *Henry V*, p. 18.

14 A. W. Pollard, *Shakespeare's Folios and Quartos: A Study in the Bibliography of Shakespeare's Plays, 1594–1685* (London: Methuen, 1909). See also his *Shakespeare's Fight with the Pirates and the Problems of the Transmission of his Text*, 2nd edn (Cambridge: Cambridge University Press, 1937), and G. I. Duthie, *The 'Bad' Quarto of Hamlet: A Critical Study* (Cambridge: Cambridge University Press, 1941), pp. 1–54.

15 Charlton Hinman (ed.), *The First Folio of Shakespeare: Based on Folios in the Folger Shakespeare Library Collection*, 2nd edn (New York and London: Norton, 1996), p. 7; 'To the great variety of readers', sig. A3.

16 The idea that Q constitutes an abridged text for provincial performance goes back at least to the Preface of Israel Gollancz's edition of 1895. Q's deliberate excision of 'The king has killed his heart' (F, 2.1.70) is a telling sign of abridgement.

17 Gurr, (ed.), *King Henry V*, pp. 221–2.

18 Ibid., pp. 217, 223.

19 Ibid., pp. 220, 223.

20 Andrew Gurr (ed.), *The First Quarto of King Henry V* (Cambridge: Cambridge University Press, 2000), pp. ix, 13.

21 Craik (ed.), *Henry V*, p. 28.

22 Gurr (ed.), *King Henry V*, p. 8.

23 Gurr, 'Maximal and Minimal Texts', p. 70.

24 A. R. Humphreys (ed.), *The Second Part of King Henry IV* (London: Methuen, 1966), p. 186.

25 Ernst Honigmann, *The Stability of Shakespeare's Text* (London: Edward Arnold, 1965), pp. 144–5.

26 Gurr (ed.), *First Quarto*, 30, my italics.

27 Gurr (ed.), *King Henry V*, p. 6. C. H. Herford and Percy Simpson (eds), *Ben Jonson*, 11 vols (1927; rpt. Oxford: Clarendon Press, 1966), vol. 3, p. 303. I have modernised spelling.

28 Ibid., p. 438.
29 Lukas Erne, *Shakespeare as Literary Dramatist* (Cambridge: Cambridge University Press, 2003), p. 220.
30 Ibid., p. 204.
31 Ibid., p. 224.
32 Ibid., pp. 194–5.
33 A. W. Verity (ed.), *Thomas Heywood* (London: T. Fisher Unwin, n.d.), pp. 78, 154, 329.
34 Erne, *Shakespeare as Literary Dramatist*, pp. 210–11.
35 Ibid., p. 215.
36 Ibid., p. 221.
37 Ibid., p. 216.
38 Ibid., p. 221.
39 Ibid., p. 222.
40 Ibid., p. 218, my emphasis; cf. p. 225.
41 Ibid., p. 218.
42 Ibid., p. 257, note 6.
43 Ibid., p. 258.
44 All, that is, except Graham Holderness and Bryan Loughrey in their edition of Q, *The Chronicle History of Henry the Fift* (London: Harvester Wheatsheaf, 1993), who courageously postulate that 'the Folio is an expanded version of the Quarto' (p. 22).
45 Taylor (ed.), *Henry V*, pp. 12–18.
46 Honigmann, *The Stability of Shakespeare's Text*, p. 133.
47 Gurr (ed.), *First Quarto*, p. 81.
48 Gary Taylor, 'Shakespeare's Leno: *Henry V* IV.v.14', *Notes and Queries*, 224 (1979), 117–18.
49 Q's reversal of scenic order for 4.4 and 4.5 suggest that the two scenes were written as separate sections and easily shuffled out of place.
50 Gurr (ed.), *First Quarto*, p. 9.
51 Taylor, *Three Studies*, p. 126.
52 Q's rendering seems less absurd in light of the fact that fraudsters would commonly be paraded through the London streets with a paper notice indicating their crime. The Repertories of the Court of Aldermen (Reps 21, 26) record Agnes Savage put into the pillory at Cheape for two hours with a paper over her head 10 July 1586, 21.445v; Richard Hewett salter 'sett upon a horse backe wth his face towards the horsetayle . . . wth a paper uppon his backe wth theys words written viz. For selling of salte wth a false measure, and so to be conveyed on horse back through all the marketts' 18 August 1588, 21.591v; Henry Rose whipped and carted with a paper on his head 30 April 1603, 26.150v.
53 On the Hostess's notorious line at 2.3.16–17 see Duncan Salkeld, 'Falstaff's Nose', *Notes and Queries*, 249 (2004), 3, 284–5. I am

grateful to Dr Irving Finkel, curator of games at the British Museum, who advises me that paint rather than baize would have been used on early modern backgammon boards but that in all other respects, nouns notwithstanding, a gaming interpretation of the line is convincing.

54 Gurr (ed.), *First Quarto*, 98.
55 Harold Jenkins (ed.), *Hamlet* (London: Methuen, 1982), p. 29.
56 Gurr (ed.), *First Quarto*, 17.
57 Ibid., p. 12.
58 Ibid., p. 9.
59 See, for example, Taylor, *Three Studies*, p. 98; Gurr (ed.) *First Quarto*, p. 9.
60 Craik (ed.), *Henry V*, p. 28.

7

Shakespeare's deletions and false starts, mark 2[1]

E. A. J. Honigmann

In the first half of the twentieth century Shakespeare's editors began to take an interest in a topic that their predecessors had largely neglected. If we consult the index to W. W. Greg's *The Shakespeare First Folio*, that monumental appraisal of the new bibliography, eight plays are listed under 'false starts and first drafts in foul papers', while others are omitted. Greg does not include *Timon*, yet he seems to agree with E. K. Chambers that some passages 'look very much like rough notes, hastily jotted down to be worked up later'.[2] Nor does he refer to *A Midsummer Night's Dream*, though he abandons the caution with which he usually treats Dover Wilson's textual theories: he agrees with Wilson's 'demonstration of revision at the beginning of Act V'.

> Here in the first eighty-four lines there are eight passages of varying length in which the line-division is disturbed. Omit these passages and a perfectly consecutive text remains. There is no escaping the conclusion that in this we have the original writing, which was supplemented by fresh lines crowded into the margin so that their metrical structure was obscured.[3]

Shakespeare's false starts, I believe, are a more important problem than Greg and others have realised. I want to approach them by way of a specific example, partly because I was the target of criticism and equally because it leads on to more fundamental questions. In 1996 I suggested that *Othello*, 4.3.62–5, looks like a false start.[4]

> *Des.* Would'st thou do such a deed for all the world?
> *Æmil.* Why, would not you?
> *Des.* No, by this Heauenly light.
> *Æmil.* Nor I neither, by this Heauenly light:
>   I might doo't as well i'th'darke.

65

Des. Would'st thou do such a deed for al the world?
Æmil. The world's a huge thing:
    It is a great price, for a small vice.

(F)

The Q version is substantially the same, except that the second 'deed' (l. 66) becomes 'thing'. I suggested that lines 62–5 ('Would'st . . . i'th'darke') were a false start. Scott McMillin commented:

> Because they were marked lightly or strangely, Honigmann surmises, the scribe and/or compositor misunderstood the intention and allowed the passages to stand in Q1 . . . [This] highlights the weakness of the 'false start' possibility, which is that a professional playwright could not cross out his lines effectively enough for the scribe and/or compositor to grasp the intention, so both versions passed through to print. Sloppiness all around is assumed in the speculation: (1) the author writes out a 'false start'; (2) he then marks it imperfectly for cancellation; (3) the scribe and/or the compositor miss the cancellation and keep the 'false start' as text.[5]

McMillin omits to mention that the suggested false start in *Othello* is not an isolated instance. Many editors have postulated false starts in other texts, both in the good quartos and the Folio. See the second quarto of *Romeo and Juliet*:

(1)
The grey eyde morne smiles on the frowning night,
Checkring the Easterne Clouds with streaks of light,
And darknesse fleckted like a drunkard reeles,
From forth daies pathway, made by *Tytans* wheeles.
Hence will I to my ghostly Friers close cell,
His helpe to craue, and my deare hap to tell.

Exit.

Enter Frier alone with a basket.

Fri. The grey-eyed morne smiles on the frowning night,
    Checking the Easterne clowdes with streaks of light:
    And fleckeld darknesse like a drunkard reeles,
    From forth daies path, and *Titans* burning wheeles:

(2.1.232ff, 2.2.1ff)

(2)
This may flyes do, when I from this must flie,
And sayest thou yet, that exile is not death?
But *Romeo* may not, he is banished.

Flies may do this, but I from this must flie:
They are freemen, but I am banished.

(3.3.41ff)

(3)
Ah deare Iuliet

Why art thou yet so faire? I will beleeue,
Shall I beleeue that vnsubstantiall death is amorous, . . .
Depart againe, come lye thou in my arme,
Heer's to thy health, where ere thou tumblest in.
O true Appothecarie!
Thy drugs are quicke. Thus with a kisse I die.
Depart againe, here, here, will I remaine, . . .
Heeres to my Loue. O true Appothecary:
Thy drugs are quicke. Thus with a kisse I die.

(5.3.101ff)

In these three fascinating instances of second thoughts, I assume that Shakespeare realised almost immediately that he hadn't got it right and tried again. He retained the four lines of (1), with some improvements ('burning wheels'); he fidgeted with (2), and even more so with (3), yet in each case seems to have gone on writing, i.e. his second thoughts were not a marginal or later insertion.

(4) The Folio text of *Troilus and Cressida* repeats three lines from 5.3 in 5.10:

Pand. Why, but heare you?
Troy. Hence brother lackie; ignomie and shame
    Pursue thy life, and liue aye with thy name.

(TLN 3328–30)

Pand. But heare you? heare you?
Troy. Hence broker, lackie, ignomy, and shame
    Pursue thy life, and liue aye with thy name.

(TLN 3569–71)

In the quarto (1609) 5.3 omits the last two of the three lines, reading '*Pand.* Do you heere my Lord, do you heere'.

(5) In *Love's Labour's Lost* Q (1598), Shakespeare quite manifestly struggled in 4.3 when he wrote the play's longest and most important speech. Again he seems to have continued writing, without any deletions, so that the compositor, failing to grasp this, set many more lines than Shakespeare could have wanted:

From womens eyes this doctrine I deriue,
They are the Ground, the Bookes, the Achadems,
From whence doth spring the true *Promethean* fire.

Then Q prints 46 lines of verse, followed by

From womens eyes this doctrine I deriue,
They sparcle still the right promethean fier,
They are the Bookes, the Artes, the Achademes,
That shew, containe, and nourish all the worlde.

I shall return to this speech below.

In these five instances, alternative versions of the same passage either followed immediately or reappeared in a later scene, because the author thought they would be more appropriate there. In addition there are textual oddities in Shakespeare's plays which also point to imperfect deletions.

Take (6), the epitaphs in *Timon of Athens*, 5.4.70ff:

Alcibiades reades the Epitaph.
Heere lies a wretched Coarse, of wretched Soule bereft,
Seek not my name: A Plague consume you, wicked Caitifs left:
Heere lye I Timon, who aliue, all liuing men did hate,
Passe by, and curse thy fill, but passe and stay not here thy gate.

The four lines come from Plutarch's account of Timon, with one word changed (*Caitifs*, from Plutarch's *wretches*). In Plutarch, though, there are two epitaphs: the first two lines, attributed to Timon himself; the next two, by Callimachus. H. J. Oliver had 'little doubt that Shakespeare copied down from North's *Plutarch two* epitaphs, each in a couplet, meaning to omit one or the other . . . on revision. As it is, they contradict each other ("Seek not my name", "Here lie I, Timon")'.[6]

'Meaning to omit one or the other, on revision': the same explanation can help us with (a) false starts where 'both versions passed through to print'; (b) textual tangles left unclear in the manuscripts used by Shakespeare's printers; (c) 'ghost' characters named in stage directions and apparently forgotten thereafter. I have in mind, of course, the revision carried out by authors of any period when they write a fair copy of their rough draft. If, as I deduce from the number of examples of (a), (b) and (c) scattered in so many texts, it was Shakespeare's habit to mark intended omissions lightly or not at all, we have to take on board a very important consequence – that it was

Shakespeare's intention to prepare his own fair copy from his foul papers, as indeed was the general practice. 'There is no evidence whatever', according to Fredson Bowers, 'that an author ever submitted for payment anything but a fair copy', and, said Bowers, we have not the slightest scrap of evidence that the actors 'required a dramatist to turn over his original foul sheets along with the fair copy'.[7] It seems reasonable to suppose that Shakespeare, having no permanent home in London, could have handed over his 'foul papers' to the company manager not because he did not want to write out a fair copy like other dramatists but merely for safe keeping, and that foul paper texts with intended cancellations were thus available for the printers when they were needed.[8]

Let us return to (5) *Love's Labour's Lost*, and then to *Othello*. In (5), as in (1)–(4), Shakespeare recognised that he had not made the most of his key idea ('From womens eyes . . .'): he expanded three lines into four, and changed the preceding or following verses. That is, he retained the gold and abandoned some of the dross. Since he did not delete his intended cancellations, editors do not know which lines of 'dross' should be kept. Some throw out 23 lines (TLN 1646–68 in the Folio text); an alternative would be to exclude a passage more than twice as long (TLN 1652–700), where the repetition of what are essentially the same ideas becomes wearisome, which would still leave a long speech of 29 lines. In either case, as also in (1)–(4), Shakespeare repeated one or more 'golden' lines and sacrificed or modified inferior lines.

Why would Shakespeare wish to cancel (7) *Othello*, 4.3.62–5? McMillin thought that 'there is no need . . . to explain the exchange between Emilia and Desdemona': 'Performers have been playing these lines as written for centuries. One way is to play Emilia's joke about doing it in the dark as an aside. That keeps the joke and protects Desdemona from having to hear it.' The truth is that performers have for centuries played lines in Shakespeare that are puzzling or incomprehensible and have got away with it. To understand what happened in *Othello*, 4.3.62–5, we have to take into account a structural development in the preceding scenes, an increasing emphasis on 'feminism'. In 3.4, 4.2 and 4.3 Emilia sides more and more positively with Desdemona and against Othello. Shakespeare took care to establish that Emilia knows about Othello's suspicions and unhesitatingly rejects them ('I durst, my lord, to wager she is honest', 4.2.12), and she knows how they devastate Desdemona (4.2.152ff).

At the same time Shakespeare unites Emilia and Desdemona in 'intimate togetherness', and in 4.3 he creates an 'emotion-packed climax of feminine tenderness and communion'⁹ – is this elaborate build-up to be sacrificed for a bawdy joke? Jokes came too easily to Shakespeare and 'sometime it was necessary he should be stopped'.¹⁰ Emilia's question, 'Why, would not you [do such a deed]?', even more than the quip about doing it in the dark, damages the 'togetherness' of the two women, was out of place and had to go. So we find: (1) a telltale repeated line, the 'gold' that Shakespeare wished to retain; (2) a repeated jest ('a great price, for a small vice', replacing 'I might do't as well i'th'dark', essentially the same idea, which is then elaborated at great length, as in *Love's Labour's Lost*); (3) a pruning of the 'dross', an improvement since Emilia's attitude is made clear by what follows.

Perhaps I may add that I did not omit 4.3.62–5 from my edition of *Othello*: at this time Shakespeare's cancellations were not properly understood and I felt that my explanation still needed to be tested.

We may now respond to McMillin's 'sloppiness all around' as follows. (1) 'The author writes out a false start'. Yes, this was Shakespeare's way: he left false starts in many other plays. (2) 'He then marks it imperfectly for cancellation'. Intending to write out his own fair copy, either he did not bother to delete or he drew a squiggle against the passage, to remind himself of his intention (sometimes he may have wished to keep his options open). (3) 'The scribe or the compositor misses the cancellation'. Yes: do other plays with obvious false starts or alternative passages (*Timon*) not prove that this could and did happen? (4) 'F prints the passage [4.3.62ff] virtually as Q1 has it', which means that the scribe who prepared F's copy 'failed to see the intended cut too, an unlikely possibility'.¹¹ Thanks to Alice Walker we know that F shares many 'common errors' with Q texts, i.e. was not an entirely independent text.¹² I assume that the F scribe of *Othello* was told to prepare a 'full' text, and added not only 160 lines that are not found in Q but also Q lines not found in the text he was given. And (5), why was the false start at 4.3.62ff not noticed for three centuries? Reply: other false starts were not noticed until the twentieth century, when the new bibliography began to take a closer interest in such textual peculiarities. If we see these problems historically in the sequence in which discoveries were made, the editorial treatment of Shakespeare's deletions and false starts is less surprising than McMillin seems to think it.

(8) Here I want to stress that when Hand D in *Sir Thomas More* got into a tangle and tried to extricate himself, he left several false starts undeleted. (I have recently presented new evidence confirming that Hand D must be Shakespeare.)[13]

> and your vnreuerent knees   110
> [that] make them your feet to kneele to be forgyven.
> [is safer warrs, then euer you can make]
>   [in in to yor obedienc.]
> [whose discipline is ryot; why euen yor warrs hurly]
>   tell me but this
> [cannot proceed[14] but by obedienc] what rebell captaine
> as mutynes ar incident, by his name[15]   115

Greg commented on lines 112–14: 'with the exception of the single word *warrs* (which he crossed out, adding *hurly* in its place) these lines were left standing by D. All the other deletions are in darker ink, presumably by C, who added the interlined words in the third line'.[16]

Humphrey Moseley's epistle in the Beaumont and Fletcher Folio of 1647 is relevant: 'now you have both All that was *Acted*, and all that was not; even the perfect full Originalls without the least mutilation'. As Greg explained, 'by "Originalls" he seems to have meant full texts, but not necessarily texts exactly as the author had written them'. Had the undeleted lines of Hand D gone to the printers we would expect 'false start' confusion very much as we find it in Shakespeare's quartos and Folio.[17]

If, as I have argued, Shakespeare sometimes did not trouble to delete lines that he thought of as cancelled, this throws a new light on the words of Heminge and Condell in the First Folio: 'His mind and hand went together: And what he thought, he vttered with that easinesse, that wee haue scarse receiued from him a blot in his papers'. Heminge and Condell probably misjudged the number of 'blots' in the plays because Shakespeare did not always cross out rejected passages; indeed, so much so that their Folio texts retain almost all the first and second thoughts that I have listed (*Romeo and Juliet, Love's Labour's Lost, Othello, Timon* and even most of the mislineation in *Midsummer Night's Dream*).[18]

(9) The muddle that results when editors (Heminge and Condell and their successors) are unaware of Shakespeare's habit of not deleting cancelled passages may be illustrated from *Measure for Measure*. Act 1, scenes 2 and 3, in the Folio, usually printed as

scene 2 in modern editions, divide into four sections. (1) (TLN 95–137) The 'gentlemen' indulge in trivial and obscene chatter; (2) (TLN 138–74) Mrs Overdone informs the gentlemen, including Lucio, that Claudio has been sentenced 'for getting Madam Julietta with child'; (3) (TLN 174–204) Mrs Overdone asks Pompey why Claudio has been sentenced, and he tells her what she has just told the others (Lucio is not present); (4) (TLN 205ff) Lucio, who has re-entered, asks Claudio the reason for his arrest. In short, both Lucio and Mrs Overdone know, and then do not know, the reason for Claudio's arrest, and this difficulty disappears if we assume that (2) – or perhaps (1), (2) and (3), viz. the whole of scene 2 in the Folio – was meant to be cancelled and was printed in error.

Were Shakespeare's second thoughts always improvements? Years ago I suggested that, when Shakespeare prepared a fair copy from his foul papers, 'little verbal changes, not necessarily always for the better', might run quite freely from his pen, and that some might be unconscious substitutions.[19] I remain of that opinion, but assume that, if he decided to change a line or lines rather than single words, some improvement is to be expected. What, then, are we to make of (**10**), the two reports of Portia's death in *Julius Caesar*: (a) 4.3.142–57 and 165, and (b) 4.3.180–94, in T. S. Dorsch's edition?[20] Dorsch thought that

> the inconsistency could be explained only by the supposition that the copy from which the Folio was printed contained two versions of the account of Portia's death, of which one was a revision, and that both were printed by mistake . . . With most recent editors, I accept these views, and take the present passage [viz. (b)] to be the original version . . . not clearly cancelled in the MS.[21]

Dorsch, like other editors, seems to have thought (a) superior to (b). If we agree with him, and I do, this would mean that, for once, the second version would not improve on the first, a surprising outcome. While it is just possible that Shakespeare wanted both versions to stand, my guess is that (a), though printed first, was written after (b) – that is, was written on a separate sheet of paper and inserted later; in short, as Dorsch said, that (b) was 'not clearly cancelled in the MS'.

(**11**) Dorsch was less positive about another inconsistency later in the same play, 5.1.98ff:

> [*Cassius*]. If we do lose this battle, then is this
> The very last time we shall speak together:

What are you then determined to do?   100
Brutus. Even by the rule of that philosophy
  By which I did blame Cato for the death
  Which he did give himself, I know nor how,
  But I do find it cowardly and vile,
  For fear of what might fall, so to prevent   105
  The time of life, arming myself with patience
  To stay the providence of some high powers
  That govern us below.
Cassius. Then, if we lose this battle,
  You are contented to be led in triumph
  Thorough the streets of Rome?   110
Brutus. No, Cassius, no: think not, thou noble Roman,
  That ever Brutus will go bound to Rome . . .

Ben Jonson complained that Shakespeare 'flowed with that facility, that sometime it was necessary he should be stopped . . . As when he said in the person of Caesar, one speaking to him, "Caesar, thou dost me wrong," he replied "Caesar did never wrong, but with just cause" and such like, which were ridiculous.'[22] Shakespeare, I believe, flowed with too much facility in *Julius Caesar*, 5.1, and stopped himself just in time. He cancelled, in his mind though not clearly enough on paper, lines 101–8. The alternative is to regard the clash of 101–8 and of 111ff as another instance of Brutus' capacity for self-deception and confusion. Once we see how often Shakespeare's intended cancellations reached print, the balance of probability, I think, favours cancellation.

(12) Elsewhere the clue we need is not self-contradiction in adjacent passages but, as in the extract from *Sir Thomas More*, incoherence. In the F text of *Troilus and Cressida*, where I noted above the false start of Troilus' farewell to Pandare in 5.3, consider Troilus' farewell to Cressida:

Troy. Heare why I speake it; Loue:
  The Grecian youths are full of qualitie,
  Their louing well compos'd, with guift of nature,
  Flawing and swelling ore with Arts and exercise . . .
                                    (4.4.76ff)

Q omits the words I have italicised: either all of them or just 'Flawing' look like a false start that reached print by mistake. Or take (13) Agamemnon's welcome to Hector:

Aga. Worthy of Armes: as welcome as to one:
That would be rid of such an enemie.
But that's no welcome: vnderstand more cleere
What's past, and what's to come, is strew'd with huskes,
And formelesse ruine of obliuion:
But in this extant moment, faith and troth
Strain'd purely from all hollow bias drawing:
Bids thee with most diuine integritie,
From heart of very heart, great Hector welcome.

(4.7.49ff)

Again, Q omits the words in italics. Why? Because Shakespeare remembered that he had written a very similar speech for Ulysses (3.3.139ff), one that also deals with the past, the instant way or this extant moment, time and oblivion: I assume that he intended to cancel the six lines in 4.7 and that in the F text they passed through into print in error. Or did he simply think the six lines too turgid?

(14) Another reason for cancelling what has already been written can be that it impedes the momentum of a scene.

Bast. I am thinking brother of a prediction I read this other day, what should follow these Eclipses.
Edg. Doe you busie your selfe about that?
Bast. I promise you the effects he writ of, succeed vnhappily, *as of vnnaturalnesse betweene the child and the parent, death, dearth, dissolutions of ancient amities, diuisions in state, menaces and maledictions against King and nobles, needles diffidences, banishment of friends, dissipation of Cohorts, nuptial breaches, and I know not what.*
Edg. How long haue you beene a sectary Astronomicall?
Bast. Come, come, when saw you my father last?

(*King Lear*, 1.2.135ff, Q)

F omits the words in italics. This could have been a 'theatrical' cut or it might indicate the author's dissatisfaction with unnecessary prolixity. The two possibilities are nicely balanced.

(15) In addition to the likelihood that many longer passages in the quartos and Folio were meant to be cancelled we must consider the possibility that single lines and half-lines were imperfectly deleted and thus passed through into printed versions. Some sound odd or awkward in their context:

Forsooth, a great Arithmetition,
One Michael Cassio, a Florentine,
A fellow almost dambd in a faire wife,

20

That neuer set a squadron in the field . . .

(*Othello*, 1.1.18ff., Q)[23]

Then there are what I call 'loose half-lines',[24] metrically superfluous words that contribute little or nothing, whether poetically or dramatically:

(i)
And spoke such scuruy, and prouoking tearmes
[Against your Houor,] that with the little godlinesse I haue,
I did full hard forbeare him: but I pray sir,

(*Othello*, 1.2.7ff, Q)

(ii)
That he you hurt is of great fame in Cypres,
[And great affinity,] and that in wholesome wisedome,
He might not but refuse you: but he protests he loues you

(*Othello*, 3.1.46ff, Q)

F repeats the loose half-lines, probably taking them from Q.

Most of the 'intended cancellations' that I have suggested so far exhibit giveaway signs such as repetition, a logical clash with what precedes or follows, almost incomprehensible obscurity, metrical irregularity or several of these together. Any writer, however, even one as 'flowing' as Shakespeare, might be dissatisfied with his own work (and we have Jonson's word for it that his facility sometimes betrayed him): would Shakespeare himself not feel, now and then, that he had written too quickly and had better start again? I am thinking of passages such as *Measure for Measure*, 1.2.1–55, which I described above as 'trivial and obscene chatter'. True, these lines have a function – they bring before us the 'witless bravery' (1.3.10) and lifestyle that the Duke wants Angelo to stamp out. Yet Shakespeare could do this kind of thing so much more brilliantly, and, compared with his other plays, where the opening scenes are usually arresting, I think he might have wanted to scrap 1.2.1–55 or 1–79 (see above). It cannot be proved, but producers of the play should be made aware of the possibility which depends on the fact – yes, let us call it the fact – that Shakespeare sometimes did not trouble to mark his cancellations.

Shakespeare's failure to delete clearly can also lead us to alternative interpretations of famous cruxes in *Hamlet*:

(16)
O this is the poyson of deepe griefe, it springs all from her Fathers death, and now behold, ô Gertrard Gertrard,

When sorrowes come, they come not single spyes,
But in battalians: first her Father slaine . . .

(4.5.74ff, Q2)

(**17**)
Come Gertrard, wee'le call vp our wisest friends,
And let them know both what we meane to doe
And whats vntimely doone,
Whose whisper ore the worlds dyameter,
As leuell as the Cannon to his blanck,
Transports his poysned shot, may misse our Name,
And hit the woundlesse ayre, ô come away,
My soule is full of discord and dismay.

(4.1.37ff, Q2)

In both passages F regularises the metre:

(**16**)
Oh this is the poyson of deepe greefe, it springs
All from her Fathers death. Oh Gertrude, Gertrude, . . .

(**17**)
Come Gertrude, wee'l call vp our wisest friends,
To let them know both what we meane to do,
And what's vntimely done. Oh come away,
My soule is full of discord and dismay.

That is, F's (**16**) omits 'and now behold', F's (**17**) omits 'Whose whisper . . . ayre'. We may choose to think that Q2 transmits the 'true text' (though it loses some words at the end of (**17**), line 3, such as 'So envious slander'.[25] The alternative is to assume that Shakespeare himself removed 'and now behold' (a false start), and for once actually deleted the missing words in (**17**), and thought that he had also cancelled 'Whose whisper . . . ayre', a passage that reminds me of Agamemnon's welcome to Hector, losing itself in pointless detail. That is, Shakespeare himself had second thoughts and regularised the metre in both instances: here, consequently, F may record Shakespeare's final intention.

Most of Shakespeare's second thoughts seem to have come to him immediately while he was writing, and to have been inserted below his first version, thus confusing inattentive scribes or compositors who were unaware of his practice of not deleting cancelled passages. Now and then, however, he wrote his second thoughts in the margin, presumably because some time had elapsed, as in the case of (**18**) *A Midsummer Night's Dream* (see above) and of (**19**) *Titus Andronicus*, 4.3.89ff:

> *Clowne.* From heauen, alas sir, I neuer came there,
>   God forbid I should be so bolde, to presse to heauen in my young daies:
>   Why I am going with my pidgeons to the tribunall
>   Plebs, to take vp a matter of brawle . . .

As Greg said, the typographical arrangement here 'suggests that this unquestionably Shakespearian sally was a marginal addition to the Clown's speech as first written'.[26] And of course a whole scene might be added years after the original composition, as probably in the case of (**20**), the 'fly scene' in *Titus Andronicus*, 3.2.

In 2003, when I wrote the first version of this chapter, I thought that small is beautiful – I had made my point, why go on? But it now occurs to me that there are other things that ought to be said. First, that editors of single plays have gone beyond Greg in arguing that Shakespeare did not make 'deletion marks so positive or clear that the compositor understood them' and pointing to interesting textual consequences.[27] Next, that commentators on single plays have also had their say, as for example Terence Spencer in a compelling short note on *Timon of Athens*.[28] Timon sends his servant to ask a supposed friend, Lucilius, 'to supply his instant vse with so many Talents' –

> *Lucil.* I know his Lordship is but merry with me,
>   He cannot want fifty fiue hundred Talents.
>
>   (TLN 1016–19)

Spencer noticed that in other parts of the play Shakespeare 'did not know, or had forgotten, how much a talent was worth', referring to reasonable requests (three or five talents) and huge and unreasonable ones (fifty or a thousand). 'The author wrote "*so many talents*" . . . because he had not made up his mind what figure to put', and fifty five hundred 'represents his manuscript indication for "*either* fifty *or* five hundred" . . . The transference of *both* the alternatives from the manuscript to the printed text is similar to the inclusion of both of Timon's epitaphs (which are contradictory).'

Textual explanations are not always so neat and irresistible. What are we to make of the following cruxes? (I quote from the Folio)

(21)
And you good Brother Father; what offence hath this man made you, Sir?
(*Measure for Measure*, the disguised Duke to Elbow, TLN 1502–3)

(22)
This wide and vniuersall Theater
Presents more wofull Pageants then the Sceane
Wherein we play in.
(*As You Like It*, Duke Senior, TLN 1115–17)

(23)
he will sell the fee-simple of his saluation, the inheritance of it, and cut th'intaile from all remainders, and a perpetuall succession for it perpetually.
(*All's Well*, Parolles of Dumain, TLN 2379–82)

(24)
I feare thou wilt once more come againe for a Ransome.
(*Henry V*, King Henry to Mountjoy, TLN 2376–7)

(25)
And like a dew drop from the Lyons mane,
  Be shooke to ayrie ayre.
Achil. Shall Aiax fight with Hector?
(*Troilus and Cressida*, Patroclus to Achilles, TLN 2079–80; Q omits
ayrie)

Do these strange readings reveal the author's indecision? Editors may prefer to blame careless scribes or compositors, yet the possibility that once again we are privileged to observe Shakespeare in the act of composition, as in so many other instances of intended deletion, cannot be ruled out.

So far my examples have ranged from the compelling to the trivial. Are there any that make a significant difference to our interpretation of a play? Let us turn back to *Julius Caesar*. At 4.3.66ff Brutus reprimands Cassius for refusing him 'certain sums of gold':

(26)
There is no terror, Cassius, in your threats;
For I am arm'd so strong in honesty
That they pass by me as the idle wind,
Which I respect not. I did send to you

For certain sums of gold, which you denied me;　　　　70
For I can raise no money by vile means:
By heaven, I had rather coin my heart,
And drop my blood for drachmas, than to wring
From the hard hands of peasants their vile trash
By any indirection. I did send　　　　　　　　　　75
To you for gold to pay my legions,
Which you denied me: was that done like Cassius?

Long ago M. W. MacCallum commented 'What does all this come to? That the superfine Brutus will not be guilty of extortion, but that Cassius may: and then Brutus will demand to share in the proceeds', so that 'his offended virtue becomes even a little absurd'.[29] Yet is it not likely that here, again, Shakespeare regarded lines 69–75 ('I did send to you . . . indirection') as deleted? Just as, in (**11**), he picked up 'If we do lose this battle', repeating 'if we lose this battle' – so now he returns to 'I did send to you / For certain sums of gold, which you denied me' in 'I did send / To you for gold . . .Which you denied me'. Editors still claim that Brutus' words are a little absurd and do not see that Shakespeare himself may have realised this (compare 'Caesar doth never wrong but with just cause'). The Arden 3 editor, David Daniell, thinks that 'Brutus deceives himself into wanting a clean conscience and the dirty money':[30] I suggest that Shakespeare decided to drop the emphasis on dirty money. And if Shakespeare intended to delete two passages in the same play (**11**, **26**) does this not make another possible deletion (**10**, Portia's death) much more probable? And is it not significant that in these three passages Brutus most gratingly plays the Infallible (MacCallum's phrase), and that their elimination from the received text, after four hundred years, unavoidably changes our conception of Brutus' character? In these three key passages the textual evidence collides sharply with the traditional psychological reading and, I must stress, the probable presence of different kinds of 'intended cancellation' in a single text brings us very close to Shakespeare rethinking his options – even closer than in the three pages of *Sir Thomas More*.

　　Another thing that should now be said is that Sir Walter Greg's interest in Shakespeare's intended deletions was greater than I indicated, and had a delayed effect, like a time-bomb. In *Two Elizabethan Stage Abridgements* (1923) he already stated that 'most manuscript plays of the [Elizabethan] period that have been prepared for the stage show cancelled passages that a printer might very

likely have retained' – quoted by Lukas Erne in 2003.[31] Perhaps I
may add that I wrote the first version of this chapter in 2003, before
I saw Erne's important book, and had already published my views
in 1996 ('Editors, I believe, have been so preoccupied with the possibility of revision coming *between* Q and F that they have failed to
pay attention to the signs of authorial alterations *within* Q') and
indeed in 1965.[32] Erne also noted that in the play *Beggar's Bush* two
versions of the same speech are printed one after the other, as in
some of Shakespeare's plays, and of course my contention that
several episodes in *Measure for Measure* were intended deletions
(see above) would support Erne's theory that some longer plays must
have existed in shorter versions as well. The search for Shakespeare's
intended deletions, in other words, has many consequences for our
understanding of the plays, not least for producers who wish to cut
outsize plays to more manageable proportions.

Next, what light does the survival of intended cancellations in so
many texts throw on Shakespeare's attitude to his plays and to their
publication? The replacement of 'bad' quartos by 'good' ones containing intended cancellations (*Romeo and Juliet*, *Hamlet* and probably *Love's Labour's Lost*) seems to me to confirm the established view
that he took little care to see that his plays were printed (or should we
say that it was a matter of indifference to him how carelessly they were
printed?). Confusing speech prefixes and stage directions, omitted
stage directions, nonsense passages and intended cancellations
printed in error all tell the same story – that neither Shakespeare nor
his colleagues supervised the printing of his plays. Nevertheless I
cannot believe that a poet who declared so confidently that

> Not marble nor the gilded monuments
> Of princes shall outlive this pow'rful rhyme
>
> (Sonnet 55)

would feel less certain about the immortality of his best dramatic
verse. How shall we resolve this paradox – a poet convinced that his
powerful rhyme will live yet willing to sanction carelessly printed
texts? The most plausible option, I think, is that Shakespeare hoped
to 'set forth and oversee' his own collected works, superseding inferior editions, as Heminge and Condell hinted in their epistle in the
First Folio:

> It had bene a thing, we confesse, worthie to haue bene wished, that the
> Author himselfe had liu'd to haue set forth, and ouerseen his owne

writings; But since it hath bin ordain'd otherwise, and he by death departed from that right . . .[33]

Most of the false starts and intended deletions that I have cited occur in texts based on what used to be called foul papers. But we now know that misinterpretations of the foul papers could be transferred to subsequent manuscripts[34] and, as this chapter has sought to confirm, to printed versions. Texts thought to have been based on promptbooks or private transcripts are not necessarily free from this kind of error.

At this point, let me say that I do not regard all the 'undeleted cancellations' discussed above as equally certain. I feel that there is no obvious alternative for (1)–(3), (4), (5), (6), (8), (9) and (18), viz. *Romeo and Juliet, Troilus and Cressida, Love's Labour's Lost, Timon, Sir Thomas More, Measure for Measure* and *A Midsummer Night's Dream*; the rest seem to me probable or very probable, but I can see that some editors may wish to defend the text as it stands. I submit, however, that, once we are aware of Shakespeare's tendency not to delete cancelled lines as evidenced by so many quarto and Folio texts, this must affect the balance of probability in all disputed passages.

Finally, a question. If the argument of this chapter is correct, and Shakespeare often left undeleted words and lines that he regarded as deleted, what light does this hypothesis throw on other texts, especially long texts (2800 lines and upwards), which may also include lines and scenes that he thought of as cancelled? It will be noticed that I have concentrated on passages that repeat the same words, or are logically inconsistent, but have mentioned some passages that are, quite simply, less brilliant than we might expect (e.g. (9), *Measure for Measure*) or where either the Folio or the quarto version omits superfluous words (e.g. (13), *Troilus and Cressida*, or (14), *King Lear*). Is it possible that other inferior passages that can be removed without damaging the play were also 'intended deletions'?

Notes

1 This is an expanded version of a paper first published in *The Review of English Studies*, New Series, 56 (2005), 37–48. I am grateful for permission to reprint.

2 W. W. Greg, *The Shakespeare First Folio* (Oxford: Clarendon Press, 1955), p. 408.

3 Ibid., pp. 241–2.

4 Honigmann, *The Texts of 'Othello' and Shakespearian Revision* (London: Routledge, 1996), p. 34. NB: In this chapter I usually change act, scene and line references to conform with Shakespeare's *Complete Works*, ed. Stanley Wells and Gary Taylor (Oxford: Clarendon Press, 1986). When quoting from the Folio 1 use Through Line Numbers (TLN).

5 *The First Quarto of Othello*, ed. Scott McMillin (Cambridge: Cambridge University Press, 2001), pp. 11–12.

6 *Timon of Athens*, ed. H. J. Oliver, Arden 2 (London: Methuen, 1959), p. 139.

7 Fredson Bowers, *On Editing Shakespeare* (1st pub. 1955; Charlottesville: University Press of Virginia, 1966), pp. 15–16.

8 For recent discussions of Shakespeare's foul papers see also my article, 'The New Bibliography and its Critics', in Lukas Erne and Margaret Jane Kidnie (eds), *Textual Performances: The Modern Reproduction of Shakespeare's Drama* (Cambridge: Cambridge University Press, 2004), pp. 77–93.

9 See my edition of *Othello*, Arden 3 (London: Thomas Nelson, 1997), p. 55.

10 See E. K. Chambers, *William Shakespeare: A Study of Facts and Problems*, 2 vols (Oxford: Clarendon Press, 1930), vol. 2, pp. 243, 268–9 (for Shakespeare's jokes), and 210.

11 See Scott McMillin, 'The *Othello* Quarto and the "Foul-Paper" Hypothesis', *Shakespeare Quarterly*, 51 (2000), 67–85, p. 76.

12 Alice Walker, *Textual Problems of the First Folio* (Cambridge: Cambridge University Press, 1953), passim.

13 Honigmann, 'Shakespeare, *Sir Thomas More* and Asylum Seekers', *Shakespeare Survey*, 57 (2004), 225–35.

14 Abbreviated in secretary hand.

15 Square brackets are used to indicate deletions in the MS.

16 *Shakespeare's Hand in the Play of Sir Thomas More*, ed. A. W. Pollard (Cambridge: Cambridge University Press, 1923): Greg's note on Hand D, pp. 112–14.

17 For Moseley see Chambers, *William Shakespeare*, vol. 1, p. 97, and Greg, *The Shakespeare First Folio*, p. 101.

18 See also my *The Stability of Shakespeare's Text* (London: Edward Arnold, 1965), ch. 3: 'The Unblotted Papers'.

19 See ibid., pp. 65–7.

20 *Julius Caesar*, ed. T. S. Dorsch, Arden 2 (London: Methuen, 1955).

21 Ibid., p. 106.

22 See Chambers, *William Shakespeare*, vol. 2, 210.

23 For attempts to explain line 20 see the Arden 3 edn (London: Thomas Nelson, 1997), p. 335.

24 Honigmann, *The Texts of 'Othello'*, p. 36.

25 See the Arden 2 edn., ed. Harold Jenkins (London: Methuen, 1982), p. 336.

26 Greg, *The Shakespeare First Folio*, p. 204.

27 E.g. Philip Edwards in the New Cambridge *Hamlet* (Cambridge: Cambridge University Press, 1985), pp. 10ff.

28 Terence Spencer, 'Shakespeare Learns the Value of Money: The Dramatist at Work on *Timon of Athens*', *Shakespeare Survey*, 6 (1953), 75–8.

29 M. W. MacCallum, *Shakespeare's Roman Plays and Their Background* (London: Macmillan, 1910), p. 264.

30 David Daniell (ed.), *Julius Caesar*, Arden 3 (London: Nelson, 1998), p. 282.

31 See Lukas Erne, *Shakespeare as Literary Dramatist* (Cambridge: Cambridge University Press, 2003), p. 180 note 23.

32 Honigmann, *The Texts of 'Othello'*, p. 34; *The Stability of Shakespeare's Text*, index ('false starts').

33 See Honigmann, *The Stability of Shakespeare's Text*, Appendix A (pp. 172–92), 'The dramatist's "rights" in his play', and cf. Erne, *Shakespeare as Literary Dramatist*, pp. 110–11.

34 See also Honigmann, 'The New Bibliography and its Critics'.

Part III

Readers

8

The First Folio: 'My Shakespeare'/'Our Shakespeare': whose Shakespeare?

George Donaldson

My concern is to enquire into the views of Shakespeare's plays expressed in the prefatory material to the First Folio, where there is a conflating of the plays – as performed and as printed – as the plays *authored* by Shakespeare.[1] Although tangential to Lukas Erne's arguments in *Shakespeare as Literary Dramatist* about the substantive differences between versions of the plays written by Shakespeare as performed and as printed, my argument will be about claims made for Shakespeare as a dramatist to be read on the page as well as seen on the stage. Before developing and investigating the issues central to his book – 'Shakespeare's attitude to the emergent printed drama, the place his plays occupy within it, and the way in which it may have affected the composition of his plays' – Lukas Erne states the importance of recognising that 'the cultural capital' that Shakespeare and his 'contemporary dramatists possess today is a product of later times': 'Scholarship has thus rightly insisted on how later ages turned the drama of Shakespeare and his contemporaries into literary and cultural entities that are substantially different from what they were in their own time'.[2] The issue to be investigated here, however, is not what the drama of Shakespeare was in his own time or was turned into by later ages but to try to establish what literary and cultural entity Shakespeare is turned into – not in his lifetime, but a few years afterwards – in the prefatory material of the First Folio of 1623.

In *Ben Jonson: A Life*, David Riggs suggests that 'the publication of *Mr. William Shakespeare's Comedies, Histories, and Tragedies* in 1623 reopened the central rivalry of Jonson's career':

> Although he had previously sneered at Shakespeare's artistry, the publication of the 1623 folio made it possible for him to view Shakespeare

as a figure rather like himself. Since his own *Works* of 1616 had set the
precedent for a book of this kind, the publication of Shakespeare's first
folio represented a triumph of sorts for Jonson. The realization that
Shakespeare's plays transcended the medium of performance and
belonged in print, bore out Jonson's life-long contention that plays are
(or should be) a serious form of literature. Moreover, the men who prepared the folio for the press (and Jonson may have been one of them)
remade Shakespeare in Jonson's image. Heminge's and Condell's prefatory letter 'To the Great Variety of Readers' echoes Jonson's Induction
to *Bartholomew Fair*, his Preface to *The Alchemist*, his epigram 'To my
Bookseller', and his *Discoveries*. The prefatory poems by Jonson,
Hugh Holland, James Mabbe, and Leonard Digges transform
Shakespeare into a specifically literary figure whose works have
achieved the status of modern classics . . .[3]

The 'central rivalry' of Jonson's career, known also to literary history
as the Stage Quarrel or the War of the Theatres, has been redefined
recently by James P. Bednarz in *Shakespeare and the Poets' War* as
a dispute not so much between theatres or of the stage as such but
between Jonson and Shakespeare as playwrights, which he describes
as 'the most important theatrical controversy of the late Elizabethan
stage', during which 'we find the first record of these writers' mutual
commentary and criticism'.[4]

I want to suggest that the reopening of this old-established rivalry
can be traced in *Mr. William Shakespeares Comedies, Histories, &
Tragedies*, but that it is not resolved in 'a triumph of sorts for
Jonson', as David Riggs suggests. It is a reopening that, on the
contrary, offers persistent resistances and challenges to Jonson,
although it does not involve his eventual defeat. The quarrel is no
longer, of course, between Jonson and Shakespeare, but among the
editors of, and contributors to, Shakespeare's First Folio: that is,
between Jonson and an opposed John Heminge and Henry Condell,
as well as others.[5] Although I would concur with Riggs that for
Jonson 'the publication of the 1623 folio made it possible for him to
view Shakespeare as a figure rather like himself', I would suggest
that for others it was an opportunity to view Shakespeare as a figure
unlike Jonson, as still indeed Jonson's mighty opposite. It is true that
'the realization' embodied in the First Folio is 'that Shakespeare's
plays transcended the medium of performance and belonged in
print'; and it is also true that this 'bore out Jonson's life-long contention that plays are (or should be) a serious form of literature'.

However, I would contend with the claim that the men who prepared the Folio for the press, although Jonson probably was one of them, 'remade Shakespeare in Jonson's image'. I think there are evidently different images of Shakespeare in the First Folio, and in only Jonson's imagining of Shakespeare is Shakespeare remade a figure like Jonson himself. Moreover, Riggs's assertion that Heminge's and Condell's address variously 'echoes' Jonson (in which he coincides with what Greg calls, in *The Shakespeare First Folio*, 'parallels' and 'points of resemblance') seems to me disputable.[6]

Sometimes it may be – as in the case of Jonson's *Discoveries* – that Jonson echoes Heminge and Condell, rather than they him. It has been a case made about the dedicatory epistle and the address 'To the great Variety of Readers' and Heminge's and Condell's roles as those who put their names to them that 'it has sometimes been doubted whether they were actually of their own writing', as Greg reports. Although 'there may be no compelling reason to deny that Heminge and Condell were capable of their composition', it is the case that 'there is a distinct literary quality in the writing that suggests a practised hand'.[7] The practised hand that has most often been proffered is Jonson's:

> The only candidate for authorship whose claims for authorship have been seriously argued is Ben Jonson. That Jonson was in some way connected with the publication appears, not so much from the noble tribute in the only considerable commendatory poem the volume contains, but by his having apparently been commissioned to write the verses on the portrait. It was George Steevens who first suggested his authorship, and the view was later supported by a formidable array of parallels.[8]

However, to call such moments – when the phrasing of the expression or the tenor of the thoughts expressed in the address are found to coincide in some way with Jonson's public or private writings – 'echoes', 'parallels' or 'points of resemblance' seems to me to misrepresent the relation of at least some of these coincidences in relatively obvious ways; and at least one of them seems to indicate how the relation between Heminge's and Condell's address and Jonson's writings is both more dynamically active and more at odds than Greg's geometrical metaphor and his literal but generalised sense of similitude convey:

> The most obvious parallel, often observed, is between the words of the address, 'His mind and hand went together: And what he thought, he

vttered with that easinesse, that wee haue scarce receiued from him a blot [i.e. erasure] in his papers', and the passage in Jonson's *Discoveries*, 'I remember, the Players have often mentioned it as an honour to Shakespeare, that in his writing, (whatsoever he penn'd) hee never blotted out line. My answer hath beene, Would he had blotted a thousand.'[9]

It is most obvious that this 'most obvious parallel' is not obviously such. In *Timber: or Discoveries; Made upon Men and Matter*, when Ben Jonson writes 'De Shakespeare nostrat[i]' ('concerning our Shakespeare'), he is, as he says, remembering, and what he is recalling and referring to seems to be – perhaps among other instances of such praise of Shakespeare – Heminge's and Condell's address:

> I remember the players have often mentioned it as an honour to Shakespeare, that in his writing, whatsoever he penned, he never blotted out line. My answer hath been, 'Would he had blotted a thousand'; which they thought a malevolent speech. I had not told posterity this but for their ignorance, who choose that circumstance to commend their friend by wherein he most faulted; and to justify mine own candour: for I loved the man, and do honour his memory, on this side idolatry, as much as any.[10]

This is not a parallel between Jonson and Heminge and Condell, but Jonson remembering that he stood at a right angle to the players' often mentioning as an honour to Shakespeare that he 'never blotted out line'. Jonson has reason to justify his candour now in remembering this and writing it down: 'I had not told posterity this but for their ignorance, who choose that circumstance to commend their friend by wherein he most faulted'. What need would Jonson have to tell posterity this, unless what the players had often mentioned to him (of which frequent mentioning there would be no record other than his remembrance) had found its way into a record for posterity – into, that is, the First Folio, where Heminge and Condell do 'commend their friend by wherein he most faulted', not as they had done often in speaking to Jonson, but once and for all in print? This supposed parallel cannot provide evidence that Jonson himself composed the address, since Jonson could never have admiringly expressed the view that he so evidently deplores in *Discoveries*.

Greg observes this problem, but his solution to it is less than persuasive. He notes that the passage in *Discoveries* 'has usually been taken as a direct allusion to the address', and is so taken by A. W.

Pollard: 'Pollard speaks of the phrase which gives rise to it . . . to prove that Jonson could not have written the same.' Against Pollard, Greg argues 'But Jonson speaks, not of what was written, but of what he had heard the players say, and of his answer, "Which they thought a malevolent speech"'. (Greg does not notice that in writing of Pollard's and Jonson's writing, he writes 'Pollard speaks' and 'Jonson speaks'; which, if he had noticed, might have made him less certain than he is that when Jonson writes of speaking, he does not also write of writing.) Greg accepts that the two passages 'may very well be contemporary – indeed, they must be', but the conclusion he thereby comes to seems to me incongruous:

> In that case it could be argued that Jonson, writing on the players' behalf, repeated what they were in the habit of alleging as evidence of Shakespeare's ease of composition, while in his common-place book he recorded his private opinion of the same as it affected the propriety of Shakespeare's writing.[11]

That Jonson would write publicly – 'on the players' behalf' – something with which he fundamentally disagreed, and would privately write of that disagreement on his own behalf, stretches possibility to improbability.

In the side-note to this account of his disagreement with the players, it is possibly significant that Jonson does not write of 'my Shakespeare', as he does in the First Folio but of 'our Shakespeare'. Donaldson notes that 'the side-notes are probably the work of Jonson himself' but his suggestion, as a gloss to Jonson's side-note, *De Shakespeare nostrat*[*i*], that Shakespeare is 'ours' 'as both colleague and fellow-countryman' does not perhaps suppose the full implication of Jonson's '*nostrat*[*i*]'.[12] The change in the possessive pronoun from the personal 'My Shakespeare' (line 19) in his elegy in the First Folio to the more than personal 'our', changes it to that of Digges's elegy, which follows his. Jonson had cast himself in his elegy as the self-conscious role of arbiter of his age and for all time; but implicit in the 'our' of 'concerning our Shakespeare' might be Jonson's intention to speak to posterity from a position in which he can present his judgement as triumphant over the ignorance of others.

The further and even more obvious ground for denying that Heminge's and Condell's address parallels or, more especially, echoes Jonson's *Discoveries* is what underlies the fact that *Discoveries* was 'first published several years after Jonson's death in the 1640–41 two-volume Folio edition of his works'. As Donaldson notes:

> In his 'Execration upon Vulcan' . . . Jonson laments the loss of what appear to be similar commonplace books – 'twice twelve years' stored-up humanity', – in the fire that destroyed his books and papers in November 1623. The present collection presumably consists in the main of writings made after that date, though it is possible that certain papers escaped the fire, or that certain notes were written from memory.[13]

Donaldson allows that 'it is possible that certain papers escaped the fire, or that certain notes were written from memory'. It may thus be the case that, in *Discoveries*, Jonson's account of what he remembers the players as saying about Shakespeare and himself as answering in rebuke to them is a retrieval of what he had written in a commonplace book, not devoured by the 'greedy flame'.[14] Or it may be a note whose remembrance was itself re-remembered and rewritten – a remembrance belonging to a period earlier than or contemporaneous with the time when Jonson was supposedly also showing his hand in writing the address for Heminge and Condell. It is, however, no less a possibility – or more probable – that Jonson's commentary 'on our Shakespeare' is written after the publication of the First Folio in November or December 1623. (Donaldson's 'the present collection presumably consists in the main of writings made after that date' supports this.[15]) A concern for the way Shakespeare is to be remembered, and a preoccupation with Shakespeare's posterity, would be predominant, it is plausible to imagine, in Jonson's thought throughout the period of the production of the First Folio.[16] Indeed, it would also be plausible to imagine that what Jonson remembers the Players as having often mentioned might most often have been mentioned by them, when the ease of reading Shakespeare's manuscripts had an especial pertinence: that is, when they were being prepared for publication in the First Folio. Of course, that claim might have been also made without a concern for Shakespeare's legibility and solely in admiration of his facility in composition, and certainly Jonson's concern is with Shakespeare's 'gentle expressions; wherein he flowed with that facility that sometime it was necessary he should be stopped'.[17] But the question remains, in what circumstances and with what considerations might the fact that it was usual for Shakespeare that 'he never blotted out line' have been a matter of observation (both of their seeing and of their commenting) by the players? The probability seems to me that Shakespeare's facility of composition would be most visible and found remarkable – and so most remarked on – when the largest number of his manuscripts were to hand and their legibility would also have been a priority.

In Riggs's supposing the transformation of Shakespeare into a Jonsonian literary figure, he does not attend to the differences between the claims made by Jonson and by other contributors to the prefatory materials of the First Folio: Heminge and Condell in the dedicatory epistle and address, and Leonard Digges, Hugh Holland and James Mabbe ('I.M.') in their elegies. 'Whose Shakespeare is Shakespeare?' is the question.

The First Folio, I would suggest, is a site both of a collective effort of remembrance and of contending views of how Shakespeare is to be remembered and what he is to be remembered for. The contention, to put it at its simplest, is between Ben Jonson's 'my Shakespeare' ('To the memory of my beloued, The Author Mr. William Shakespeare: And what he hath left vs', line 19) and Leonard Digges's 'our Shakespeare' ('To the Memorie of the deceased Authour Maister W. Shakespeare', line 21). It is visible in the difference between singularity and plurality of view not only in the identified difference between Ben Jonson's 'my' and Digges's 'our', but also in the difference with which readers are conceived, the difference, that is, between Ben Jonson's poem 'To the Reader' which simultaneously singularises and generalises, and Heminge's and Condell's address 'To the great Variety of Readers', which, in seeming emphatic resistance to Jonson's one-and-all representative and definitive 'Reader', addresses not merely 'Readers' but 'the great Variety of Readers', conveying not only such readers' multiplicity but their extreme diversity, and perhaps, in that, a figural or even actual relation to a playhouse audience.

Of course, there is undoubtedly, on Heminge's and Condell's part, a necessary commercial concern: the address to a broad readership suggests their ambition to secure for the First Folio not only many readers but, more particularly, many purchasers, as they frankly specify at the very start of their address:

Well! It is now publique, & you wil stand for your priuiledges wee know: to read and censure. Do so, but buy it first. That doth best commend a Booke, the Stationer saies. Then, how oddesoeuer your braines be, or your wisdomes, make your licence the same, and spare not. Iudge your sixe-pen'orth, your shillings worth, your fiue shillings worth at a time, or higher, so you rise to the iust rates, and welcome. But, whateuer you do, Buy.

Heminge's and Condell's imperative appeal is supported by a surety that arises from Shakespeare's proven popularity. Their subsequent statements make it plain that the future success of the Folio is connected to the past success of the public performances of the plays contained in it:

> Censure will not driue a Trade or make the Iacke go. And though you be a Magistrate of wit, and sit on the Stage at *Black-Friers*, or the *Cock-pit*, to arraigne Playes dailie, know, these Playes haue had their triall alreadie, and stood out all Appeales; and do now come forth quitted by a Decree of Court, then any purchas'd Letters of commendation.

There is here, I think, a not altogether covert reference to the 'Poets' War' and a distinction being drawn between the popular success of Shakespeare's plays at the Globe and Ben Jonson's relative lack of such at the Blackfriars theatre. The general reference to the fact that at the Blackfriars wealthier members of the audience were able to occupy seats at the side of the stage, and thus act as arbiters of taste is particularisable, in that Jonson seems an especially apt candidate for the title, 'Magistrate of wit'. As Greg suggests:

> Sitting in judgement on plays is almost an obsession with Jonson: for the phrasing compare *The Magnetic Lady*, 'I shall have just occasion to beleeve My wit is magisterial' [1.1.12–13], and 'unlesse like a solemne Justice of wit, you will damne our Play, unheard' [1. chorus, 40–1], and the Ode on *The New Inn*, 'Vsurpe the chaire of wit! Indicting, and arraigning euery day Something they call a Play' [ll. 4–6].[18]

Jonson gains further right to this title in his prefatory poem in the First Folio, 'To the Reader', and his wishing that Droeshout could have drawn more than Shakespeare's physical features – 'O, could he but haue drawne his wit' (line 5) – and in the magisterial beginning of his elegy, in which Jonson establishes himself as writing on Shakespeare not out of '*seeliest Ignorance*', or '*blinde Affection*', or '*crafty Malice*', but out of an authority invested in his judgement of *his* Shakespeare's worth: '*Soule of the Age! / The applause! delight!*'

the wonder of our stage! / My Shakespeare rise' (lines 7–19). The address invokes against Jonson's 'magisterial wit' an altogether public arbitration, bypassing Jonson's right to (and rightness of) magisterial judgement.

The contention is between a Jonsonian Shakespeare to be admired for his wit as a poet and Shakespeare the playwright of popular success. It is not, and should not be mistaken for, a contention between the stage and the page, since Heminge and Condell are seeking purchasers of the Folio who will be readers of Shakespeare:

> But it is not our prouince, who onely gather his works, and giue them you, to praise him. It is yours that reade him. And there we hope, to your diuers capacities, you will finde enough, both to draw, and hold you: for his wit can no more lie hid, then it could be lost. Reade him, therefore; and againe, and againe: And if then you doe not like him, surely you are in some manifest danger, not to vnderstand him. And so we leaue you to other of his Friends, whom if you need, can bee your guides: if you neede them not, you can leade your selues, and others. And such Readers we wish him.

Here, where their address comes to its end, Heminge's and Condell's emphasis again falls on the diversity of such a readership. They leave some readers to be guided by other friends of Shakespeare. Is this another reference to Jonson, whose elegy follows? Other readers are to be led by their own independent selves. And Shakespeare's 'wit' – in what might be an appropriation rather than an accommodation of Jonson's favoured term – is declared available to all.

A full discussion of the prefatory material of the First Folio would entail a detailed analysis of each page and its relations to all the others. I can now instance only a few features of these pages, immediately relevant to my argument. In their 'Epistle Dedicatorie' to the Earls of Pembroke and Montgomery, Heminge and Condell anticipate the position they adopt in their address to the great variety of readers, in laying claim to the Earls' patronage: although Heminge and Condell write of the rashness of their enterprise and the fear of its success, they simultaneously offer grounds for its success in what are claims for the proven value of what they attempt. The elaborately depreciatory acknowledgement that the dignity of the Earls is greater than '*to descend to the reading of these trifles*', and their own depriving themselves of their defence in naming as trifles what they publish to be read – at least, by the Earls – is countered by another acknowledgement that places the evaluation of these identified '*trifles*' on their Lordships' previous experience of them and previous valuing of them: '*since your L.L. haue beene pleas'd to thinke these trifles some-thing, heeretofore; and haue prosequuted both them, and their Authour liuing, with so much fauour*'. The First Folio is thus privileged:

> *There is a great difference, whether any Booke choose his Patrones, or finde them: This hath done both. For, so much were your L.L. likings of the seuerall parts, when they were acted, as before they were published, the Volume ask'd to be yours.*

The plays as printed coincide and are commensurate with their performance in the theatre. That this is so is further enforced in the phrasing '*as before they were published*', which identifies their theatrical performance as their first publication. Further still, the way that theatrical performance is described attends to what is written as well as to what is performed: '*the seuerall parts, when they were acted*' describes performance distinctively as the acting of parts – of, that is, the words assigned by an author to the persons of the play and thereby to the actors charged to perform those persons on the public stage.

The last page of the prefatory material is no less interesting than these first pages in terms of the relation implied between stage and page. But, before looking at that last page, I want to attend to a larger consideration of the First Folio. The publication of *The Workes of Benjamin Jonson* in folio in 1616 is a singularly significant occasion in the history of the printing of texts in the early modern period: 'Jonson was the first Elizabethan dramatist to publish a collected edition of his works.'[19] Further to that: 'The Folio of 1616 . . . set a precedent which was followed by the First Folio of Shakespeare in 1623 and the First Folio of Beaumont and Fletcher in 1647.'[20] That there is a precedent in folio publication, set by Jonson's Folio of 1616, is indisputable; but to consider in what ways the Folio of *Mr. William Shakespeares Comedies, Histories, & Tragedies* does and does not follow the precedent set by *The Workes of Benjamin Jonson* is another matter.[21]

There are many observations that could be made about the titles and the title-pages of these Folios in their differences, even of typography, that suggest that the Shakespeare Folio does not straightforwardly follow the precedent of Jonson's Folio, and, on the contrary, is deliberately differentiated from it. There is not space to make more than one observation here: the largest capitals on the title-page of Jonson's Folio are used for *Workes*, the largest capitals on the title-page in Shakespeare's Folio are used for Shakespeare's surname. These differences may distinguish these two publications, as one overseen by its living author and one commemorating its dead author, with Jonson's emphasis on his writings and Heminge's and Condell's repeated emphasis on the writer of the plays in their Folio, and their responsibility to Shakespeare as the executors of his writings. One may, nevertheless, be struck by Jonson, as the prototype of possessive authorship, showing typographical caution or modesty with regard to his name and Heminge and Condell showing a relatively reckless, or reckoned, immodesty with regard to, and probably in regard for, Shakespeare – and with a glance at Jonson.

In Jonson's Folio, the table of contents, or 'The Catalogue', lists not only the titles of the plays but the titles of the collections of poems and of other writings included in the Folio ('Epigrammes, The Forrest, Entertaynments, Panegyre, Masques, and Barriers'). In Shakespeare's Folio, the table of contents is 'A Catalogue of the seuerall Comedies, Histories and Tragedies contained in this Volume', repeating from the title-page the three types of play specified there. There are, of course, no writings of Shakespeare's other than his plays in the Folio of 1623. To state the obvious is not necessarily to state the insignificant. To say that 'Jonson was the first Elizabethan dramatist to publish a collected edition of his works' states the fact of the matter in such a way as to fail to present the crucial truth: Jonson was the first Elizabethan poet to publish a collected edition of his works, in which plays were considered worthy of inclusion with poems, traditionally more highly valued writings. It is Shakespeare, not Jonson, who is the first Elizabethan dramatist to have published (by others) a collected edition – not of his poems and plays – but of his plays and only his plays. As Peter Blayney puts it, the First Folio 'was the first folio book ever published in England that was devoted exclusively to plays'.[22] The significance of this can be imagined: the reception of Jonson's *Workes* by some of his contemporary playwrights and poets is well documented, and that reception identifies the perceived indecorous departure of Jonson from usual publishing practice in his treating his plays as worthy of folio publication. This may also suggest the particular extraordinariness of Heminge's and Condell's Shakespeare Folio. Its title does not follow Jonson's precedent; but, more importantly, there is no precedent in the contents of Jonson's *Works* for the contents of Heminge's and Condell's Shakespeare Folio. They dared not to call his plays works but to publish nothing but his plays in the Folio, and to declare the fact explicitly in their title: *Mr. William Shakespeares Comedies, Histories, & Tragedies.*

To rehearse briefly the contemporary or near-contemporary reception of Jonson's *Workes*, the information provided on 'The Folio of 1616' in the Herford and Simpson edition of Ben Jonson suffices. The editors cite, among other criticisms of Jonson, two epigrams, published in *Wits Recreations* in 1640, but written earlier, in which Jonson is questioned and answered for:

> *To Mr. Ben. Johnson demanding the reason why he call'd his playes works.*
>
> Pray tell me *Ben*, where doth the mystery lurke,
> What others call a play you call a worke.
>
> *Thus answer'd by a friend in Mr. Johnsons defence.*
>
> The authors friend thus for the author sayes,
> *Bens* plays are works when others works are plaies.[23]

A concern with Shakespeare's 'works' and 'plays' also appears in Leonard Digges's poems, in the First Folio and in the 1640 edition of Shakespeare's poems. Among the commemorative and commendatory verses of the First Folio, Digges's 'To the Memorie of the deceased Authour Maister W. Shakespeare' alone names Shakespeare's plays as his works:

> Shake-speare, *at length thy pious fellowes giue*
> *The world thy* Workes: *thy* Workes, *by which, out-liue*
> *Thy Tombe, thy name must: when that stone rent,*
> *And Time dissolues thy* Stratford Moniment,
> *Here we aliue shall view thee still. This Booke,*
> *When Brasse and Marble fade, shall make thee looke*
> *Fresh to all Ages: when* Posteritie
> *Shall loath what's new, thinke all is prodegie*
> *That is not* Shake-speares; *eu'ry Line, each Verse*
> *Here shall reuiue, redeeme thee from thy Herse.*

The awkwardness of the syntax of '*thy Workes, by which, out-liue / Thy Tombe, thy name must*' of lines 2 and 3 has no other evident *raison d'être* beyond its producing the second line's emphatic repetition at its mid-point: '*thy Workes: thy Workes*'. Here is someone who sees no impropriety in calling Shakespeare's plays 'works'; or, rather, perhaps seeing the impropriety of it to some eyes, seizes the opportunity to assert the propriety of it to all eyes by unabashed avowal. As a coda to the above arguments about the contendings within the prefatory materials of the First Folio, Leonard Digges's poem has an epitomising interest.

The second half of Digges's poem identifies the nature of that interest further:

> Nor Fire, nor cankring Age, as Naso said,
> Of his, thy wit-fraught Booke shall once inuade.
> Nor shall I e'ere beleeue, or thinke thee dead
> (Though mist) vntill our bankrout Stage be sped
> (Impossible) with some new straine t'out-do
> Passions of Iuliet, and her Romeo;
> Or till I heare a Scene more nobly take,
> Than when thy half-Sword parlying Romans spake.
> Till these, till any of thy Volumes rest
> Shall with more fire, more feeling be exprest,
> Be sure, our Shake-speare, thou can neuer dye,
> But crown'd with Lawrell, liue eternally.

Digges's Shakespeare is 'our Shakespeare', not 'my Shakespeare'; and he is not Jonson's Shakespeare in that he is a Shakespeare of the theatre as much as of the book, whose absence from the stage has left it bankrupt. Jonson, one has to suppose, is one among those whose plays provide evidence for the impoverishment of the contemporary stage.

The full implication of Digges's position is made clear only in another and later poem of commemoration and commendation. This is ostensibly 'Upon Master William Shakespeare, *the deceased Authour, and his* Poems', and first appears in the edition of Shakespeare's *Poems* of 1640, five years after Digges's death. John Freehafer suggests that the title of these commendatory verses 'may have been altered to excuse their appearance in a volume of poems where they are shown to be out of place by the fact that they deal entirely with the plays'.[24] It is his evinced conclusion that the appropriate place for the poem would have been not the First Folio of 1623 as has sometimes been suggested but the Second Folio of 1632; and that, in all probability, it was excluded from that volume because of its attack on Jonson.

Having emphatically called Shakespeare's plays 'works' in his poem in the Folio of 1623, Digges now makes a point of not doing so. The poem begins:

> Poets are borne not made, when I would prove
> This truth, the glad rememberance I must love
> Of never dying *Shakespeare*, who alone,
> Is argument enough to make that one.
> First, that he was a Poet, none would doubt,
> That heard th'applause of what he sees set out
> Imprinted; where thou hast (I will not say
> Reader his Workes for to contrive a Play:
> To him twas none) the patterne of all wit,
> Art without Art unparaleld as yet.[25]

Digges pointedly does not call Shakespeare's plays 'works', I would suggest, not because he succumbs to a sense of the doubtful propriety of describing plays as 'works' but primarily to address what Freehafer sees as a secondary concern:

> the fact that this description was a Jonsonian innovation helps to explain Digges's refusal to refer to Shakespeare's plays as 'Workes' in 1632, as he had done in 1623. Jonson's description of his plays as 'Workes' also helped to develop the copybook contrast between Shakespeare, the effortless writer who followed Nature, and Jonson, the laborious writer who followed classical precedents and practised 'Art'; and this contrast was fostered by no one more than by Ben himself.[26]

This contrast is, here, also fostered by Digges, who asserts at the start of this poem the truth, proved by Shakespeare, that 'Poets are borne not made'.

That this is a reference to Jonson's elegy in the First Folio intensifies that contrast:

> *Yet must I not give Nature all: thy Art*
>   *My gentle* Shakespeare, *must enioy a part.*
> *For though the* Poets *matter, Nature be,*
>   *His Art doth giue the fashion. And, that he,*
> *Who casts to write a liuing line, must sweat*
>   *(Such as thine are) and strike the second heat*
> *Vpon the* Muses *anuile: turne the same,*
>   *(And himselfe with it) that he thinkes to frame;*
> *Or for the lawrell he may gaine a scorn,*
>   *For a good* Poet's *made, as well as borne.*

In the sequence of the prefatory materials of the First Folio, Jonson's elegy follows Heminge's and Condell's address; and, as we have already seen, they affirm that the plays in the First Folio are presented by a Shakespeare

> Who, as he was a happie imitator of Nature, was a most gentle expresser of it. His mind and hand went together: And what he thought, he vttered with that easinesse, that we haue scarce receiued from him a blot in his papers . . .

The lines in Jonson's elegy, quoted above, are thus a refutation of Heminge's and Condell's claim, in his also laying claim to Shakespeare as 'a most gentle expresser' in 'My gentle Shakespeare' – with the emphasis perhaps falling on 'my', once again, as a word expressive not only of possession but also of distinction – 'my gentle Shakespeare, not your gentle Shakespeare'. Distinguishing his Shakespeare from Heminge's and Condell's, Jonson 'must . . . not give Nature all':

> *thy Art*
> *My gentle* Shakespeare, *must enioy a part.*
> *For though the* Poets *matter, Nature be,*
> *His Art doth giue the fashion.*

The gentleness of Shakespeare's expression is the result of creative effort and artful working and re-working.

The contrast between Shakespeare and Jonson is further developed and detailed by Digges (as the poem repeats elements and extends the concerns of his earlier elegy), in his describing Jonson's failure, not in print, but in performance:

> I doe not wonder when you offer at
> Blacke-Friers, that you suffer: tis the fate
> Of richer veines, prime judgements that have far'd
> The worse, with this deceased man compar'd.
> So have I seene, when Cesar would appeare
> And on the Stage at halfe-sword parley were,
> *Brutus* and *Cassius*: oh how the Audience
> Were ravish'd, with what wonder they went thence,
> When some new day they would not brooke a line,
> Of tedious (though well laboured) *Catilines*;
> *Sejanus* too was irksome, they priz'de more
> Honest *Iago*, or the jealous Moore.
> And though the Fox and subtill Alchimist,

Long intermitted could not quite be mist,
Though these have sham'd all the Ancients, and might raise,
Their Authours merit with a crowne of Bayes.
Yet these sometimes, even at a friends desire
Acted, have scarce defrai'd the Seacoale fire
And doore-keepers: when let but *Falstaffe* come,
Hall, *Poines*, the rest you scarce shall have a roome
All is so pester'd: let but *Beatrice*
And *Benedicke* be seene, loe in a trice
The Cockpit Galleries, Boxes, all are full
To heare *Maluoglio* that crosse garter'd Gull.

Digges's claim for Shakespeare's art is not that it is justified in the
'literary' printing of his writings, but that the printing is justified by
the success of the 'theatrical' art: the then heard and applauded playhouse performance of what is now seen 'set out / Imprinted'. As
Freehafer states:

> Although Digges's views are not without precedents or successors, they
> are in sum so partisan and so prophetic of later viewpoints towards
> Shakespeare that his poem qualifies as the first published expression of
> Shakespeare idolatry. It also speaks of the popularity and staging of
> Shakespeare's plays before 1632, and it joins forcefully in the contin-
> uing argument over the relative places of Nature and Art in the pro-
> duction of great poetry – an argument in which Shakespeare and
> Jonson came to be, for their age at least, the paradigm of the opposing
> principles, so that the success or failure of one of these men could be
> virtually equated with the success or failure of a whole philosophy of
> artistic creation, over which men like Digges and Jonson were pre-
> pared to quarrel bitterly, even if Shakespeare himself seemingly was
> not.[27]

Heminge and Condell and Leonard Digges, as opposers of Jonson,
in an argument that still continues over the relative places of Nature
and Art in the creation of great poetry and great plays, are not,
however, precursors of the stage-versus-page opposition and
impasse, but hearers in the theatre who, having heard and
applauded, wish to publish as seers of printed text: in another word,
as readers. Shakespeare is for the page *because* he is of the stage, and
only on the page can what he was on the stage become 'the glad
rememberance . . . / Of never dying *Shakespeare*'.
    In the First Folio, the fact of its being a volume of plays is not
only explicitly stated on the title-page but restated in the title of the

table of contents, 'A Catalogue of the seuerall Comedies, Histories and Tragedies contained in this Volume', and in the subdivisions of the listings under the headings, 'Comedies', 'Histories' and 'Tragedies'. But after that repetition in the Catalogue, there is another one, in a context that is striking. On the last page of the prefatory material, immediately before the first page of *The Tempest*, the generic names of the title-page and the catalogue are repeated again. What precedes this is the page's title that affirms the substance of the Folio as 'The Workes of William Shakespeare'. 'Workes' here does, of course, echo the title of Jonson's Folio. Its belated echo may not convey continuing doubt as to the propriety of such naming of plays; but may, more plausibly, display confident audacity. For what follows below on the page is not any further reference to the plays themselves or their titles but 'The Names of the Principall Actors in all these Playes'. Listed first among these names, with a decorated capital W, is the name, 'William Shakespeare'. Both these features of the page merit comment, as having no precedent in Jonson's *Works*; and their appearance on a page titled 'The Workes of William Shakespeare' seems to me a provocative divergence from Jonson, in its valuation of the stage. The naming of the principal persons who performed in 'all these plays' – or to return to the phrasing of the dedicatory epistle – the persons who played '*the seuerall parts, when they were acted*', now presented to be read, commemorates the plays' performances in the theatres of Elizabethan and Jacobean London.

Moreover, this naming – with Shakespeare's own name foremost among those of his fellow-actors – immediately before the texts of the plays that he had authored, and that had provided them with their employment and their reputation, takes an extraordinary leap from stage to page. The named performers are 'the Principall Actors in all these Playes': yet 'these plays' are obviously not plays in performance, or – given Lukas Erne's arguments in the latter half of his book – even Shakespeare's plays as performed. Yet the actors are in 'all these plays'. I suggest that they share the plays' textual existence, in so far as reading these plays might involve for some readers – the great variety of readers in addition to the Earls of Pembroke and Montgomery – remembering the principal actors in their '*seuerall parts, when they were acted*'. This is not to give the performance of plays priority, except in a temporal sense, over the reading of them. In the larger pattern of the prefatory material to the Folio, it actually suggests the priority of Shakespeare as author of these works that are plays, both performed and printed. That leap from stage to page speaks not of recognition of the difference between the two media but of indifference to that difference. The realm of remembered performance, after all, is not the stage, just as the realm of reading is not the page: their realms are the mind and its memory and imagination.

The claim of the First Folio's title-page had been that the plays were 'Published according to the True Originall Copies'. It is repeated here on this page: 'The Workes of William Shakespeare, containing all his Comedies, Histories, and Tragedies: Truely set forth, according to their first Originall'. If one looks beyond the seeming oxymoron of 'original copies', and the tautology of 'first original', there is in the First Folio an emphasis on a point of origin beyond previous imperfect printings, or performance, to Shakespeare's writing of his plays, or even to their existence 'absolute in their numbers, *as he conceiued them*'. In this most un-Jonsonian moment of the address, there is no distinction drawn between Shakespeare's conceiving and writing. On the contrary: 'His mind and hand went together: And what he thought, he vttered with that easinesse, that wee haue scarce receiued from him a blot in his papers'. The First Folio's full audacity is to claim that it puts its readers directly in touch not only with his hand, but also with Shakespeare's mind.

Notes

1 The prefatory materials are reproduced in full photographic facsimile in *The Riverside Shakespeare*, edited by G. Blakemore Evans (Boston: Houghton Mifflin, 1974), pp. 57–76. I have used this facsimile for my text. There are incomplete transcripts or truncated photo-facsimiles of the front matter of the First Folio in a number of other readily available editions of Shakespeare's works, including the Oxford edition, *William Shakespeare: The Complete Works*, and *The Norton Shakespeare*. The front matter is also in full in *The First Folio of Shakespeare: The Norton Facsimile*, prepared by Charlton Hinman, with a new introduction by Peter W. M. Blayney, 2nd edn (New York and London: W. W. Norton, 1996).

2 Lukas Erne, *Shakespeare as Literary Dramatist* (Cambridge: Cambridge University Press, 2003), pp. 10–11.

3 David Riggs, *Ben Jonson: A Life* (Cambridge MA and London: Harvard University Press, 1989), p. 276.

4 James P. Bednarz, *Shakespeare and the Poets' War* (New York: Columbia University Press, 2000), p. 1. See also his 'Introduction: The Elizabethan Dramatists as Literary Critics', pp. 1–18.

5 According to Greg, '"Heminges" is perhaps the more correct form of the name (which appears as "Hemminges" in the actor-list among the preliminaries), but it is natural, in a work about the First Folio, to use the spelling he himself adopted [Heminge] in signing the dedication and address' (W. W. Greg, *The Shakespeare First Folio* (Oxford: Clarendon Press, 1955), p. 1 note 1). Surprisingly, Greg errs here: the name 'Hemminges' does not appear in the list of principal actors; the name 'Hemmings' does. Although there is not a complete consensus among scholars about how the name should be spelt, Greg's reasoning seems to me sound enough explanation for the preference of one form of the name above the others.

6 Greg, *The Shakespeare First Folio*, pp. 18–19.

7 Ibid., pp. 17–18.

8 Ibid., p. 18.

9 Ibid., p. 19.

10 Ian Donaldson (ed.), *Ben Jonson*, The Oxford Authors (Oxford and New York: Oxford University Press, 1985), p. 539.

11 Greg, *The Shakespeare First Folio*, p. 19 note 1.

12 Donaldson (ed.), *Ben Jonson*, p. 742.

13 Ibid., p. 735.

14 'The Underwood', 43, 'An Execration upon Vulcan', l. 3, in Donaldson (ed.), *Ben Jonson*, pp. 365–70 (p. 365).

15 Donaldson (ed.), *Ben Jonson*, p. 735.

16 The First Folio was 'expected to be on the market by October 1622, whereas we know that in fact it did not appear till near the end of 1623' (Greg, *The Shakespeare First Folio*, p. 4).

17 Donaldson (ed.), *Ben Jonson*, p. 359.

18 Greg, *The Shakespeare First Folio*, p. 20.

19 *Ben Jonson*, ed. C. H. Herford and Percy and Evelyn Simpson rpt. (Oxford: Clarendon Press, 1966), vol. 9, p. 13.

20 Ibid.

21 The relationship between Ben Jonson and Shakespeare's Folio collections is also addressed by Jane Rickard in Chapter 9, below.

22 Peter W. M. Blayney, *The First Folio of Shakespeare* (Washington DC: Folger Library Publications, 1991), p. 1.

23 *Ben Jonson*, ed. Herford and Simpson, vol. 9, p. 13.

24 John Freehafer, 'Leonard Digges, Ben Jonson, and the Beginning of Shakespeare Idolatry', *Shakespeare Quarterly*, 21 (1970), 63–75 (p. 64). In this article, Freehafer comprehensively discusses Digges's 'rejection of the words [and] methods of Jonson' (p. 71).

25 The text I have used is that in *The Riverside Shakespeare*, ed. G. Blakemore Evans (Boston: Houghton Mifflin, 1974), pp. 1845–6.

26 Freehafer, 'Leonard Digges, Ben Jonson, and the Beginning of Shakespeare Idolatry', p. 67.

27 Ibid., p. 75.

9

The 'First' Folio in context: the folio collections of Shakespeare, Jonson and King James

Jane Rickard

Polonius. What do you read, my lord?
Hamlet. Words, words, words.
Polonius. What is the matter, my lord?
Hamlet. Between who?

(2. 2.191–5)[1]

The book Hamlet is here appearing to read could be anything; it is, like any book, a sequence of words to be interpreted by its reader. Polonius would like the book – and indeed Hamlet himself – to be composed of a singular and describable 'matter'. But as Hamlet wilfully misunderstands the questions, exposing in his play on 'matter' that even Polonius' words escape the notion of meaning as singular and fixed, the Prince reveals nothing, either about himself or about the book. The opacity and complexity on which he here insists reminds us of the opacity and complexity of the text of which this moment forms a part. In printed form, the connection between the book Hamlet holds and the book that holds *Hamlet* is still more striking; *Hamlet* too consists of 'words, words, words' that beg but yield no simple answer to the question 'What is the matter?' In 1623 the book of *Hamlet* would become part of Shakespeare's book, and here too, its representation of the relationship between books and readers stands for the whole book of which it forms a part.

This chapter will consider how distinctive the so-called *First* Folio was, particularly with regard to how it represents the relationship between books and readers, by comparing it to other collected editions of the Jacobean period. The two most significant folio collections of the Jacobean period before 1623 are the *Workes* of Ben Jonson (1616), the importance of which has been recognised by a large number of critics, and the *Workes* of the patron of Shakespeare's playing company, King James, of the same year, which has attracted very little critical attention.[2] Each of these three collections is in its own way unprecedented and an attempt to redefine the format of the collected edition: no monarch before James had published their works as a collection; no collected edition before that of Jonson had included plays written for the public stage; and no collected edition before that of Shakespeare had been entirely devoted to plays. Despite being to a large extent unprecedented, however, the two earlier collections also situate themselves firmly within existing literary traditions. While Shakespeare's Folio was of course very different in that it represents a dead author constructed by other people, rather than someone constructing himself as an author, comparing it to these two earlier collections both suggests how it evolved from earlier developments and innovations, and highlights the ways in which it was even less precedented than the two 1616 collections. More specifically, I will argue that Shakespeare's Folio more fully realises not only some of what Jonson and James tried to achieve for their *Workes*, but also what they tried anxiously to deny and resist. I will also suggest that, while the role of Jonson's *Workes* in enabling the publication of Shakespeare's Folio seven years later has been acknowledged, more consideration needs to be given to the role of King James in the literary culture he inhabited.

Ever since the sixteenth century the collected edition has been central to the construction of authorial identity, literary reputation and the canon of individual authors, as well as the literary canon as a whole. Though it may not entirely determine an author's reputation, the production of a collected edition is a way of attempting to shape how posterity will view an author and his or her work. A collected edition creates, Andrew Nash suggests, 'an air of finality and completeness; a sense of personal and artistic investment and embodiment'; we might also add a sense of personal and artistic *achievement*. While any collected edition may have these associations, Nash speculates that Jonson may have been the first major author consciously to attempt to use his collected edition in this way.[3]

The late Elizabethan and Jacobean periods produced several folio editions of the works of the revered poets of the past. These include works from the relatively recent past, such as *The Workes of Our Ancient and Learned Poet, Geffrey Chaucer* (1598 and 1602) and Sir Philip Sidney's *The Countesse of Pembroke's Arcadia*, which is supplemented by his other works (1598). Kevin Pask suggests that the Chaucer edition 'marked a watershed in the authorization of Chaucer as well as of the English poet altogether', and that the Sidney edition was a 'best seller' in elite circles.[4] Collections of the works of ancient writers were also produced in this period, including the *Workes* of Seneca, translated by Thomas Lodge (1614), and *The Whole Works of Homer in his Iliads and Odysses*, translated by George Chapman (1616?). In both of these editions, the translator justifies producing his translation partly on the basis of what these classical writers can teach their readers.[5] The proliferation of editions such as these four both emphasises the role of the collected edition in the preservation of a writer's work for future generations, and suggests that the production of such an edition confirms a writer's greatness.

This period also saw writers beginning to publish collected editions of their *own* work, reflecting the growing status of contemporary literature. These tended to be confined to poetry and in quarto rather than folio size, and include *The Workes of John Heywood* (1562; republished 1566, 1576, 1587 and 1598) and *The Whole Workes of George Gascoigne* (1587). Samuel Daniel was the first to publish his *Works* in folio (1601; republished in 1602, and in 1623 as *The Whole Workes of S. Daniel in Poetrie*). This was an age in which much writing was collaborative and many publications were anonymous, or at least did not emphasise the identity of their authors, but each of these publications gives the individual author's name prominence in the very title of the book, suggesting that the name is its greatest selling point.[6] At the same time, these collections tend to emphasise the patronage connections of their writers or translators. Several are dedicated to the monarch. Daniel's *Works*, for example, was originally dedicated to Elizabeth, and its dedication emphasises the favour he has already won with her, claiming he has received 'That comfort which my Muse and me hath blest'. At the top of the title-page is the royal coat of arms, topped with a crown and encircled with the royal motto.[7] In 1605 Joshua Sylvester dedicated to James *Du Bartas His Deuine Weekes and Workes Translated and Dedicated to the Kings Most Excellent Maiestie*, and this was republished in 1606, 1608, 1613 and 1621. Such editions were, the frequency of republication would suggest, popular with their market, and therefore attractive both to publishers and to writers seeking to reach a large audience.

Collected editions were thus associated with the notion of a singular author, with posterity, with literary greatness, with the educative function of literature and with classical and monarchical authority. Both 1616 collections seek to exploit all of these associations. Yet there is within these associations a contradiction: while the author is represented as transcending the contemporary moment and entering the realm of posterity, he is also tied to specific contexts of patronage, politics and classical precedent. Shakespeare's Folio, as we shall see, largely escapes this tension, but in both 1616 collections it results in attempts to separate texts from contexts that are partial and ambivalent.

James's *Workes*, in particular, embodies the tension between the literary and the political because he is simultaneously an author and a source of authority, that which is representing and that which is represented. On the one hand, his very act of publishing a collected edition of writings stretching back to the 1580s under the title 'Workes' constitutes a claim that these writings transcend their contexts of production, are relevant beyond their immediate political moment and warrant being treated as literary texts, to be reread and preserved for posterity. One of the most striking features of the volume in this regard is its inclusion of speeches to Parliament spanning the whole of James's English reign to date: the interest of political speeches, then as now, was primarily topical, and until James's *Workes* royal speeches were never published more than a year after being delivered. By including in his *Workes* speeches as much as thirteen years old, James was making an unprecedented claim that their interest extends beyond the topical into the historical, and perhaps even the literary. The collection intensifies this separation of texts from their contexts of production by ordering the works generically rather than strictly chronologically, and by removing from some extra-textual material that ties them to specific contexts.[8] On the other hand, the political responsibility and sensitivity of James's position made it crucial that his texts be interpreted in accordance with his royal authority. The collection therefore insists that James's writings be read in the context of the divine authority from which royal authority derived. The frontispiece depicts James with the Bible at his side, the title-page intertwines royal and divine imagery, the preface is contributed by a bishop, James Montague (who also assisted in the preparation of the volume), and the first work is James's *Paraphrase vpon the*

Reuelation. This opening implies that all of the writings in the collection are founded upon divine authority.

If the attempt of the collection to separate texts and contexts is thus rather selective – removing texts from their specific political moment but nevertheless presenting them within a framework of divine and royal authority – it is also unachievable. As much as James may have attempted to construct himself as an author, he was to be read primarily as a king, his writings scrutinised for evidence of his political beliefs and intentions, not only amongst his contemporaries but also amongst succeeding generations of critics and historians who have not attended to the literary properties and aims of his writings. As Montague's preface to James's *Workes* attempts to justify the very fact of the King writing books, it returns his work to a context of the King's actions being judged by his subjects and of resistance to his literary aspirations:

> *But while I am collecting workes one way, I heare others scattering wordes as fast an other way, affirming, it had beene better his Maiestie had neuer written any Bookes at all; and being written, better they had perished with the present, like* Proclamations, *then haue remayned to* Posterity.
>
> (sig. B2v)

Here we get a strong sense that many of James's subjects did not share his desire that his writings be preserved for posterity, but rather saw writing books as inappropriate in a king, and maintained that his utterances should be confined to those that engage with and do not outlive the present, such as proclamations. This emphasises that it was particularly difficult for James to separate his texts from their contexts not only because of the inevitably political nature of his writings but also because of specific public expectations that a king's utterances should exist only within their immediate context.

Jonson, like his king, is somewhat selective in his attempts to separate texts and contexts, and unable to achieve fully the kinds of separation he seems to want. He tries to claim that his texts transcend some of their contexts of production and to limit their topical specificity. For example, as Martin Butler points out, 'the generic organisation [of Jonson's *Workes*] helps to de-emphasise his texts' dependence on the world of ordinary contingency, and omissions in the poems and masques elide uncomfortable traces of Jacobean politics'.[9] The collection also elides the dips in fortune and success that characterised Jonson's career; its organisation and consistencies of presentation create an impression of a smooth progression. The plays he had written collaboratively are not included while the information that *Sejanus* had been co-authored is suppressed.[10] In several cases, the masques republished in the Folio cut from their original printed editions lists of noble participants and references to contributions by others, such as Inigo Jones. Those masques first printed in the Folio 'contain no cast lists, few stage directions, virtually no descriptions of scenery, no mention of Jonson's collaborators'.[11] The volume as a whole has no dedicatee or patron. Jonson's *Workes* thus makes a bold claim of sole authorship and suggests the relative independence and self-sufficiency of the author.

At the same time, however, Jonson's position by 1616, the year in which he received a royal pension, as 'in all but name Poet Laureate',[12] resulted from and required him playing the patronage game. His collection thus includes, for example, the dedications to patrons of the original editions of the plays and the Epigrams. This, in addition to the insertion of title-pages before most of the works, diminishes the impression that the *Workes* is one coherent corpus and reminds us that it is in fact a series of individual texts written and performed at different times. In particular, Jonson frequently employs the King's name as a source of patronage and the audience for many of the entertainments and masques that appear in the collection. His *Workes* is closely related to that of the King in the extent to which it draws upon royal authority and continues that other collection's project of reflecting an – at least ostensibly – ideal image of the King.[13] Whatever the practical advantages of this engagement with aristocratic and royal authority, Jonson insisted that it had moral justification on the grounds that the poet has political and ethical responsibility and should play the role of reformer, exposing and correcting folly and vice. In his commonplace book, *Timber, or, Discoveries*, for example, he wrote that 'he which can feign a commonwealth, which is the poet, can govern it with counsels, strengthen it with laws, correct it with judgements, inform it with religion and morals'.[14] Yet this engagement tied Jonson's work to contexts that not only enabled but limited his work; as Butler observes, Jonson's Folio 'could partly efface' the political and professional tensions to which he was subject but 'could not escape altogether' from them.[15]

The context that Jonson is most keen to emphasise for his work is that of classical precedent. His employment of the work of classical writers as an external authority is analogous to James's use of the Bible – it provides a context within which his work is to be interpreted. As Richard C. Newton suggests, Jonson 'labors throughout his writing, through allusion and imitation, to appropriate to himself the epithet "classical"', and 'in the 1616 *Workes*, his translation of the Latin *opera* specifically makes the claim that Jonson as a writer is a classic'.[16] The title-page of his *Workes* depicts classical theatre, while the engraved portrait of Jonson that appears as a frontispiece in some copies portrays him as a classical poet, complete with laurel wreath, with books at either side, and an inscription in Latin that presents this picture as the 'true image of the greatest teacher of English poetry'.[17] One of the implications is that as the work of classical writers has lasted into Jonson's present, so will his work remain to posterity. This desire for posterity is in itself a reason for putting work into print: Jonson says in the preface to his first masque, *The Masque of Blacknesse* (1605), 'I adde this later hand, to redeeme [these solemnities] as well from Ignorance, as from Enuie' (p. 893), and when included in his *Workes* this idea of print as redemptive stands for the collection as a whole. Yet the collection's invocation of classical authority also works against this desire for posterity by locating it within specific styles of writing and reading practices, and within an age in which the classical was held in a particular regard.

Shakespeare's Folio, however, more fully achieves the separation of texts from both the specific contexts in which they were produced, and general contexts of authority and literary tradition.[18] The plays are not only transferred from stage to page but also almost entirely separated from their contexts of production and performance: nowhere in the volume are we given specific information about individual plays, such as when, where, and by which particular actors they were first performed. The fact that we get one list of the 'Principall Actors in all these Playes', like the fact that the plays are ordered generically and lack individual title-pages, presents the texts as one coherent corpus rather than a series of texts written and performed at different times. This fuller separation of texts from specific contexts is possible because of the collection's comparative lack of concern with external sources of authority. There is one dedication to noble patrons and a brief sequence of poems by contemporary writers, but the title-page does not draw on any external sources of authority and after the prefatory material there is no further mention of any external authorities.

As Leah Marcus has pointed out, 'nowhere in the First Folio is it mentioned that Shakespeare or Heminge or Condell or any of the others included in "The Names of the Principall Actors" belonged to a company called the King's Men'.[19] Mentioning the name of the company would have been an obvious and effortless way to do what Jonson does, and authorise the collection through drawing upon the most important patron and political figure of the time. That those preparing the collection did not exploit this opportunity suggests they were making a concerted attempt to separate the writing from any specific and transient context.

The second of Jonson's two contributions to Shakespeare's Folio, 'To the memory of my beloued, The Author Mr. William Shakespeare: And what he hath left vs', suggests his more ambivalent attitude towards the issue of patronage versus literary transcendence. It famously claims that Shakespeare is *'not of an age, but for all time'*, but it also gives the only direct mention in the collection of the two monarchs that presided over Shakespeare's lifetime (it imagines seeing him *'make those flights vpon the bankes of* Thames, / *That so did take* Eliza, *and our* Iames!'*), subtly reminding the reader of Shakespeare's political, temporal and geographical context. The possessive 'our' emphasises the relationship of Jonson, Shakespeare, everyone involved in the collection, and everyone reading it in 1623, to the King, but this is a relationship that, as we have seen, the collection otherwise refuses. This poem's famous dig about Shakespeare's lack of classical learning also relates the collection to the context of classical authority that was so important to Jonson. The title and title-page of Shakespeare's Folio make no claim that this is a collection of works in the classical sense. For Jonson, the failure of the collection – a 'Workes' that, unlike Jonson's own or that of his king, refuses that classical name – to ground itself in classical tradition is a basis for criticism. Yet it is also another way in which Shakespeare's Folio goes beyond the two earlier collections in transcending specific contexts.

Marcus suggests that the Shakespeare represented in his Folio corresponds to a Jonsonian ideal: 'The Bard generated by the First Folio is a figure for Art itself as Renaissance humanists like Ben Jonson wished to imagine it, existing in lofty separateness from the vicissitudes of life, yet capable, from its eminence, of shedding influence, "cheere", and admonition.'[20] This does not take into account, however, the ways in which Jonson's contribution to the collection tries to lessen the gap between Shakespeare and the context in which he wrote, and underestimates the extent of Jonson's concern with a poet's political and ethical involvement in his society. In so far as Shakespeare's Folio represents a transcendent Shakespeare, it does not accord exactly with what seems to have been Jonson's view of art. Richard Dutton gives a rather more nuanced view of how the 1623 Folio constructs Shakespeare, suggesting it represents a split between the attempts of Heminge and Condell to construct him as a man of the theatre, albeit gentrified, and the attempts of Jonson to construct him as an author, taking his place in the literary canon.[21] As many of the chapters in the present book suggest, such distinctions between the theatre and literary authorship may be overstated. Beyond this, the split seems more to concern Jonson trying to position Shakespeare in relation to specific contexts of monarchical authority and classical tradition, and Heminge and Condell trying to separate him from any such contexts. In this regard, Heminge and Condell seem more in tune with the plays themselves, in that the plays too lack the kind of dedications, prologues and epilogues Jonson often provided as a way of situating his plays within contexts of authority and tradition, and, as various critics have recognised, resist specific topical readings.[22]

The different ways in which these three collections represent the relationship between texts and contexts shape, as we can begin to see, the ways in which they construct the relationship between the author and authority. Both James and Jonson try to authorise their work not only by drawing on external authorities but also by implying their proximity and even comparability to them, and this is reflected in the presentation of their collections. For example, the frontispiece of James's *Workes* not only depicts the Bible but implies a parallel: God is represented through a book as James is here representing himself through a book. The parallel is emphasised by the verses below the picture which conclude '*knowledge makes the KING most like his maker*'. The frontispiece that, as noted above, appears in some copies of Jonson's *Workes* claims in Latin that Jonson is 'the greatest teacher of English poetry', and this suggests not only that his works draw on classical authority but also that they are of the same exemplary status. While this frontispiece was not part of Jonson's collection as originally constructed but added later, it thus seems, like James's frontispiece, to reflect some of the claims the collection implicitly makes.

In the same way, when Jonson draws on James as an external source of authority, he also appropriates that authority to serve his own ends. In particular, James wrote and published poetry himself, thereby validating poetry and suggesting that the roles of poet and king were complementary.[23] Jonson appropriates this aspect of James's self-representation in order to present himself as poet as though on a level with the King. For example, Jonson's *Panegyre, on the Happie Entrance of Iames, our Soveraigne, to His first high Session of Parliament in this his Kingdome, the 19 of March, 1603*, included in his *Workes*, ends 'Solus Rex, aut Poeta non quotannis nascitur [only the King and the Poet are not born every year]' (p. 868). Despite such attempts to appropriate different types of authority for themselves, James and Jonson remain intimately tied to the sources upon which they draw and cannot claim to be the originators of their own authority. In this sense, the authority of both writers as represented in their collections is less immediate – it remains the product and reflection of sources of authority that exist elsewhere.

One effect of the 1623 Folio's relative freedom from external sources of authority is that what authority it has derives almost entirely from its author. This is highlighted by the positioning of the picture of Shakespeare on the title-page, not on a separate page. Tellingly, the position Shakespeare occupies here is occupied in the collections of James and Jonson by invocations of their sources of authority – symbols of and quotations from the Bible and classical writings respectively – while the pictures of James and Jonson appear on separate pages. In the earlier collections, then, authors and authorities remain subtly separate, while in Shakespeare's Folio the author is the authority. The picture of Shakespeare is unusually lacking in elaboration and embellishment, breaking with the conventions for such works that had been established in recent times of placing the author in visual relation to his position and work.[24] This simplicity further emphasises the degree to which Shakespeare's Folio is able to rely more on its author, without situating him amongst a complex of associations. Thus the effect James and Jonson sought to achieve through their employment of divine and classical authority, namely that of equating author and authority was an effect that Shakespeare's Folio achieves more fully.

The three collections also differ in terms of the extent to which they appear to represent or embody the author. Both James and

Jonson are voices in their own collections, writing about themselves in the first person and addressing the reader directly. Indeed, in all of the texts included in the King's collection, except the opening *Paraphrase vpon the Reuelation* where he assumes the persona of John, James writes as himself. Jonson appears at various points in his *Workes* and addresses the reader as himself in prefaces, prologues, epilogues and marginal notes. He is even a voice in Shakespeare's Folio, his 'To the memory of my beloued, the Author' firmly establishing a persona in the first person; as John Lyon suggests, this poem, though generous, is also motivated by a concern for his own reputation.[25] Yet, in different ways, both 1616 collections complicate the idea that the author is embodied in the text.

For James, the issue is complicated by his position in the political limelight. *Basilikon Doron*, his political treatise and handbook for princes, first published in 1599, republished in 1603, and included in his *Workes*, seems to reflect his hopes for the fate of his writings when he advises Prince Henry that 'your writes will remaine as true pictures of your minde, to all posterities' (p. 184). This suggests a desire for writing to be seen as an unmediated representation of the author, and James indeed often makes rhetorical claims of transparency and sincerity, particularly in his speeches to Parliament, several of which, as noted above, were included in his *Workes*. At the end of his first speech to the English Parliament, for example, he claims that 'as farre as a King is in Honour erected aboue any of his Subiects, so farre should he striue in sinceritie to be aboue them all, and that his tongue should be euer the trew Messenger of his heart' (p. 497). This is an attempt to portray royal speech as unmediated, but the metaphor of tongue as messenger admits a distance between thought or belief and expression. Claims of royal sincerity were of such obvious political value as to invite scepticism, and James indeed had somewhat of a reputation as a dissembler.[26] Moreover, the notion that James's texts did give access to his thoughts was in tension with his desire to maintain royal mystique, preserve his authority from the encroachments of his subjects and avoid overexposure. This desire is evident in, for example, the speech to the Star Chamber of 1616, which concludes his *Workes*, when he asserts that what 'concernes the mysterie of the Kings power, is not lawfull to be disputed; for that is to wade into the weakenesse of Princes, and to take away the mysticall reuerence, that belongs vnto them that sit in the Throne of God' (p. 557). In this regard, the metaphor of the tongue as messenger does serve his purposes in that it allows for a space between inner and outer, thought and expression; a space where the mystery of kingship could be preserved. What we get overall, then, is an equivocal claim that royal texts could, but did not necessarily, represent all of the thoughts of the king. We may surmise that James wanted his Folio to be regarded as a sincere reflection of his beliefs, but not as an embodiment of himself in which he was available to unlimited scrutiny.

Jonson, meanwhile, was not concerned to claim that his writings represented his unmediated thoughts, and indeed advocated taking painstaking care with writing: 'For a man to write well . . . he must first think, and excogitate his matter; then choose his words, and examine the weight of either. Then take care in placing . . . No matter how slow the style be at first, so it be laboured, and accurate.' This advocates effort rather than inspiration, and suggests that the relationship between thoughts and words is not immediate but considered. Jonson therefore criticised Shakespeare for not doing more to revise his work: seemingly thinking of Heminge and Condell's claim in Shakespeare's Folio that they have 'scarse receiued from him a blot in his papers', he retorts 'the players have often mentioned it as an honour to Shakespeare, that in his writing, whatsoever he penned, he never blotted out a line. My answer hath been, "would he had blotted out a thousand".'[27] Jonson also allegedly commented 'that Shakespeare wanted art'.[28] In keeping with his advice on writing well and such criticisms of Shakespeare, Jonson's use of 'art' seems to maintain a distance between Jonson the man and his work. In his direct addresses to the reader, he is primarily concerned to discuss literary and critical issues, with the effect that his Folio reads as a series of examples of his art, rather than expressions of himself. Even one of the commendatory verses in his collection, 'To Ben Ionson, *on his workes*' concludes with Edward Heyward telling Jonson he is paying his due 'To your iust worth, not you', further separating the work from the man. In both 1616 collections, then, the authors may address the reader on their own behalf, but those addresses seem mediated by politics and art respectively.

While the authority of Shakespeare's Folio derives from his name and image, he is not a voice in the collection in the ways that James and Jonson are in theirs. The plays do not incorporate extra-textual material in which Shakespeare speaks on his own behalf, and, as has preoccupied many critics, do not give us any clear insight into his views or beliefs. At the same time, however, Shakespeare's Folio more fully achieves a sense that the author is embodied within the book; that the book is an authentic and unmediated representation of him. The fact that Shakespeare was already dead meant that the book became more fully a representation of him, or even a substitute for him, as indicated in the title of Jonson's poem, 'To the memory of my beloued, The Author Mr. William Shakespeare: And what he hath left vs'; in the play on 'remaines' in the dedication (*'we most humbly consecrate to your H. H. these remaines of your seruant* Shakespeare'); and on the repeated insistence throughout the prefatory materials that the book is a monument in which *'we aliue shall view thee still'*. The very positioning of his picture on the title-page implies that Shakespeare is in and of the text. Moreover, as George Donaldson also emphasises in the present book, the prefatory material tries to create the impression that this book gives access not only to the plays as 'he conceiued them' but to the very thoughts of its writer; that what Shakespeare 'thought, he vttered', and that this is what his Folio represents. This phrase suggests the direct correlation between inner thought and outward expression that James's metaphor of the tongue as a messenger of the heart fails entirely to evoke. The notion of Shakespeare's Folio as an unmediated representation of his thought was for a long time persuasive, and enables this folio to make a fuller claim of being authoritative, in the sense of authentic, than the *Workes* of James and Jonson were able to make. Paradoxically, the Shakespeare here represented is thus both the main source of the collection's authority and, to borrow Marcus's phrase, 'almost an abstraction'.[29]

Perhaps what is most distinctive of all about Shakespeare's Folio, however, is the extent to which it appears to give itself to its readers and leave itself open to their interpretations. In the sixteenth and early seventeenth centuries reading was increasingly being understood as an active process in which multiple meanings can be perceived, and there are a number of factors that contributed to this understanding. Renaissance educational theory emphasised the arts of reading, and humanism recognised 'the independence and power of readers, as well as authors, to construct their own meanings'.[30] At the same time, the rise of Protestantism and religious division had exposed the fact that even the Bible could be interpreted in a range of ways, to a large extent undermining the notion that a text dictates its own fixed meaning. This awareness led to considerable anxiety in political and religious spheres, and reverberated through all forms of writing as authors engaged with the pressures involved in seeking patronage or commercial success and avoiding conflict with authority. Anxiety about interpretation is evident, for example, in the prefaces often added to printed versions of plays.[31] Such anxiety is reflected and crystallised in the *Workes* of James and Jonson, but is notably absent in Shakespeare's Folio.

James's anxiety about the misinterpretation of scriptural and royal texts is evident throughout the writings that were gathered into his *Workes*. In a speech to Parliament delivered in 1610, for example, he asks Parliament: 'peruert not my words by any corrupt affections, turning them to an ill meaning, like one, who when hee heares the tolling of a Bell, fancies to himselfe, that it speakes those words which are most in his minde' (pp. 547–8). Here James acknowledges that interpretation may be subjective, and rejects such interpretation as perverting the meaning he wishes to impose. His language echoes a warning he had given his own son eleven years earlier in *Basilikon Doron*, but there his concern was with what he claims is widespread misinterpretation of Scripture: 'beware ye wrest not the word to your owne appetite, as ouer many doe, making it like a bell to sound as ye please to interprete' (p. 149). Again we see a strong sense that texts are susceptible to manipulation by their readers, and an equally strong desire to prevent such manipulation by teaching readers how to read. This echo, particularly in the context of the *Workes* in which both texts appear, reinforces the implication that the King's word should be read as God's word should be read – within the bounds of authority. In the preface James added to the second edition of *Basilikon Doron* in 1603, he further reveals his anxiety that the publication of his work means uncontrollable and universal judgement of it: now it is in the public view, it is '*subiect to euery mans censure*' (p. 142). He goes on to reject criticisms of his text and to explain his intention and meaning, concluding, in his most emphatic statement of desire for singular and fixed interpretation, '*that this is the onely meaning of my Booke*' (p. 144). These extracts reflect the interplay between religion, politics and writing that centred on the figure of the King, and his desire to predetermine and limit interpretation of the texts on which his authority was based and through which his authority was represented. The emphasis in his *Workes* on royal and divine authority provides a framework for interpretation, furthering this attempt to control the reader.

The desire to control interpretation is also evident in Jonson's work, to an exceptional degree.[32] It appears within his plays as performed. For example, in the 'Induction on the Stage' of *Bartholomew Fair* (1614) he states that he does not want 'any *State-decipherer*, or politique *Picklocke* of the *Scene*' to try to work out who is meant by each of the play's characters.[33] By publishing his work, however, Jonson could assert still more authorial control through prefaces, notes and marginalia which guide the reader, and, in the case of plays, respond to claimed misinterpretation of the performed version.[34] His dedication to *Volpone* (1605) attacks 'inuading interpreters', suggesting that 'nothing can bee so innocently writ, or carryed, but may be made obnoxious to construction' and insisting upon his own 'innocence' (p. 444). While some extra-textual materials were omitted from the plays when they were republished in the *Workes*, this contentious dedication was included with only minor revisions.[35] Jonson does not deny the right of a reader to censure, but suggests that this right depends upon the knowledge and learnedness of that reader. In Epigram 17, for example, he claims to welcome the censure of the 'learned critick', but in the following epigram he satirises 'my meere English censurer' (p. 773). He is thereby trying to censure his censurers, to maintain control over who judges his texts. Like James, by publishing his works as a collection Jonson was able to further this attempt to control interpretation.

As Shakespeare's Folio largely frees itself from the contexts of politics, patronage and classical precedent, and from any direct authorial voice, so it appears to hand itself over to the reader. This is reflected in the unusual placing of the address 'To the Reader' on the very first page, even before the title of the work. The preface, 'To the great Variety of Readers', begins by embracing the full spectrum of readers, 'From the most able, to him that can but spell'. This echoes Jonson's epigram 'To My Booke-Seller', but lacks the bitterly satiric tone of that poem's acknowledgement that his book may be advertised to 'some clarke-like seruing-man, / Who scarce can spell th' hard names: whose knight lesse can' (p. 769).[36] 'To the great Variety of Readers', while insisting upon the inherent value of the texts, does not attempt to dictate 'the only', or indeed any, meaning of the book, but rather accepts the role of the reader in determining meaning and suggests the plurality of interpretation. Unlike the earlier collections, it does not even claim the works have an educative function. Here we get an acknowledgement that now that the book is in the public

domain, its readers have the right to judge it: 'It is now publique, &
you wil stand for your priuiledges wee know: to read, and censure'.
This is of course largely a conventional gesture, not a genuine invi-
tation of criticism, but there seems to be a confidence here, a sense
that the censure of readers does not pose a threat, which contrasts
with James's and Jonson's more anxious treatments of this issue.
When the preface proposes that 'it is not our prouince, who onely
gather his works, and giue them you, to praise him. It is yours that
reade him', the slight indeterminacy of the second 'it', and the fact
that 'It is yours that reade him' is given emphasis by standing as a
separate sentence, stresses that both the book and the right to judge
it are now possessed by the reader. Moreover, the prefatory materials suggest that it is the reader who, by reading Shakespeare 'againe,
and againe', realises the promise that Shakespeare is alive in his book.

    The openness of Shakespeare's Folio to the interpretation of its
readers – its refusal to tell us 'what is the matter' – is in keeping
with what critics have long recognised to be the resistance of
Shakespeare's plays to single interpretations, and with Shakespeare's
own approach to writing and publication. It seems that for
Shakespeare the relationship between texts and their readers was
a source not of anxiety but of creative potential. As we saw in
the moment from *Hamlet* with which this discussion began,
Shakespeare's plays are interested in what books are, how people
want to be able to interpret them and how they resist single or fixed
interpretations. Even if, as Lukas Erne has argued, Shakespeare was
concerned with publication, he does not insert prefaces, notes and
marginalia in his publications as Jonson and other contemporary
playwrights do.[37] The 1609 edition of *Troilus and Cressida* does
have a preface, but even this, which is of unknown authorship and
was not included in his Folio, is not concerned to tell the reader what
the text means. The brief dedications Shakespeare wrote to his two
narrative poems similarly make no attempt to tell the reader what
the poems mean. If we accept that Shakespeare was concerned with,
and involved in, the publication of his plays, then we may take the
lack of such extra-textual material as an indication that Shakespeare
was content to let the authority to interpret his texts lie with his
readers. The very titles *As You Like It* and *Twelfth Night, or What
You Will* suggest this willingness to let the power to interpret lie
with the recipients, not the creators, of a performance or text. The
prologue of *Troilus and Cressida* renders this still more explicit,

instructing 'Like or find fault; do as your pleasures are' (line 30). The appeals to audience judgement at the ends of *The Tempest* and *All's Well that Ends Well* also work on the page as an acknowledgement that, once a text is published, the authority to judge it lies with its readers. These Shakespearean moments are all echoed when Heminge and Condell tell the readers of Shakespeare's Folio that 'the fate of all Bookes depends vpon your capacities'.

It would of course be simplistic to suggest Shakespeare allows his readers utter interpretative freedom; rather his texts shape our readings in more subtle ways, and even dramatise some of the ways in which texts work on us. For example, in *Titus Andronicus*, Act 4, scene 1, Lavinia exploits her reading of Ovid's *Metamorphoses* to tell her father her own tale, but this moment of remarkable authorial self-consciousness also reveals the extent to which she is herself constructed by Ovid's *Metamorphoses*. Shakespeare seems to be here displaying the fact that the book to which Lavinia draws attention is able to tell her tale precisely because it is one of the main sources he used in writing that tale. He draws further attention to this by having Titus respond that their actions have been 'Patterned by that the poet here describes' (4.1.56); within the fiction the characters are constructed by the books they have read and without the fiction they are constructed by those the playwright has read. The poet to whom Titus refers could equally be Ovid or Shakespeare. This onstage scene of reading, one of the few moments in Shakespeare when a named book is brought onstage, gives a picture of the relationship of Shakespeare – or any writer – to the sources they read: a new text both constructs its own meanings from, and is constructed by, its sources. It may also provide a model for Shakespeare's sense of the relationship between his texts and their readers: readers may construct their own meanings from the texts they read, but they are also the products of those texts.

As each of these three collections engages with its readers, so too is each engaging with a profit-driven market. Publishing was a business, which removed texts from such lofty contexts as those of aristocratic pastime and coterie circulation, and turned them into commodities to be bought. Both 1616 collections express anxiety about this even as they participate in it. In the preface to James's *Workes*, Montague's project of trying to dismiss popular objections to royal books involves him in reproducing those objections, including the view that '*since that Booke-writing is growen into a Trade; It is as dishonorable for a*

King *to write bookes; as it is for him to be a Practitioner in a* Profession' (sig. B2v). This reveals a contemporary perception that the commercialisation of the book has demeaned book-writing to the level of a profession, the implication being that it does not require a particular talent or status but might be practised by anyone.[38] It is therefore doubly dishonourable for the King: it involves him in a sphere that is a commercial one and that does not reflect his privileged position.

For Jonson it seems that the commodification of literature was, at best, a necessary evil. His collection of Epigrams, included in his *Workes*, begins with a sequence of three epigrams, 'To the Reader', 'To My Book' and 'To my Booke-Seller' respectively. 'To my Booke-Seller' questions the equation of literary merit with marketability, beginning 'Thou, that mak'st gaine thy end, and wisely well, / Call'st a booke good, or bad, as it doth sell' (p. 769). After bemoaning this tendency to judge books by their marketability, Jonson suggests that he does not want his book to be advertised, as though only those who can recognise its intrinsic value should buy it: he asks that it may 'lye vpon thy stall, till it be sought; / Not offer'd, as it made sute to be bought' (p. 770). Jonson must have been aware, however, of the contradictions here: his book would not be read if it were not bought, and it would not be bought if people did not know it was available. These contradictions reflect – perhaps self-consciously – his ambivalent attitude towards print culture.

The preface to Shakespeare's Folio, by contrast, simply acknowledges that the book is a commodity and implores people to buy it. Whether or not we read the tone as grudging, this preface acknowledges that 'the fate of all Bookes depends vpon your capacities: and not of your heads alone, but of your purses'. In this regard, however, the prefatory material faintly echoes a moment from the plays it introduces in such a way as to gently undermine its attempt to seduce the reader. In *The Winter's Tale* Shakespeare comically satirises belief in the authority of print:

> *Clown.* What hast here? Ballads?
> *Mopsa.* Pray now, buy some. I love a ballad in print, alife, for then we are sure they are true.
> *Autolycus.* Here's one to a very doleful tune . . .
> *Mopsa.* Is it true, think you?
> *Autolycus.* Very true, and but a month old.
>
> (4.4.250–7)

The emphasis is on the simplicity and gullability of the clowns and we are made to laugh at their unquestioning belief that if the ballads are printed they must be true. Yet this moment also speaks to the claim in the Folio that it contains the 'True Originall Copies' of Shakespeare's plays, and is a replacement for the 'diuerse stolne, and surreptitious copies' with which readers have previously been abused. The parallel suggests the extent to which this claim is a marketing ploy designed to make the reader buy the book. It has proved to be an effective strategy.

Shakespeare's First Folio was thus, in many ways, an unprecedented collection, yet, as critics such as Dutton have claimed, it 'would probably have been an unthinkable publication if Jonson's own 1616 *Workes* had not paved the way'.[39] This assertion may require qualification in the light of Lukas Erne's argument in *Shakespeare as Literary Dramatist* that Jonson was less unique in terms of his concern with publishing than has previously been thought.[40] It does, however, given the connections identified between the two 1616 collections, raise the question of whether Jonson's *Workes* itself was at all indebted to the interests and activities of the King. Jonson certainly read James carefully, and many of his writings were shaped by the King's preferences and ideologies in so far as they were written for him. But how far might James's self-styling have influenced or enabled Jonson's construction of authorship? The relationship of word and image in the Renaissance is a vast topic and it has long been suggested that the Jacobean court was in the main more word-centred than the Elizabethan, and that Jonson shared and supported this preference.[41] Jonson's *Workes* exemplifies his representation of the word as superior to the image, most obviously in the verses below his engraved portrait which claim '*O could there be an art found out that might / Produce his shape soe lively as to* write'. Jonson would carry such representation of the relationship of word and image into his contribution to the opening of Shakespeare's Folio, where his verse concludes by telling the reader 'looke / Not on his Picture, but his Booke'. But these Jonsonian frontispieces also echo James's prioritisation of the verbal over the visual, in his *Workes* as elsewhere. Of course these claims of the superiority of the word are far from unique, but the fact that Jonson felt the need to make the claims indicates that this was the subject of ongoing debate, not a widely accepted truism. Perhaps Jonson's construction of himself, and subsequently of Shakespeare, as an author whose words were far more valuable than pictures, was facilitated and validated by a king who preferred to write than to sit to have his portrait taken. Yet this issue is complicated, and Sara van den Berg's assertion that Jonson was able to publish his *Workes* partly because James had replaced a performative version of royal self-representation with a literary and print-orientated one may accord James too much agency.[42] Moreover, we must remember the criticisms with which this change in styles met, as reflected, for example, in Montague's preface to James's *Workes*. I would suggest rather that James and Jonson were drawing on similar values and developments, resisting analogous objections, and, whether consciously or not, reinforcing each other's authority. In this regard, James's *Workes* may also have been a factor in enabling the publication of Shakespeare's Folio in 1623.

That it was Shakespeare's book that became the more lasting monument, while within a century or two of his death Jonson was seen as a poet of his age but *not* for all time,[43] and James's writings continue to be neglected, is ironic, given that Jonson and James more explicitly express a concern with posterity in their collections than Shakespeare does in the texts gathered in the 1623 Folio.[44] Yet the very fact that Shakespeare was already dead when his Folio was produced, and that he had not publicly expressed a desire for his plays to be preserved for posterity, may be one factor in the greater success of his collection: as early as the fourteenth century Petrarch had suggested that death was a necessary condition for winning literary praise, for then 'you cease being an obstacle to yourself'. The Romantic poets later recognised that 'the narcissistic concern to survive in the future might itself be the cause of one's inevitable neglect in that future'.[45] More importantly, however, Shakespeare's Folio differs from the collections of James and Jonson in that it seems to transcend immediate exigency and specificity, it resists topical reading, and it presents itself as susceptible to the various interpretations of its readers. In these ways, it accords more with – and perhaps helped to shape – subsequent notions of 'literariness'.[46]

The difference in the fates of Jonson's *Workes* and Shakespeare's Folio is, as several critics have noted, particularly ironic, given not only Jonson's 'great faith in the judgement of posterity' but also the fact that he contributed to the monumentalisation of Shakespeare in the 1623 Folio.[47] What has not been given much consideration, however, is the further irony where James is concerned. Shakespeare's Folio, by more fully achieving the effect of an author who self-authorises, not only surpasses the earlier collections but exists beyond the limits of royal authority. As Marcus has noted, it constructs 'Shakespeare not as the King's Man but as his own man, not "authored" by a higher power but Author in his own right'.[48] It thereby prevents the continuation of James's project of being an author in the sense of authoriser, which had included authorising the King James Bible of 1611. Perhaps in publishing his own folio collection in an attempt to assert his authority through his authorship, James had, inadvertently, contributed to a process whereby authors could increasingly claim an authority that lay outside his bounds. But the seemingly autonomous author that emerges from the prefatory material of Shakespeare's Folio is of course a construction of the people who prepared the collection. What it creates is a Shakespeare that, like his book, is a construction of 'words, words, words'.

Notes

1 All references to Shakespeare's plays are to Stephen Greenblatt, Walter Cohen, Jean Howard, and Katherine Maus (eds), *The Norton Shakespeare* (New York: Norton, 1997). Act, scene and line numbers follow in parentheses.

2 On Jonson's *Workes* see, among others, Richard Helgerson, 'The Elizabethan Laureate: Self-Presentation and the Literary System', *English Literary History*, 46 (1979), 193–220; Richard C. Newton, 'Jonson and the (Re-)invention of the Book', in Claude J. Summers and Ted-Larry Pebworth (eds), *Classic and Cavalier: Essays on Jonson and the Sons of Ben* (Pittsburgh: University of Pittsburgh Press, 1982), pp. 31–55; David Riggs, *Ben Jonson: A Life* (Cambridge MA and London: Harvard University Press, 1989); Jennifer Brady and W. H. Herendeen (eds), *Ben Jonson's 1616 Folio* (Newark: University of Delaware Press, 1991); Richard Dutton, *Ben Jonson: Authority: Criticism* (London: Macmillan Press, 1996); Martin Butler (ed.), *Re-Presenting Ben Jonson* (London: Macmillan Press, 1999); and Joseph Loewenstein, *Ben Jonson and Possessive Authorship* (Cambridge: Cambridge University Press, 2002). King James was a prolific writer in a range of genres and formats, and brought together all his major prose works, including scriptural exegeses, and social and political treatises, for his folio collection. His writings have until recently been subjected to little critical analysis, but a number of critics are beginning to recognise their literary and cultural significance, as evidenced by the publication in 2002 of Daniel Fischlin and Mark Fortier (eds), *Royal Subjects: Essays on the Writings of James VI and I* (Detroit: Wayne State University

Press), the first collection of essays devoted to this topic. For further discussion of the full range of James's writings, see my *Authorship and Authority: The Writings of James VI and I* (Manchester: Manchester University Press, 2007); for further discussion of his *Workes* in particular see *Authorship and Authority*, chapter 4.

3 Andrew Nash, 'Introduction: The Culture of Collected Editions: Authorship, Reputation and the Canon', in Nash (ed.), *The Culture of Collected Editions* (Hampshire: Palgrave Macmillan, 2003), pp. 1–18 (p. 2). See this collection of essays for a range of perspectives on collected editions from Jonson to the present.

4 Kevin Pask, *The Emergence of the English Author: Scripting the Life of the Poet in Early Modern England* (Cambridge: Cambridge University Press, 1996), pp. 6, 73.

5 See the *Workes* of Seneca (London: William Stansby, 1614), preface 'To the Courteous Reader', and *The Whole Works of Homer* (London: Nathanial Butter, 1616?), verse dedication to Prince Henry. The date of the latter work is conjectural, but, if this collection was indeed published in the same year as Jonson's *Workes* it intensifies the contrast between Jonson's aspirations and those of his contemporaries and rivals: while Chapman was translating a classical writer into English, Jonson was trying, as we will consider further below, to translate his work into a classical format.

6 For a discussion of collaboration as a normal mode of Renaissance writing see Jeffrey Masten, *Textual Intercourse: Collaboration, Authorship, and Sexualities in Renaissance Drama* (Cambridge: Cambridge University Press, 1997). For a recent consideration of the role of authors' names on the title pages of playbooks see Lukas Erne, *Shakespeare as Literary Dramatist* (Cambridge: Cambridge University Press, 2003), esp. pp. 34–41.

7 Samuel Daniel, *The Works of Samuel Daniel* (London: Simon Waterson, 1601).

8 The most notable example of this concerns two scriptural exegeses that James published in Scotland in the late 1580s, which both originally included a preface written by Patrick Galloway, a Minister of the Scottish Church. These prefaces, which tie the texts to a specific Scottish political and religious context, are removed for the *Workes*. All references to James's works and to the prefatory materials contained in his *Workes*, are to James I, *The Workes of the Most High and Mighty Prince, Iames* (London: Robert Barker and John Bill, 1616). Italics are reproduced as they occur in the original text. Page and signature numbers follow in parentheses.

9 Martin Butler, 'Introduction: from *Workes* to Texts', in Butler (ed.), *Re-presenting Ben Jonson*, pp. 1–20 (p. 11).

10 Martin Butler, 'Jonson's Folio and the Politics of Patronage', *Criticism*, 35 (1993), 377–90 (p. 377).

11 Joseph Loewenstein, 'Printing and "The Multitudinous Presse": The Contentious Texts of Jonson's Masques', in Brady and Herendeen (eds), *Ben Jonson's 1616 Folio*, pp. 168–91 (p. 186).

12 Richard Dutton, 'Jonson: Epistle to Volpone', in *Licensing, Censorship and Authorship in Early Modern England: Buggeswords* (Basingstoke: Palgrave Macmillan, 2000), pp. 114–31 (p. 127).

13 Recent studies of Jonson's court masques in particular have suggested that the praise offered may be qualified by subtle criticism and satire, and that agendas at odds with that of the king may also be at play. For further discussion see, among others, Lesley Mickel, *Ben Jonson's Antimasques: A History of Growth and Decline* (Aldershot: Ashgate, 1999); David Bevington and Peter Holbrook (eds), *The Politics of the Stuart Court Masque* (Cambridge, Cambridge University Press, 1998), esp. Martin Butler, 'Courtly Negotiations', pp. 20–40, and Butler, 'Ben Jonson and the Limits of Courtly Panegyric', in Kevin Sharpe and Peter Lake (eds), *Culture and Politics in Early Stuart England* (Stanford: Stanford University Press, 1993), pp. 91–116.

14 Jonson, *Timber, or, Discoveries*, lines 1045–8, in Ian Donaldson (ed.), *Ben Jonson* (Oxford: Oxford University Press, 1985), p. 549.

15 Butler, 'Jonson's Folio and the Politics of Patronage', p. 390.

16 Newton, 'Jonson and the (Re-)invention of the Book', pp. 39, 37.

17 This portrait was produced in the mid-1620s and subsequently bound in to some copies of Jonson's *Workes* (Mark Bland, 'William Stansby and the Production of *The Workes of Beniamin Jonson*, 1615–16', *The Library: The Transactions of the Bibliographical Society*, 20 (1998), 1–33 (p. 24n)). For the portrait see the first leaf of some copies of Ben Jonson, *The Workes of Beniamin Jonson* (London: William Stansby, 1616). All subsequent references to Jonson's works refer to this edition unless otherwise specified. Page numbers follow in parentheses.

18 All references to Shakespeare's Folio are to *Mr William Shakespeares Comedies, Histories, & Tragedies* (London: Isaac Jaggard and Edward Blount, 1623).

19 Leah S. Marcus, *Puzzling Shakespeare: Local Reading and Its Discontents* (Berkeley, Los Angeles, London: University of California Press, 1988), p. 106.

20 Marcus, *Puzzling Shakespeare*, p. 24.

21 Dutton, *Ben Jonson: Authority: Criticism*, pp. 159–61.

22 This resistance is the focus of, for example, Marcus, *Puzzling Shakespeare*.

23 As King of Scotland, James published two collections of poetry: *The Essayes of a Prentise, in the Diuine Art of Poesie* (Edinburgh: Thomas

Vautroullier, 1584) and *His Maiesties Poeticall Exercises at Vacant Houres* (Edinburgh: Robert Waldegrave, 1591). He continued writing poetry and circulating it in manuscript during his English reign.

24 Marcus, *Puzzling Shakespeare*, p. 19.

25 John Lyon, 'The Test of Time: Shakespeare, Jonson, Donne', *Essays in Criticism*, 49 (1999), 1–21 (p. 11).

26 This reputation predated James's accession to the throne of England. For example, the Dean of Durham, Tobias Matthew, wrote to the Lord Treasurer, Burghley, on 9 April 1594: 'I pray God the King's protestations be not over-well believed; who is a deeper dissembler, by all men's judgements that know him best, than is thought possible for his years' (quoted in preface to *Basilikon Doron*, reprinted by Charles Butler for Roxburghe Club (London, 1887)).

27 Jonson, *Timber, or, Discoveries*, lines 1713–22, 658–61, in Donaldson (ed.), *Ben Jonson*, pp. 566, 539. Cf. George Donaldson's detailed discussion of the relationship between these two comments in Chapter 8, above.

28 Jonson, *Conversations with William Drummond*, line 37, in Donaldson (ed.), *Ben Jonson*, p. 596.

29 Marcus, *Puzzling Shakespeare*, pp. 24–5.

30 Kevin Sharpe, *Reading Revolutions: The Politics of Reading in Early Modern England* (New Haven and London: Yale University Press, 2000), p. 40. See this study for an exploration of the nature and conception of reading in the period.

31 See Paul D. Cannan, 'Ben Jonson, Authorship, and the Rhetoric of English Dramatic Criticism', *Studies in Philology*, 99 (2002), 178–201. This article emphasises that Jonson was not alone amongst his contemporary playwrights in experimenting with prefatory writing.

32 Cannan suggests that while other contemporary playwrights also attempted to control and limit interpretation, John Marston, for example, asking in the dedication to *The Fawn* that his peruser '*be pleased to be my reader, and not my interpreter*', Jonson offers a 'dictatorial ethos that is unprecedented in prefatory addresses' and privileges authorial interpretation to a level unmatched until the work of Dryden ('Rhetoric of English Dramatic Criticism', pp. 182, 193–4).

33 C. H. Herford and Percy and Evelyn Simpson (eds), *Ben Jonson*, 11 vols (Oxford: Oxford University Press, 1925–52), vol. 6, Induction, lines 137–39.

34 For a discussion of Jonson's dramatic prefaces see Cannan, 'Rhetoric of English Dramatic Criticism'. For a study of Jonson's use of marginalia see Evelyn B. Tribble, *Margins and Marginality: The Printed Page in Early Modern England* (Charlottesville and London: University Press of Virginia, 1993), pp. 130–57.

35 Cannan, 'Rhetoric of English Dramatic Criticism', pp. 195–6.

36 Some critics have suggested that Jonson may have in fact written 'To the great Variety of Readers' on the basis of parallels with the induction to *Bartholomew Fair*, but I would agree with Marcus that this is unlikely because of the marked differences between the two, particularly in terms of Jonson's insistence on a hierarchy of audience members or readers (*Puzzling Shakespeare*, p. 22).

37 Cannan suggests that so many of Shakespeare's contemporaries experimented with prefatory writing as a means of legitimising the printed text that it is Shakespeare's texts that are unusual, even going so far as to propose that 'A play text completely devoid of textual apparatus – as is the case with Shakespeare's quartos – was suspect' ('Rhetoric of English Dramatic Criticism', p. 187).

38 For a discussion of the history of the book trade see H. S. Bennett, *English Books and Readers, 1558–1603* (Cambridge: Cambridge University Press, 1965) and *English Books and Readers, 1603 to 1640* (Cambridge: Cambridge University Press, 1970).

39 Dutton, *Ben Jonson: Authority: Criticism*, p. 159.

40 See Erne, *Shakespeare as Literary Dramatist*, esp. p. 34.

41 For a survey of some of the main differences between the cultures of the Elizabethan and Jacobean courts see Linda Levy Peck, 'The Mental World of the Jacobean Court: An Introduction', in Peck (ed.), *The Mental World of the Jacobean Court* (Cambridge: Cambridge University Press, 1991), pp. 1–20. Of course, as this collection of essays emphasises, the 'court' is not a homogenous or monolithic entity, particularly in the Jacobean period when there was not one court but several, grouped around the King, Queen and heir respectively.

42 Sara van den Berg, 'Ben Jonson and the Ideology of Authorship', in Brady and Herendeen (eds), *Jonson's 1616 Folio*, pp. 111–37 (p. 117). See Douglas A. Brooks, *From Playhouse to Printing House: Drama and Authorship in Early Modern England* (Cambridge: Cambridge University Press, 2000), pp. 104–39, for a refutation of such claims.

43 Ian Donaldson, '"Not of an Age": Jonson, Shakespeare, and the Verdicts of Posterity', in *Jonson's Magic Houses: Essays in Interpretation* (Oxford: Oxford University Press, 1997), pp. 180–97 (p. 189).

44 Shakespeare does, of course, contemplate immortality in his sonnets, but even here the emphasis is more on poetry as a way of preserving the subject recorded in the verse than on poetry as a way of preserving its writer. For a consideration of the ways in which later critics and writers responded to and modified Renaissance notions of posterity, with particular regard to Shakespeare, see Andrew Bennett, *Romantic Poets and the Culture of Posterity* (Cambridge: Cambridge University Press, 1999), esp. pp. 28–37.

45 Bennett, *Culture of Posterity*, pp. 29, 35.

46 Frank Kermode suggests that 'the books we call classic possess intrinsic qualities that endure, but possess also an openness to accommodation which keeps them alive under endlessly varying dispositions' (*The Classic* (London: Faber and Faber, 1975), p. 44). It is precisely this 'openness to accommodation' that Shakespeare's Folio seems more in possession of than the two 1616 folios, but there is of course a possible circularity here; such systems of value may be less a response to such books as Shakespeare's Folio, as Harold Bloom maintains (see *The Western Canon* (London: Macmillan, 1995)), than produced by them. However we might understand the relationship between Shakespeare and literary value, 'all the evidence we have to date confirms', as John Lyon suggests, 'that Ben Jonson was and/or is right' to claim Shakespeare was 'not of an age but for all time' ('The Test of Time', p. 1).

47 Donaldson, *Jonson's Magic Houses*, p. 189. Writers and critics have measured Jonson against Shakespeare and found Jonson lacking; Jonas A. Barish begins the introduction to a 1963 collection of essays on Jonson by noting that 'probably no major author has suffered such a catastrophic decline in popularity since his own day as has Ben Jonson. Certainly none has been so punished for the crime of not being Shakespeare' (Barish (ed.), *Ben Jonson: A Collection of Critical Essays* (Englewood Cliffs NJ: Prentice-Hall, 1963), p. 1). Lyon notes the further irony that Jonson had helped to make 'the very argument for Shakespeare's immortal greatness' in which he became a 'pawn to be denigrated' ('The Test of Time', p. 16).

48 Marcus, *Puzzling Shakespeare*, p. 106.

10

A new early reader of Shakespeare

Stanley Wells

During 2003 I was invited to inspect a manuscript, previously unexplored by scholars, which adds to the corpus of Elizabethan literature a new work of exceptional interest, not least in that it reveals a previously unknown reader of, and commentator upon, writings by Shakespeare. The property of a family trust, the manuscript is housed in a private collection, and I was asked not to disclose its whereabouts. It was first shown to me as a matter of interest incidental to the main purpose of my visit, and on that occasion I examined it in only a cursory way which was, however, enough to reveal that closer study would be profitable. On a later visit I was able to devote more time to it, though by no means as much as it deserved. (This was the result of practical considerations, not of any inhospitality on the part of the owner.) I should have liked to make a full transcript, but in the event the most I could do was to read it aloud to my colleague Paul Edmondson, who kindly accompanied me, and to ask him to keyboard selected passages. This chapter is based on the notes taken on that occasion.

Made up of 98 closely written, unnumbered pages in a fine italic hand, probably scribal, the manuscript is a fair copy with a few corrections and alterations. Its title page, slightly damaged but skilfully repaired, reads '[The Model] of Poesy or the Art of Poesy drawn into a short or summary discourse', and it carries an unattributed epigraph of lines from the Prologue to Terence's play *Eunuchus*. An elaborately Ciceronian dedication to Sir Henry Lee identifies the author as 'Willm Scott' and his treatise as 'the first fruits of my study'. (Quotations from the manuscript here are given largely in modern spelling, partly for ease of reading, but also because it is not readily available for checking.)

Sir E. K. Chambers referred in passing to Scott's work in 1936 in

his biography of Lee, who lived from 1533 to 1611, and it is also
mentioned, by way of Chambers, in the entry on Scott in the *History
of Parliament*.[1] The owner first told me that he had found it in an
envelope of the early twentieth century marked 'Inland Revenue'.
Later however he discovered that the envelope actually emanated
from the Department of Education. Since this is where Chambers
worked for much of his life, it looks as if he actually handled the
manuscript but did not think it worthy of detailed examination, presumably because he thought it would tell him little about his object
of primary interest, Henry Lee.

Lee (whose portrait hangs in the National Portrait Gallery) was
Queen Elizabeth's first champion, an office which he occupied from
1559 to 1590 and which gave him the privilege of defending her
honour against all comers in an annual tournament held on her
birthday. He was also High Steward of New Woodstock. When, to
the Queen's regret, he retired as champion because of advancing
years, the occasion was commemorated by George Peele in the well-
known lines beginning 'His golden locks time hath to silver turned'.
Lee was a relative of Scott, who refers to himself as 'a sharer in
[Lee's] blood as well as in many his honourable favours'. Scott
was to witness Lee's will and to write the long and informative
eulogy once inscribed on Lee's monument in Quarrendon,
Buckinghamshire. Scott refers to Lee's achievements in the body of
the newly revealed work. Discussing emblems, for instance, he for-
bears to enlarge upon the subject 'especially before one so nobly
famous for his accomplished skill in feats of arms and chivalry . . .
in this age in which the sweet sunshine of our blessed peace, under
the happy reign of a most sacred majesty [i.e. Elizabeth] has gilded
so many wits that have brought forth so great plenty of devices of
this kind as for variety, subtlety and grace of invention they
deserved to be conveyed in fame's golden records to all posterity'.
(Sadly the device of this kind that we should most like to have been
conveyed in fame's golden records, the impresa composed by
Shakespeare for use by the Earl of Rutland in a tournament of 1613,
is lost to posterity.)

William Scott himself was born about 1579; we do not know how
long he lived after writing Lee's epitaph in 1611. Poetry was in his
blood: he was a great-grandson of the poet Sir Thomas Wyatt. He
entered the Inner Temple in June 1595 and represented New
Woodstock in Parliament in 1601. His treatise includes a number of

clues as to the date at which he wrote it, most significantly a reference to the Earl of Essex in the course of a discussion of poetic epithets: 'What honour, or rather dishonour, should I do to that famous general of the army of the most famous prince [i.e. Elizabeth], of whom one says he is the true image of the Achilleian virtues, to call him "swift-footed" Essex, though perhaps he can run as fast as Achilles could, except there be some occasion to use that particular active quality.' As Scott uses the present tense, this must have been written before Essex's execution, in 1601, and the epithet 'swift-footed' may have been directly suggested by Essex's 1599 journey from Dublin to London in the space of four days.

William Scott appears, like another of Lee's relatives, to have obtained a post in the Ordnance Office; at any rate, someone of the same name was a servant to the secretary of the Office, Sir John Davies, and gave evidence in the enquiry into the Essex rebellion on 10 February 1601.[2] Davies, described by Sir Robert Cecil as 'that traitor knave . . . a conjurer and Catholic, who in Oxford occupied himself in the idle art of figure casting', was deeply implicated in the rebellion, whereas Scott played only a minor part at his master's behest. By 1611 Scott was grand enough to send a man to Lee's funeral.

In the same collection as the manuscript of *The Model of Poesy* is an incomplete and damaged verse translation of the first and second days of the strongly Protestant poem by Guillaume de Salluste du Bartas (1544–90), *La Sepmaine; ou, Creation du monde* (1578) and the unfinished *La Seconde Sepmaine* (1584), dedicated 'to the worthy gentleman my very good uncle George Wyatt Esq.'. George Wyatt, a learned man, was the grandson of Sir Thomas Wyatt. In his dedication, Scott (still in his early twenties) describes the translation as having been written in his 'very young years' and revised in much haste, 'as only having one vacation to spend about it and my discourse of the Art of Poesy', 'as being besides [i.e. apart from] the main scope and bent of my necessary more fruitful studies'. In other words, this was no way to earn a living. The first instalment of Joshua Sylvester's translation of du Bartas's poem had appeared in 1595, but Scott's is an independent version, previously unknown. It is not, for example, mentioned in the list of translations given in Susan Snyder's Clarendon Press edition of Du Bartas.[3] A later instalment of Sylvester's translation includes a eulogy of Sir Henry Lee.

The scope and purpose of Scott's treatise is best defined in his own words:

> in our MODEL of POESY we must proceed (if we will proceed orderly) first to lay the foundation, to define it in general, which explained we may show by division how all several kinds of poetry, as the diverse rooms and offices are built thereon, how the general is dispensed into the particulars, how the particulars are sundered by their special differences and properties, that as walls keep them from confounding one in another, and lastly what dressing and furniture best suits every subdivided part and member, that thereby direction how to work in which of the kinds our nature shall inform us we are most apt for; and this is the period of discipline, and farthest scope, to assist and direct nature to work as being ordained to reduce man to his former state of moral and civil happiness, whence he is declined in that unhappy fall from his original understanding and righteousness.

The treatise is well organised and scholarly, highly derivative in its use of classical sources but also showing real independence of thought, and distinguished from many related works of the period by numerous references to contemporary English writers and their works, along with illustrations derived from everyday life. So for example Scott writes of having 'seen in some colleges . . . bringing up the boar's head at Christmas and in the inns of court some such thing'; and remarks that 'To add a light and loose epithet on to so grave a substantive were as seasonable as to set a pied feather on a minister's hat, which I confess I have seen and farther I confess how ridiculous the wearer was'.

Though Scott may have relied to some extent on secondary sources, he was unquestionably well read in both classical and vernacular writings. Indeed the depth of his learning at so early an age is a remarkable tribute to the rigours of the educational system available to young men in the Elizabethan period. His work abounds in allusions to 'those great fathers of science Plato and his scholar Aristotle', to Homer and Ovid, Virgil and Quintilian, Seneca, Terence and Plautus, and of course to the Bible. Closer to his own time he shows knowledge of Petrarch (translating part of one of his sonnets), of Chaucer and of Sir Thomas More's *Utopia*.

Unsurprisingly, if justly, Scott praises the work of his great-grandfather Sir Thomas Wyatt: none has bettered him 'for prose or verse of comparable sweetness and fullness, saving my Lord of Surrey, who hath written in this kind'. Scott is a great admirer of the works of Sir Philip Sidney, and his treatise forms a major contribution to the history of Sidney's reputation. He places *Arcadia*, as an 'absolute pattern of decorum', on a par with Virgil. He knows *Astrophil and Stella* and frequently cites the *Apology for Poetry*, published posthumously in 1595, only a few years before Scott was writing. He knows Heliodorus's *Aetheopica*, the popular Greek romance published in an English translation by Thomas Underdown in 1569 (?) etc., and Samuel Daniel's *Complaint of Rosamund* (1592) and *The Civil Wars between the Two Houses of Lancaster and York* (1595). A broader admiration for the arts, and an indication of Scott's willingness to think of his contemporaries in the same terms as the ancients, is shown by his laudatory mention of the great miniaturist Nicholas Hilliard (1547–1619): 'all painters', he says, 'may be said to labour to be like Apelles or Hilliard'. A degree of contempt, resembling Sidney's, for the popular drama may be indicated by his reference to 'our clowns, antikes or Giggs [*sic*] in plays; but I reckon these scum unworthy the countenance of poesy'.

Scott demonstrates independence of judgement in criticising the writings of some of his contemporaries. Spenser's 'Shepherd's Calendar', a kind of 'low comedy', 'imitates the ancients so well that I know not if he come behind any for apt invention; only for his affecting old words and phrases'. Scott is an acute critic of style, particularly good at close criticism. He has read with censorious care the Senecan tragedy *Gorboduc*, attributed on its first publication in 1565 to Thomas Norton and Thomas Sackville: 'Especially you must avoid repetition of the same conceit; as in that commended tragedy of *Gorboduc* you may in one leaf observe to the same person the story of Phaethon twice to be alluded unto, as if the world afforded no other example to show the unhappy success of rash aspiring; or as if it could be proved no other way but by example.'[4] Samuel Daniel is not above blame: 'Surely if Lucan be faulty for too lofty a proposition our Mr Daniel that treads in Lucan's steps even in this particular is not unreprovable.'

Perhaps of greatest interest to modern readers are a number of previously unrecorded allusions to the drama, and especially to Shakespeare. Scott never refers to him by name, but quotes directly from his writings. Here too he is not always unequivocally laudatory, offering the first known criticism of Shakespeare's versification in a reference to *The Rape of Lucrece*, first published in 1594: 'you must not have idle attributes only to fill up your metre (saith

Scaliger)'. And, objecting no doubt to the tautology in 'endless' and 'never-ending', he quotes line 935 of Shakespeare's poem, 'The endless date of never ending woe[s]', describing it as 'a very idle [*interlined* stuffed] verse in that very well-penned poem of Lucrece her rape'. Lines from *Richard II*, first published anonymously in 1597 but reprinted with Shakespeare's name on the title-page in the following year, come in for only qualified praise in a discussion of the commonest grace

> of our speeches and affections . . ., perspicuity – when our words are as it were thorough clear and transparent to convey the meaning or conceit to our understanding (as the object to our sense is carried by a convenient medium, as the school term is) which is by well-sorted usual words (as we showed before) and by fit and natural knitting of them, so as having no ambiguous or obscure phrase the reader proceeds without let or rub to understand what is delivered; the contrary to this may be seen in him that thus lays down ambiguously a good conceit:
>
> > That when the searchinge eye of heaven is hid
> > Behinde the globe that lightes the lower worlde
> >   (*Richard II*, 3.2.33–4)

This is faulty because 'One would take it by the placing his words that he should mean that the globe of the earth enlighteneth the lower hemisphere'. These comments are not merely the first examples of precise close criticism of Shakespeare's style; they are, if the *Shakspere Allusion Book* (Oxford, 1909; admittedly an out-of-date work) is anything to go by, unparalleled before 1700 at the earliest, even in the writings of John Dryden.[5] Even more interestingly, Scott's criticism anticipates an emendation first made by Sir Thomas Hanmer, in 1744, and accepted by many subsequent editors who, perceiving the logical incongruity noticed by Scott, attempt to remove it by emending 'that' in the final line to 'and'. It is however quite possible that this improves rather than corrects what Shakespeare wrote.

Elsewhere Scott is less equivocally admiring of *Richard II*. At one point he takes up words from the play into his own prose: 'besides there is much sweetness in the witty conceits, apt sentences, proper allusions and applications to be dispersed in your poem, like so many goodly plots of lilies and violets strewed all over the new-springing meadows'. This adapts words spoken by the Duchess of York: 'Where are the violets now / That strew the green lap of the new-come spring.' (5.2.46–7) And he refers again to the play in a comparison with Chaucer: 'Chaucer's *Canterbury Tales* (for aught I see) are to be counted with these [i.e. rustic poems, eclogues] and may be named of travellers or pilgrims, for the vulgar persons and for their manner is much after this. The gardener in like sort is with a passing good decorum brought on the stage in that well conceited tragedy of *Richard II*.'

At other points Scott finds the play useful as a source of illustrative quotations: 'Sometime the person shall be so plunged into the passion of sorrow that he will even forget his sorrow and seem to entertain his hardest fortune with dalliance and sport, as in the very well-penned Tragedy of Rich. the 2d is expressed in the King and the Queen whilst "They play the wantons with their woes."' This adapts Richard's words at 3.3.163, 'Or shall we play the wantons with our woes?' And a longer passage from the play comes in handy in a discussion of amplification:

> Sometime our amplification is by heaping our words, and as it were piling one phrase upon another of the same sense, to double and re-double our blows that by varying and re-iterating may work into the mind of the reader:
>
>> Shorten my dayes thou canst with sullen sorrowe,
>> And plucke nightes from me but not lende [me *struck through*] a
>>   morowe
>> Thou canst helpe tyme to furrowe me with age
>> But stoppe noe wrinkle in his pilgrimage;
>> Thy worde is currant with him for my death,
>> But deade, thy kingedome cannot buy my breath
>>
>> (1.3.220–5)

It is perhaps not surprising that Scott the literary theorist should have been attracted particularly to *Richard II*, one of the most literary of Shakespeare's plays, and one of the few written entirely in verse. But Scott's interest in the play takes on an added dimension in view of his declared interest in Essex, and of his probable, if minor, involvement in the Essex rebellion. We know that Richard's reign was seen by many of Elizabeth's subjects as an uncomfortable parallel to the political situation as her reign drew to a close. The belief that the play about the reign performed by the Lord Chamberlain's Men on the eve of the 1601 rebellion was Shakespeare's has been questioned, reasonably enough, in an article by Blair Worden.[6] But

Scott's references show at least that it was familiar to one of the men involved, if only in a small way, in the rising.

In spite of all the thought that he had expended on verse composition, no published works by Scott are known. This sketch of his previously unknown treatise is far from exhaustive of its multi-faceted interest to scholars of the literature and language of the period, or even of Shakespeare. It is a major addition to the considerable corpus of Elizabethan literary criticism, represented by writers such as Roger Ascham, Thomas Wilson, Stephen Gosson, William Webbe and George (or Richard) Puttenham, to name only some of those who had written before Scott. And it adds significantly to the story of Shakespeare's reputation: Scott may with justice be called Shakespeare's first serious critic. It is to be hoped that his work will soon enter the public domain and appear in a thoroughly annotated edition.[7]

Notes

This chapter is a revised version of 'By the Placing of His Words', *Times Literary Supplement*, 26 September 2003, pp. 14–15.

1 P. W. Hasler (ed.), *The House of Commons, 1558–1603* (London: Published for the History of Parliament Trust by H.M.S.O., 1981), vol. 3, pp. 358–9.

2 *Calendar of State Papers Domestic*, 1598–1601, p. 549.

3 See *The Divine Weeks and Works of Guillaume de Saluste Sieur de Bartas*, translated by Joshua Sylvester, ed. Susan Snyder, 2 vols (Oxford: Clarendon Press, 1979), vol. 1, pp. 70–1.

4 There are allusions to Phaethon on facing pages of the edition conjecturally dated 1570, reprinted by Scolar Press, sigs C1 verso and C2 recto.

5 Perhaps Ben Jonson comes closest in the comment in his *Timber, or Discoveries*, that 'Many times he [Shakespeare] fell into those things could not escape laughter, as when he said in the person of Caesar, one speaking to him, "Caesar, thou never didst wrong", he replied "Caesar never did wrong without just cause", and such like, which were ridiculous', in Ian Donaldson (ed.), *Ben Jonson*, The Oxford Authors (Oxford: Oxford University Press, 1985), p. 540. This may have been true of the play as first acted, but in the published text of 1623 Caesar says 'Caesar doth not wrong, nor without cause / Will he be satisfied' (3.1.47).

6 Blair Worden, 'Which Play Was Performed at the Globe Theatre on 7 February 1601?', *London Review of Books*, 25:13 (10 July 2003), pp. 22–4.

7 Since this chapter went to press the manuscript has been bought by the British Library. It is catalogued as *The Model of Poesy*, Additional MS 81083.

11

'Too long for a play': Shakespeare beyond page and stage

John Lyon

> *Ros.* I mean, what exactly do you *do*?
> *Player.* We keep to our usual stuff, more or less, only inside out. We do
> on stage the things that are supposed to happen off. Which is a
> kind of integrity, if you look on every exit being an entrance some-
> where else.
>
> Tom Stoppard[1]

One of the play's editors describes it as 'the greatest shock in
Shakespeare'.[2] The comedy of courtship that is *Love's Labour's Lost*
is drawing to a close when Mercadé enters with news of the death
of the French King, father of the play's principal female character.
Such untimely news, encroaching on the action from a world elsewhere, puts paid to the possible resolution of betrothals which the
play had seemed to promise as *Love's Labour's Lost* now goes on,
self-consciously, to tease and toy with ideas of closure and genre.
Instead of ending we have at best deferral:

> *Biron.* Our wooing doth not end like an old play.
>   Jack hath not Jill. These ladies' courtesy
>   Might well have made our sport a comedy.
> *King.* Come, sir, it wants a twelvemonth an' a day,
>   And then 'twill end.
> *Biron.* That's too long for a play.[3]

Critical attention to the reflexive or metadramatic in Shakespeare
has long been familiar to us. The seminal study of the phenomenon
by Anne Righter (or Barton) begins with an encomium to the
theatre, elaborating Hamlet's 'the play's the thing' into the idea that
[theatrical] illusion has 'power over reality'.[4] Yet manifestations
of the theatrical *within* Shakespeare's works typically disappoint,
seeming never to complete nor resolve. Perhaps this is part of a

rhetorical strategy designed to enhance, by contrast, the effective-
ness of the Shakespeare play in which these failed theatricals
momentarily appear. Perhaps it is a critique of unappreciative,
largely aristocratic, onstage audiences, the failures resting as much
with them as with the players. None the less the Pageant of the
Worthies is dismissed here in *Love's Labour's Lost* as unworthy; *The
Mousetrap*, a play uncertainly poised as a reflection of Denmark's
past or Denmark's future, aborts equivocally before, and receives
but a lukewarm reception from, its valued audience, Horatio; the
Mechanicals' performance proves an unintentionally comic fiasco,
leaving its audience with little taste for encores; and Prospero's
insubstantial pageant suddenly fades. Certainly Shakespeare's antitheatricality – if such it is – is a very different thing from that of Ben
Jonson, whose often expressed, textually defensive scorn and fear
of the theatre are testimony to *his* belief in theatre's power, a
power which Jonson typically sought to control and constrain.
Shakespeare, by contrast, seems more drawn to theatre's impotence.
At least twice in Shakespeare – in the Prologue to *Henry V* and at
the conclusion of *A Midsummer Night's Dream* – we are told that
true power resides in the imagination, in our 'imaginary forces',
forces which 'amend' the inadequate. In what follows I want to
come at a tangent to the current quarrel between Shakespeare on the
page and Shakespeare on the stage and to suggest that Shakespeare,
our largest author, is dominated by the before, after and elsewhere
as much as by the here-and-now, whether that here-and-now be theatrical or textual. The Shakespearean work is 'too long for a play',
whether play as text or play as performance, and extends beyond
both page and stage into the creative and critical imagination. In
other words, Shakespeare's imagination, though clearly affected by
the contingencies of both print and performance, is finally constrained by neither.

   Some specificity may be brought to that suggestion by way of an
initial examination of what Biron might mean when he declares
'That's too long for a play'. This idea, a kind of double-take which
becomes odder the more one ponders it, is simultaneously and self-
evidently true and false: no play – not even Wagner's music dramas –
can endure for anything approaching 'a twelvemonth and a day' yet
many plays, and pre-eminently Shakespeare's, can easily accommodate the passing of such a time and of times much longer. In the case
for Shakespeare as a literary dramatist, argument has focused on the

first, more extrinsic and theatrical sense of what it means for a play to be over-length. Thus Lukas Erne devotes the second part of *Shakespeare as Literary Dramatist* to the perceived 'wide gap' between performing time and the length of surviving Shakespearean texts. He argues that the lengthy quartos were intended to be read rather than performed and that texts were habitually abridged radically for the stage. In mounting such an argument Erne complicates current orthodoxies regarding Shakespeare as reviser, puts in question recent editorial practice, centred on theatrical performance and stage history, and undermines an important premise of most stage-centred criticism, that Shakespeare wrote solely for the stage and had no interest in print.[5]

By contrast my interest lies in what it might mean for a play to be 'too long' in the second, more intrinsic sense. The neoclassicist Ben Jonson adheres to what he calls the 'needful rule[s]'[6] regarding the unities of place and time. Thus *The Alchemist* confines itself to one day and one house in Blackfriars and attempts to elide any imaginative gap between theatrical and extratheatrical place and time: Jonson's focus is on the present in all senses. In *The Alchemist* whatever is needful to our understanding but extraneous to that time and place – the fact of and reason for the master Lovewit's absence and the circumstances of Face and Subtle's meeting, for example – are concisely and conclusively delivered to us. The play then derives much of its comic power from there being so little time and there being nowhere else to hide so that the dupers face, at every minute, inadvertent encounters in this one small, inescapable place, encounters which will explode their plot. A reading which looks beyond the defined and confined Jonsonian plot would thus be very odd: in *Volpone*, for example, to look beyond the conservative Jonson's satirical point in suggesting that the dwarf, eunuch and hermaphrodite are Volpone's own 'abnormal' children and to enquire about the circumstances, long past, in which Volpone got such children would be a misreading – indeed a Shakespearean reading. Contrariwise, Shakespeare's *The Comedy of Errors* appears exceptional in the Shakespearean canon, Jonsonian in the way that, after a lengthy and coherent initial narration contextualising the play's events, the play fulfils the unities of place and time. Yet it also outrages Jonsonian verisimilitude by its Shakespearean excess, affording us not one but two sets of twins in despite of Jonson's belief that 'he [Jonson] could never find two so like others that he could persuade the spectators they were one';[7] and Egeon's initial narration of events long past opens that characteristic Shakespearean 'wide gap', weighs the action with an emotional burden and transforms a light comedy of mistakings and misunderstanding into a play which, at its close, is intense and moving in ways comparable to the endings of Shakespeare's late plays. Hence *The Comedy of Errors* is less exceptional than it appears and sits quite comfortably with the Shakespeare who typically has no need of those unities of place and time so 'needful' to Jonson.

It would be tedious to rehearse here all the various diversities of place and of timespan covered by Shakespeare's plays, but it is astonishing how early in his career, in *Love's Labour's Lost*, Shakespeare is toying with the possibility of taking such freedom to excess to produce works that are 'too long for a play'. *Antony and Cleopatra*, which ranges over the then known world, and *The Winter's Tale*, with its 'wide gap' of sixteen years, are but extreme examples of a tendency throughout Shakespeare to make works out of a gathering of elsewheres, befores, afterwards, gaps and absences – 'absences' here understood in the straightforward sense rather than in any specifically post-structuralist or postmodern way. Reading Shakespeare or watching him performed we encounter the presence of a series of tips of icebergs. The works imply worlds, times, events and characters which are largely unseen and unwritten, and Shakespeare is an especially large author in that the relative proportions of, on the one hand, the comparatively few actions and events presented or even merely described and, on the other, the plethora of actions and events simply implied are especially extreme.

One mundane example, less geographically extreme than *Antony* and less chronologically stretching than *Winter's Tale*, must do here. A good critic and editor, R. A. Foakes, is setting up a distinction between *Hamlet* and *King Lear*. *Hamlet*, he tells us, is a play 'obsessed with memory, but there is no memory in *King Lear*, except of vague injustices and neglect of the poor. Lear has no history in spite of his great age . . . the past is a blank, and the present is all that matters.'[8] We can allow Foakes's distinction between the plays to stand provided we think in broad terms. Certainly much of the past of *King Lear* is a blank to be 'discovered' only by the resisting reader: here one thinks pre-eminently of the notoriously absent mother which concerns recent political and psychoanalytic criticism, a mother to be found in the play only as metaphor, if at all. Yet when we begin to attend to the particulars of the play, *King Lear* does call our attention to a past, albeit a more immediate past, and a past which complicates our responses to the immediate present enacted before us. The past is overtly there in the play's opening lines:

> *Kent.* I thought the King had more affected the Duke of Albany than Cornwall.
> *Gloucester.* It did always seem so to us, but now in the division of the kingdom it appears not which of the Dukes he values most . . .
> (*The Tragedy of King Lear*, 1.1.1–5)

Even when we think in terms of Shakespearean proportions, 'always' is hyperbolic, but this opening sketches in a past and a sudden great change from that past which must press on the reactions of those involved to Lear's subsequent actions. Edmund too is revealed to have a past – 'He hath been out nine years, and away he shall again' (1.1.31–2) – a past which, for example, Tate's simplifying Restoration redaction of the play, introducing the Bastard fixed in soliloquy at his play's opening, works to obliterate. Cordelia too is involved in past actions and is the object of concern of another scene, a scene of rivalry, playing itself offstage as the division of the kingdom unfolds before us: Lear tells Gloucester to 'Attend the lords of France and Burgundy' at line 34 in the Oxford text and tells us a few lines later that these two have 'Long [too long?] in our court . . . made their amorous sojourn'; Cordelia refers again obliquely but insistently to the offstage presence of France and Burgundy in asking 'Why have my sisters husbands if they say / They love you all? Haply when I shall wed / That lord whose hand must take my plight shall carry / Half my love with him, half my care and duty. / Sure, I shall never marry like my sisters, / To love my father all';[9] Lear calls for France and Burgundy at line 126; their appearance onstage is announced at line 187. We think of the first scene of *Lear* as the division of the kingdom but it might just as easily be the betrothal of Cordelia: these two actions, related though distinct, slip on and off stage, in and out of the text, and press on one another in complicating ways. Moreover, if we do think of this scene as the betrothal of Cordelia then we notice it is a scene intent on determining Cordelia's dowry in advance, and perhaps even as a precondition of her marriage. Thus we notice too a distinction, a division, between the circumstances of the youngest daughter and the circumstances of her long-married sisters – and their husbands. These couples have, it seems, waited long with the uncertainties of which husband Lear has 'more affected', uncertainties which are only now being resolved: Cordelia, in saying she 'shall never marry like my sisters', is right in a sense she does not intend since she shall never marry, as her sisters had done, in a state of uncertainty over dowry and inheritance. In *King Lear* the past is far from the 'blank' which R. A. Foakes describes, and past matters weigh heavily in the present.

Tom Stoppard's *Rosencrantz and Guildenstern Are Dead* is a play which suffers under the shadow of Samuel Beckett, its routines too obviously derivative, the relationship between its two principal characters sentimentalised and domesticated, its philosophising homespun. The true wit of Stoppard's play, however, lies in its making explicit its location in the spaces opened up by the gaps in the Shakespearean text: Stoppard's note thus records that 'The action takes place within and around the action of *Hamlet*', and Stoppard's Player, insisting on the integrity of his dramatic practice, 'every exit being an entrance somewhere else',[10] recognises that life and Shakespeare alike are always *in media res*. In this play Stoppard's relation to Shakespeare is explicit but typical rather than exceptional: to risk a claim of Bloomian proportions, the history of literature in English after Shakespeare is to a large extent the history of Shakespeare's reception in subsequent writers' creative imaginations.

The truth of the claim that the Shakespearean work exceeds its realisation on stage or page is borne out by the ways in which so many critics, of diverse critical persuasions and approaches, repeatedly are drawn to remark on the fact. Two monographs are devoted to this issue. Anthony Brennan's *Onstage and Offstage Worlds in Shakespeare* (1989) is an impressive accumulation of evidence from every Shakespearean genre. However, Brennan is a committed stage-centred critic and his analysis often disappoints, offering too many explanations of absences from the stage in terms of the need to give the actors a rest: Brennan's assumption that actors welcome cuts in their parts is questionable at least.[11] Francis Berry's earlier *The Shakespeare Inset* (1965), a finer if more idiosyncratic study of narrative moments set within the dramatic action, reveals how readily we read into Shakespearean gaps and absences the concerns of our own times: considering the narrative of Hamlet's appearance in Ophelia's closet, for example, Berry is influenced by the cinema and television to argue that 'Wordless "close-ups" were impossible on the Elizabethan stage, but Shakespeare, by means of Ophelia's narration, enables the audience to possess a "close-up" view of Hamlet's gestures and demeanour'.[12]

When we move back to the nineteenth century we find the Victorian actress Helena Faucit considering the final act of *The Winter's Tale*: 'It is here the first hint is given that Hermione is still alive. How this could be, and how the secret could have been so well kept, Shakespeare gives no hint. One is thus driven to work out the problem for one's self.'[13] And, with a lack of caution which many would presently deem naive, Faucit indeed proceeds to do so. Yet a more sophisticated and self-aware critic, E. A. J. Honigmann, considering in particular Hamlet's relation with Ophelia, argues:

> Having heard that Hamlet importuned Ophelia with love, gave her remembrances and so on, spectators need not, after all, apologise if they catch themselves wondering about the couple's previous relations, as Shakespeare himself directs attention to the past *inside the play*. Unlicensed speculation would be futile, but, on the other hand, to refuse to take account of what is inside the play seems no less irresponsible. [Honigmann's italics][14]

More recently still, Michael D. Bristol has written in defence of 'Vernacular Criticism and the Scenes Shakespeare Never Wrote'. Bristol rejects the before and after, limiting himself to 'scenes that happen during the course of the narrative action, but which are not performed on stage so that we don't see what the characters are doing or hear what they are saying'.[15] Yet Bristol may be at once too tentative and too confident of what constitutes 'the course of the narrative action', too sure of when it begins and when it ends: by contrast Shakespeare's plays typically work to erode our sense both of any fresh start and of any completion or closure. Moreover, if Bristol's self-denying ordinance were observed in the case of *The Tempest*, limiting ourselves to 'the course of the narrative action', then it would prove exceptionally difficult to say anything intelligible about that play.

Theoretically inflected criticism also registers its sense of absences from stage and page. Writing on the deconstruction of presence in *The Winter's Tale*, Howard Felperin notes the tendency of the Shakespearean text to make reference to what he terms 'prior or off-stage or, in the most general terms, unrepresented action'.[16] Celia R. Daileader begins her study entitled – with a somewhat misleading preposition – *Eroticism on the Renaissance Stage* with the rhetorical flourish: 'The trouble began when I noticed a hole in a text.'[17] Daileader then goes on to find in such holes, absences and spaces the Renaissance's treatment of female sexuality and of divinity, particularly in (or not in) the plays of Middleton and Shakespeare. Taking his cue from Daileader, Gary Taylor, in a contribution to the argument for Shakespeare's Catholicism, also discusses the divine in Shakespeare and challenges any sharp distinction between the present and the absent: divinity in Shakespeare, like the voice from the burning bush which Moses heard, 'is not simply absent, or simply present, but almost present, or present in some ways and absent in others'.[18] Taylor's example usefully illustrates how the boundaries between different categories discussed in this chapter – offstage, onstage, enacted action, reported action, implied and inferred action, beginnings, endings – become, on inspection, less and less distinct.

Shakespeare's imaginative reach exceeds his grasp and his plays reveal a rhythm of complication and containment, continually reaching out to take in yet more complex material so that the plays characteristically suggest possibilities, times, events and actions beyond those fully realised, whether on page or stage. Shakespeare's works ask us to be mindful of the gaps of which they are made, but should we attempt to fill those gaps? And if so, how? Readers and actors are at one in attempting to reclaim what is withheld from them. Shakespeare, it seems, kept some of his best scenes offstage. The death of Falstaff is an extreme example, not merely offstage, but indeed beyond the play in which we hear of it; the reunion of Leontes and Perdita, Cleopatra's encounter with Caesar, the murder of Duncan, Oliver's conversion are others. The following example of theatre's reclaiming of such offstage scenes is a quirky novelistic one, but telling none the less. It comes from Charles Dickens, who rarely goes to the theatre in his writings without some unsympathetic comedy directed against theatrical doubling. It is a joke of which he never tires, the novel, especially his novels, being capable of a seemingly never-ending profusion of new characters which, by contrast, proves difficult to match on stage because of the constraints of the professional theatre. Dickens conveniently forgets, of course, that Shakespeare can proliferate characters offstage – Claribel, the King of Tunis and Sycorax in (or not in) *The Tempest*; Yorick and the pirates; Marcus Luccicos. And Dickens's incessant joke betrays an anxious rivalry: near the end of his life Dickens took on the theatre more directly, in a series of readings, himself playing *all* the parts, an undertaking which hastened his death.

The Dickensian comedy of doubling is much in evidence when in *Great Expectations* Pip goes to see a performance of *Hamlet*:

> The noble boy in the ancestral boots, was inconsistent; representing himself, as it were in one breath, as an able seaman, a strolling actor, a gravedigger, a clergyman, and a person of the utmost importance at a Court-fencing match . . . This gradually led to a want of toleration for him, and even – on his being detected in holy orders, and declining to perform the funeral service – to the general indignation taking the form of nuts.[19]

But there are other oddities in this theatrical performance and an audience all too willing to help Mr Wopsle fill in the gaps in his rendition of Hamlet:

> Whenever that undecided Prince had to ask a question or state a doubt, the public helped him out with it. As for example; on the question whether 'twas nobler in the mind to suffer, some roared yes, and some no, and some inclining to both opinions said 'toss up for it;' and quite a Debating Society arose. When he asked what should such fellows as he do crawling between earth and heaven, he was encouraged with loud cries of 'Hear, hear!' When he appeared with his stocking disordered (its disorder expressed, according to usage, by one very neat fold in the top which I suppose to be always got up with a flat iron), a conversation took place in the gallery respecting the paleness of his leg, and whether it was occasioned by the turn the ghost had given him.[20]

Here we have an audience out of a stage-centred critic's worst nightmare, an audience paradoxically of careful readers who *do* produce, in the words of Harry Berger, Jr, voicing the New Histrionicists' case, 'commentary on minute details no theater audience could be expected to unpack without stopping the play and starting an inhouse seminar'.[21] But what is Mr Wopsle doing on stage as Hamlet 'with his stocking disordered'? Certainly Dickens, intent on deflating the great expectations of aristocratic tragedy, has transformed Mr Wopsle as Hamlet into Mr Wopsle as Malvolio, a love-sick Malvolio whose amatory disorder is neatly, prissily expressed by 'his stocking disordered (its disorder expressed, according to usage, by one very neat fold in the top . . .)'. Note Dickens's 'according to usage' however. Fictional though he is, Mr Wopsle is not exceptional but part of an otherwise real, long and (dis)honourable theatrical tradition which presents Hamlet's encounter with Ophelia in her chamber *onstage*, typically in dumb show. The scene, it seems, is too good a theatrical opportunity for thespians to miss. Yet, in the text, the scene is emphatically offstage, described by Ophelia in what we have already seen Frances Berry call, long ago, a Shakespearean Inset. (And hence it is appropriate that this scene should be enacted onstage in the 'inside out' world of Stoppard's *Rosencrantz and Guildenstern Are Dead*.)

Ophelia, unlike both her father and Mr Wopsle, refuses to interpret Hamlet's peculiar behaviour. Careful readers can ask many contradictory questions about that behaviour. Does Hamlet's sartorial disarray signify, according to convention, the unrequited lover? Or does the disarray, his stockings not merely disordered but 'fouled', suggest not the love-sick but the sick, the mentally sick? Is such madness real or feigned? Is Hamlet taking a fond leave of Ophelia? Or is this an angry rejection? Is it a farewell at all? And, for a moment thinking metadramatically and in theatrical time, is this the behaviour ('his knees knocking') of a man who has just seen a ghost? Bringing the scene onstage simplifies and impoverishes it, but Mr Wopsle's audience will have none of such simplification, recouping, despite Mr Wopsle's theatrical efforts, some of the scene's readerly complexity: 'When he appeared with his stocking disordered (its disorder expressed, according to usage, by one very neat fold in the top . . .), a conversation took place in the gallery respecting the paleness of his leg, and whether it was occasioned by the turn the ghost had given him.'

In the brief but fascinating final chapter of *Shakespeare as Literary Dramatist*, Lukas Erne has shown how abridging the Shakespearean text for the stage involves simplification of Shakespeare in print. Shakespeare aimed not only for the audience but for the reader. Citing Walter Ong, Erne relates this to a shift from orality to literacy, from oral performance to literary print, and, in terms of character, from 'flat' to 'round'.[22] Thus Shakespeare's move into print is part of a culturally and historically contingent move towards the fullness of the novel and invites a return, in Shakespearean studies, of character criticism in the manner of A. C. Bradley. To this one may offer a qualified welcome. Certainly Erne does damage to the old objection that in thinking of Shakespeare as a novelist one is thinking ahistorically and retroactively. But character criticism too, like stage performance, may diminish the Shakespearean text if it merely allows readers to reclaim too confidently what the gaps in the Shakespearean text withhold from them. Certainly the novelists are Shakespeare's heirs in so far as they are entering the wide gaps of before, after and elsewhere which Shakespeare's large imagination has opened up. In so far as the novel enters such gaps interrogatively it is profoundly Shakespearean. More usually, however, its engagement is expansive and explanatory and, as such, the anti-Shakespeareanism of an ungrateful child, trifling with terrors, making the mysterious modern and familiar and ensconcing itself into a seeming knowledge. A particularly sorry recent example is *A Thousand Acres*, Jane Smiley's modish novelisation of *King Lear* published in 1991 (which is not to say, of course, that child abuse, Smiley's 'explanation' of the chaos that afflicts the Lear family, is itself a trifling matter). In contrast, as the philosopher Hans-Georg Gadamer has it, 'Only a person who has questions can have knowledge',[23] and Shakespearean criticism is at its most adequate, its most Shakespearean, when it conducts itself in interrogative mode. It is no accident that Shakespeare's finest critics over the past few decades are those who have described Shakespeare's scepticism, perspectivism or pluralism.

The potent myth of *The Tempest* as Shakespeare's last play has long been disabled but this late, if not last, play shows how little Shakespeare is interested in explanation or in closing the gaps. Or, as Louis MacNeice puts it, here Shakespeare is 'hardly bothering / To be a dramatist'.[24] It may be by mere chance that the early text of *The Tempest* which we have is remarkably short, only 2015 lines, but, whether on page or on stage, *The Tempest* is barely there at all, yet, in respect of the pasts, 'the dark backward and abyss of time' (1.2.50), the futures and the elsewheres it implies, it is a truly large work. *The Tempest* begins in what, for other plays, would be Act 5. It does not end: the text affords no warrant for the breaking of staff and drowning of book we see in many productions and Ariel's freedom remains just around the corner. The story, such as it is, is to be retold in Prospero's 'poor cell' before the magician guarantees 'calm seas, auspicious gales' for the return to Naples. Ellipsis is the very texture of the play, as seen in Prospero's initial partial and disjointed narrative, a marked contrast to Egeon's lucid exposition at the outset of *The Comedy of Errors*. Yet, like *The Comedy of Errors*, *The Tempest* observes the 'needful rules' of place and time or, rather, it baffles such laws: set on a Mediterranean island just off the coast of America, the play's present, its duration coextensive with its playing time in the theatre, is none the less overwhelmed by past actions and actions yet to come, 'looking before and after'. With the *coup de théâtre* of its realistic shipwreck, as with the coming to life of a statue in *The Winter's Tale*, each great theatrical moment revealed in retrospect to be a non-event, *The Tempest* mocks the theatre's (and the text's) here-and-now and their claim to authenticity.

We are seeing the return of Shakespeare the author. But what is an author? Common sense suggests that this is the agency which puts meaning into a literary work, but Foucault sees the author as keeping meaning out, and defines the author as 'the principle of thrift in the proliferation of meaning'.[25] Such a definition might seem to sit comfortably with, for example, Ben Jonson, who hedges his printed work around with prefatory materials which suggest that he fears theatrical realisation as embellishment and distortion, and who ensures that his writing is anything but 'loose' or in need of stop-gaps.[26] Or with Samuel Beckett, another dramatic author with a complex relation to the theatre and a miminalist, ever resistant to interpretative embellishment, whose characters worry 'We're not beginning to . . . to . . . mean something?'[27] By contrast the Shakespearean author seems bafflingly profligate or indeed excessive, a characteristic which Frank Kermode has described as Shakespeare's patience before his interpreters.[28] Certainly it is an odd position to argue for the realisation of the Shakespearean text or script, whether that realisation be on stage and or in critical expla-nation, when that realisation entails diminution. Such diminution accords with the long history of Shakespeare's readers' dissatisfac-tion with Shakespeare onstage, a dissatisfaction too often and too diversely expressed to be dismissed as unthinking antitheatrical prej-udice. Indeed such dissatisfaction may accord with the dissatisfac-tion of a literary author who himself always knew his works were 'too long for a play'.

Notes

1 Tom Stoppard, *Rosencrantz and Guildenstern Are Dead* (London: Faber, 1967), p. 19.
2 John Kerrigan, 'Introduction' to *Love's Labour's Lost* (Harmondsworth: Penguin, 1982), p. 20.

3 William Shakespeare, *Love's Labour's Lost*, in *The Complete Works*, ed. Stanley Wells and Gary Taylor (Oxford: Clarendon Press, 1988), 5.2.860–4. All quotations from Shakespeare are from this edition and subsequent references are given in the body of the text.
4 Anne Righter, *Shakespeare and the Idea of the Play* (London: Chatto and Windus, 1962), p. 13.
5 Lukas Erne, *Shakespeare as Literary Dramatist* (Cambridge: Cambridge University Press, 2003), pp. 131–244.
6 Ben Jonson, Prologue to *Volpone*, in Ian Donaldson (ed.), *Ben Jonson*, The Oxford Authors (Oxford: Oxford University Press, 1985), p. 7.
7 Ben Jonson, 'Conversations with William Drummond of Hawthornden', *Ben Jonson*, p. 604.
8 R. A. Foakes, *Hamlet versus Lear: Cultural Politics and Shakespeare's Art* (Cambridge: Cambridge University Press, 1993), p. 181.
9 The text quoted here is that of *The History of King Lear*, based on the quarto, 1.1.91–6. The final half line is omitted in the Folio version.
10 Stoppard, *Rosencrantz*, note following cast list, p. 19.
11 Anthony Brennan, *Onstage and Offstage Worlds in Shakespeare's Plays* (London: Routledge, 1989).
12 Francis Berry, *The Shakespeare Inset: Word and Picture* (London: Routledge and Kegan Paul, 1965), pp. 8–9.
13 Helena Faucit, Lady Martin, *On Some of Shakespeare's Female Characters*, 5th edn (Edinburgh, 1893), p. 383.
14 E. A. J. Honigmann, *Shakespeare: Seven Tragedies – The Dramatist's Manipulation of Response* (London: Macmillan, 1976), p. 6.
15 Michael D. Bristol, 'Vernacular Criticism and the Scenes Shakespeare Never Wrote', *Shakespeare Survey*, 53 (2000), 89–102 (p. 96).
16 Howard Felperin, '"Tongue-tied our queen?": The Deconstruction of Presence in *The Winter's Tale*', in Patricia Parker and Geoffrey Hartman (eds), *Shakespeare and the Question of Theory* (New York and London: Methuen, 1985), pp. 3–18 (p. 4).
17 Celia R. Daileader, *Eroticism on the Renaissance Stage: Transcendence, Desire, and the Limits of the Visible* (Cambridge: Cambridge University Press, 1998), p. 1.
18 Gary Taylor, 'Divine [ ]sences', *Shakespeare Survey*, 54 (2001), 13–30 (p. 30). I am grateful to Gary Taylor for bringing Daileader's study and his own article to my attention.
19 Charles Dickens, *Great Expectations*, ed. Charlotte Mitchell (Harmondsworth: Penguin, 1996), p. 254.
20 Dickens, *Great Expectations*, p. 254.
21 Harry Berger, Jr, *Imaginary Audition: Shakespeare on Stage and Page* (Berkeley and Los Angeles: University of California Press, 1989), p. xi.

22 Erne, *Shakespeare as Literary Dramatist*, pp. 220–44.

23 Hans-Georg Gadamer, *Truth and Method*, 2nd edn (London: Sheed and Ward, 1979), p. 328.

24 Louis MacNeice, 'Autolycus', in *Selected Poems*, ed. Michael Longley (London: Faber and Faber, 1988), p. 115.

25 Michel Foucault, 'What Is an Author?' in Josué V. Harari (ed.), *Textual Strategies: Perspectives in Post-structuralist Criticism* (London: Methuen, 1980), pp. 141–60 (p. 159).

26 'Nor hales he in a gull, old ends reciting, / To stop gaps in his loose writing' (Ben Jonson, Prologue to *Volpone*, in *Ben Jonson*, p. 7).

27 Samuel Beckett, *Endgame*, in *The Complete Dramatic Works* (London: Faber and Faber, 1990), p. 108.

28 Frank Kermode, 'The Patience of Shakespeare', in *Shakespeare, Spenser, Donne: Renaissance Essays* (London: Routledge and Kegan Paul, 1971), pp. 149–63.

Afterword

Lukas Erne

'*Shakespeare's Book*'. The evocative title of this collection raises the question of when and where Shakespeare first encountered a book that was clearly marked as his, with his name on the title-page: Shakespeare's book. The title-pages of the narrative poems, *Venus and Adonis* (1593) and *The Rape of Lucrece* (1594), contained no authorship attribution, nor did his earliest playbooks.[1] But when *Richard II*, *Richard III* and *Love's Labour's Lost* were reprinted in 1598, they all mentioned his name. Did Shakespeare find out about his title-page appearance through Andrew Wise, the publisher of *Richard II*, *Richard III*, *1 Henry IV* and *Much Ado about Nothing*, with whom the Lord Chamberlain's Men (including their in-house playwright?) must have had direct dealings? Or did he discover the book, *his* book, when browsing the bookstalls in St Paul's Churchyard, some time in 1598? What other books did Shakespeare read that year? Perhaps Sir John Harington's translation of Ariosto's *Orlando Furioso* and Edmund Spenser's *Faerie Queene*, two likely sources of *Much Ado about Nothing*, which Shakespeare seems to have written that year. Quite possibly Holinshed's *Chronicles*, in preparation for *Henry V*, written the following year.[2] Probably many more, considering that Shakespeare is known to have been an avid reader.[3] After all these other books, here was his book, Shakespeare's book. Did he buy a copy, or several, and offer them to friends and acquaintances in London and Stratford? Or did he receive a few copies from the publisher? Did he read the book? And how did Shakespeare feel about seeing his name on the title-page? 'What's in a name'? Was Shakespeare reminded of sonnets he might recently have written: 'And yet to times in hope my verse shall stand' (60.13); 'Not marble, nor the gilded monuments / Of princes shall outlive this powerful rhyme' (55.1–2)?

Given our limited knowledge of Shakespeare's life, it is unsurprising that there are no definitive answers to these questions. Yet this book suggests that the time may have come to raise them. So do recent publications, which indicate that Shakespeare, at the turn of the century, was concerned about his authorial reputation: he emerges as competitive and self-consciously literary from James Bednarz's examination of his involvement in the Poets' War.[4] MacD. P. Jackson argues that he wrote the Rival Poet sonnets in c. 1598–1600 out of 'a general sense of rivalry fuelled by Francis Meres's [*Palladis Tamia*]', adding that Shakespeare must have 'read attentively' Meres's 'glib inventory of England's top poets and playwrights', including Shakespeare.[5] What this suggests is that Shakespeare was a man of books as well as a man of the theatre, who not only read and owned books but witnessed and was receptive to how his own texts were published in book format in the course of his lifetime, not just a few of them but a great many: 45 editions of plays and 15 of poetry – a total of 60 editions between 1593 and 1616.[6] During the same period, Edmund Spenser's writings received no more than eleven editions, and Philip Sidney's eight.[7] It has too often been lost from sight that Shakespeare had an astounding bibliographical presence in London during his own lifetime.

There is little hope of recovering what exactly he made of that presence, but it is of some importance to remember that he knew about it, that it must have mattered to him, and that he may well have responded to it in his writings. Important evidence that Shakespeare cared not only about the theatre but about both theatrical and bibliographical culture, the page and the stage, as well as their conjunction, can be found in Shakespeare's plays, as several contributors to this book demonstrate. It has long been clear that Shakespeare's writings show considerable self-reflexivity, but the form this self-reflexivity takes according to past criticism is chiefly that of metadrama. Retrospectively, it is striking how the insistence on Shakespearean metadrama in the second half of the twentieth century went hand in hand with the rise of performance criticism. John Russell Brown's *Shakespeare's Plays in Performance* was published in 1966, *Shakespeare's Stagecraft*, by J. L. Styan, the year after, and by 1977 Styan – in his manifesto of Shakespeare performance criticism – was proclaiming *The Shakespeare Revolution*.[8] While Anne Righter's *Shakespeare and the Idea of the Play* (1962) had slightly preceded these publications, many other studies followed while performance criticism was establishing itself: James L. Calderwood's three monographs, *Shakespearean Metadrama* (1971), *Metadrama in Shakespeare's Henriad* (1979) and *To Be and Not to Be: Negation and Metadrama in 'Hamlet'* (1983), Jackson I. Cope's *The Theatre and the Dream: From Metaphor to Form in Renaissance Drama* (1973), Robert Egan's *Drama within Drama: Shakespeare's Sense of His Art in 'King Lear', 'The Winter's Tale', and 'The Tempest'* (1975), Thomas F. Van Laan's *Role-Playing in Shakespeare* (1978) and Sidney Homan's *When the Theatre Turns to Itself: The Aesthetic Metaphor in Shakespeare* (1981).[9] By 1986, the field had gained such proportion that Richard Fly was publishing an overview of critical work on Shakespearean metadrama.[10] The emphasis on Shakespeare's plays as plays for performance may well have been related to criticism that considered the plays to be *about* performance.

The current reassessment of Shakespeare's authorial standing, to which this book contributes, suggests that the past critical focus on metatheatricality largely blended out an important part of Shakespeare's artistic self-reflexivity: to quote from three chapters to this collection, Shakespeare's plays combine 'a discourse of the book and a discourse of the theatre' (Cheney, p. 31); the 'works themselves explore the relationship between text and performance' (Meek, p. 97); they show that Shakespeare was 'an engaged member of a textual culture hovering on the boundary of print and orality' (Smith, p. 60). In other words, while many of Shakespeare's plays are certainly metadramatic, they are also metatextual and metabibliographical, dramatic texts published as play-books which are recurrently concerned – at times almost obsessively concerned – with texts and books. It seems difficult to resist this conclusion in the light of not only the evidence presented in this book but also three important recent monographs: Patrick Cheney's *Shakespeare, National Poet-Playwright* (2004) and *Shakespeare's Literary Authorship* (2008), and Charlotte Scott's *Shakespeare and the Idea of the Book* (2007).[11] Shakespeare's writings register a sustained preoccupation with the oral medium in which the plays found their theatrical realisation in fleeting moments of performance as well as with the literate medium which has assured Shakespeare's immortality: the book.

Past resistance to such a view is exemplified by the editorial history of Sonnet 23 in which the speaker, who compares himself to 'an unperfect actor on the stage', is unable to express his love in speech, but affirms that his true eloquence is apparent in his books: 'O let my books be then the eloquence'. Starting in the early eighteenth century, editors regularly changed 'books' to 'looks', despite the unambiguous evidence in the 1609 quarto. Stephen Booth is surely right in arguing that 'books' needs no emendation and that, given the theatrical context of the opening lines, that Shakespeare may well be thinking of play-books.[12] Significantly, as Helen Smith shows above, when an eminent scholar did register Shakespeare's preoccupation with not only the stage but also the scripted and printed page, as Jonas Barish did in 1991, he considered it a 'paradox' that Shakespeare, 'so notoriously indifferent to the printing of his plays', should, in his plays, be 'so endlessly and inventively preoccupied with written communication of all kinds'.[13] Recent work suggesting that Shakespeare was not as uninterested in the publication of his plays as we had been made to assume, to which my *Shakespeare as Literary Dramatist* contributed, indicate that Barish's paradox is more apparent than real. Once we dismantle the time-honoured myth of a Shakespeare warbling 'his native woodnotes wild', growing 'immortal in his own despight',[14] indifferent to publication, literary fame and posterity, we are able to see that there is no contradition between Shakespeare's interest in texts and books in the fiction of his plays and poems on the one hand, and his interest in the publication and readerly reception of his writings on the other.

This does not mean that Shakespeare was as visibly and aggressively protective of his published writings and authorial persona as Ben Jonson was. As Jane Rickard's contribution to this book helps us see, the real opposition between Shakespeare and Jonson was not between an author invested in the publication of his plays and a playwright indifferent to it. Rather, the difference seems to have resided in their different degrees of possessiveness. In contrast to Jonson, Shakespeare, in keeping with almost all the other playwrights of the time, did not oversee the printing of any of his playtexts, nor did he provide them with an epistle or dedication. Jonson did what he could to inscribe his keenly possessive authorship into his publications; Shakespeare did not, but entrusted them to the care of his publishers and readers, without ensuring, as Ernst Honigmann's chapter suggests, that 'false starts' were not left imperfectly deleted in his manuscripts. Whereas Jonson mistrusted his readers and tried to shape the reception of his texts as best he could,

Shakespeare did not. Rather, as Rickard puts it, for Shakespeare 'the relationship between texts and their readers was a source not of anxiety but of creative potential' (p. 222), a point which may find support in the choice of titles like *As You Like It* and *Twelfth Night, or What You Will*. Patrick Cheney has identified in Shakespeare a self-effacing authorship which he terms 'counter-laureate', in contrast to the self-advertising laureate authorship of Jonson and Edmund Spenser, a form of authorship which Cheney finds in the fiction Shakespeare's writings, but which also applies remarkably well to what we can gather about Shakespeare's authorial persona.[15]

Cheney rightly insists that a full account of Shakespeare's authorial status needs to take account of not only the plays but also the poems, and terms Shakespeare a 'literary poet-playwright' (p. 31). By recalling the place occupied by the poems in Shakespeare's writings, we realise that his career took a decisive turn after the closure of the theatres in 1593 and 1594 occasioned by the plague. During the plague break, Shakespeare wrote the two narrative poems, *Venus and Adonis* and *The Rape of Lucrece*; after the plague break, Shakespeare became a shareholder and the in-house playwright of the Lord Chamberlain's Men. Richard Wilson's contribution to this book reminds us what a radical, potentially traumatic turning-point this must have constituted for Shakespeare, which Wilson finds inscribed into *Richard II*, quite possibly Shakespeare's first play after joining the Lord Chamberlain's Men. What may therefore underlie King Richard's abdication is, as Wilson argues, Shakespeare's own 'professional abdication, as the dramatist disavows everything he himself previously said' (Wilson, p. 114). It seems also striking, however, that while Shakespeare opted for radical institutional change by 'exchanging his private patron for a paying public' (Wilson, p. 114), he refused to change by continuing to write poetry. For what characterises Shakespeare's plays after he joined the Lord Chamberlain's Man – *Richard II*, *Love's Labour's Lost*, *A Midsummer Night's Dream* and *Romeo and Juliet* – is precisely the amount and sophistication of their poetry. E. K. Chambers commented on this group of plays, which earlier scholars labelled 'the lyric phase', by writing that 'it is most reasonable to suppose that at some date Shakespeare decided to make a deliberate experiment in lyrical drama. A very natural stimulus would be afforded by his experience of lyrical work in the narrative poems.'[16] It seems significant that by the turn of the century, all four plays mentioned above were in print, suggesting that, in one sense at least, Shakespeare, after 1594, refused to change by continuing to write elaborate poetry which became available to the reading public, as his narrative poems had done.[17]

This last point illustrates what the contributions to *Shakespeare's Book* bear out more generally, which is that the current reconsideration of Shakespeare's authorial standing demonstrates the interrelatedness of areas in Shakespeare studies which are all too often kept safely apart: criticism, textual studies, bibliography, theatre history, reception history, as well as biography. Textual studies, in particular, might all too easily be considered a self-contained subfield, yet I argued in 2003 that they can yield vital insights into the working practices of Shakespeare and his company, especially if we reassess the origins and purposes of the variant versions of Shakespeare's multiple-text plays.[18] Duncan Salkeld's chapter turns to one of these plays, ostensibly departing from my view of Q1 *Henry V* by insisting that 'some process of memory' (p. 154) may partly lie behind it, a view which I in fact share, arguing in *Shakespeare as Literary Dramatist* that 'it should not be excluded that faulty memory may account for some of the differences between the "good" and the "bad" quartos'.[19] I believe, as Salkeld does, that Shakespeare first wrote a version close to F, of which an abridgement was made, that 'this (or a similar) shorter version provided the copy for Q' (p. 160), and that 'a performance script does indeed lie somewhere behind Q' (p. 160). I am no less pessimistic than he is about our ability to recover with any greater precision the genesis of a text like Q1 *Henry V*.[20] Yet what is important for the current revaluation of Shakespearean authorship is not that we understand in every detail how Q1 *Henry V* came into existence (we never will) but that we realise the importance, as Andrew Gurr and others have done, of the performance script which Q1 *Henry V* imperfectly reflects.[21] The prefatory material to the 1623 quarto of *The Duchess of Malfi* distinguishes between 'the Play' (A2r; the script as it was performed) and 'the Poem' (A3r; the dramatic text as it was printed), the poem containing 'diuerse things . . . that the length of the Play would not beare in the Presentment', as the title-page puts it. The evidence suggests that the extant versions of *Henry V* give us access to something similar, an (imperfectly recorded) version of 'the play' (Q1) and 'the poem' (F). The excessive length of the 'poem' for the purposes of the stage, implying a potentially excessive time of representation, is of course a feature of many of Shakespeare's plays and finds its fictional correspondence, as John Lyon's chapter shows, in the excessive represented time, the plays' fictional 'before, after and elsewhere' which Shakespeare so suggestively dramatizes (Lyon, p. 242). What a dramatic text that was too long for 'the Presentment' means for the dramatic practice of Shakespeare and his fellow players is that the plays seem to have been considerably abridged – and that Shakespeare knew they would be considerably abridged – before reaching the stage.

If the correlative of the routine abridgement of Shakespeare's plays is that the long original versions were written with readers in mind, as I have argued in *Shakespeare as Literary Dramatist*,[22] then it seems of some importance to evaluate what early reception the printed playtexts had. Fredson Bowers held the long prominent opinion that play-books were considered 'ephemeral entertainment reading', to be consumed and then discarded.[23] This view now seems increasingly dated and is even more difficult to sustain in the light of Stanley Wells's chapter about 'A new early reader of Shakespeare'. William Scott, an early literary theorist and a contemporary of Shakespeare, offers 'precise close criticism of Shakespeare's style' (p. 238) based on the poetry and the drama alike, praises 'the very well-penned Tragedy of Rich. The 2d' and draws on *Richard II* to discuss rhetorical amplification (p. 239). Wells's chapter may profitably be considered in the context of other recent work that sheds light on the status of early playbooks. Alan H. Nelson has examined numerous early libraries with books by Shakespeare and come to the conclusion, 'against the grain of much modern criticism, that Shakespeare's poems and plays ought to be approached, if we are to respect history . . . as verbal and dramatic art, as – dare I think it? – English Literature'.[24] Henry Woudhuysen, in his British Academy Shakespeare Lecture of 2004, has similarly argued that printed play-books were not the 'ephemeral items' they have often been taken to be.[25] Woudhuysen presents his case more fully in an essay published the preceding year, in which he reminds us that paper was the single most expensive item in book production and points out that early modern playbooks often contain blank pages or leaves at the beginning and at the end: 'The presence of these blanks . . . might be taken to challenge received ideas about the relative value placed on printed plays. If they were the unconsidered trifles they are generally taken to have been, it is strange that printers or publishers were so often willing to leave blank paper in them.'[26] If book collectors were willing to preserve and catalogue Shakespeare's playbooks and if publishers were willing to invest expensive paper in them, we may more easily understand why William Scott engaged with a Shakespeare play in a way which we hitherto believed did not exist prior to the eighteenth century.

If we reconsider Shakespeare from the many perspectives which this book opens up – early readers, publishers and book collectors; the engagement with books and texts in Shakespeare's writings; the shape of Shakespeare's career; the likely origins and purposes of Shakespeare's texts – then 'Shakespeare's book' looks increasingly like the kind of item Shakespeare himself had every reason to care about.

Notes

1 *Venus and Adonis* (1593) and *The Rape of Lucrece* (1594) do mention Shakespeare's name at the end of the dedication, though not on the title-page.

2 See Geoffrey Bullough, *Narrative and Dramatic Sources of Shakespeare*, 8 vols (London: Routledge, 1957–75), vol. 2, pp. 61–112; vol. 3, pp. 347–408.

3 See Stuart Gillespie, *Shakespeare's Books: A Dictionary of Shakespeare's Sources* (London: Continuum, 2005).

4 See James P. Bednarz, *Shakespeare and the Poets' War* (New York: Columbia University Press, 2000).

5 MacD. P. Jackson, 'Francis Meres and the Cultural Contexts of Shakespeare's Rival Poet Sonnets', *The Review of English Studies*, 56 (2005), 224–46, in particular 243, 236.

6 See Lukas Erne, *Shakespeare as Literary Dramatist* (Cambridge: Cambridge University Press, 2003), pp. 245–49. *Shakespeare as Literary Dramatist* was published in paperback in 2007.

7 See STC 23076–95, 22534–44. 'STC' is short for Alfred W. Pollard, G. R. Redgrave, W. A. Jackson, F. S. Ferguson and Katharine F. Pantzer, *A Short-Title Catalogue of Books Printed in England, Scotland, and Ireland and of English Books Printed Abroad, 1475–1640*, 2nd ed, 3 vols (London: The Bibliographical Society, 1976–91). The data are now also accessible online via the electronic *English Short Title Catalogue* (*ESTC*) at http://estc.bl.uk.

8 John Russell Brown, *Shakespeare's Plays in Performance* (London: Edward Arnold, 1966), J. L. Styan, *Shakespeare's Stagecraft* (Cambridge: Cambridge University Press, 1967), and J. L. Styan, *The*

Shakespeare Revolution (Cambridge: Cambridge University Press, 1977).

9 Anne Righter, *Shakespeare and the Idea of the Play* (London: Chatto and Windus, 1962); James L. Calderwood, *Shakespearean Metadrama: The Argument of the Play in 'Titus Andronicus', 'Love's Labour's Lost', 'Romeo and Juliet', 'A Midsummer Night's Dream', and 'Richard II'* (Minneapolis: University of Minnesota Press, 1971), *Metadrama in Shakespeare's Henriad: 'Richard II' to 'Henry V'* (Berkeley: University. of California Press, 1979), and *To Be and Not to Be: Negation and Metadrama in 'Hamlet'* (New York: Columbia University Press, 1983); Jackson I. Cope, *The Theatre and the Dream: From Metaphor to Form in Renaissance Drama* (Baltimore: Johns Hopkins University Press, 1973); Robert Egan, *Drama within Drama: Shakespeare's Sense of His Art in 'King Lear', 'The Winter's Tale', and 'The Tempest'* (New York: Columbia University Press, 1975); Thomas F. Van Laan, *Role-Playing in Shakespeare* (Toronto: University of Toronto Press, 1978); Sidney Homan, *When the Theatre Turns to Itself: The Aesthetic Metaphor in Shakespeare* (Lewisburg: Bucknell University Press, 1981).

10 Richard Fly, 'The Evolution of Shakespearean Metadrama: Abel, Burckhardt, and Calderwood', *Comparative Drama*, 20 (1986), 124–39.

11 See Patrick Cheney, *Shakespeare, National Poet-Playwright* (Cambridge: Cambridge University Press, 2004) and *Shakespeare's Literary Authorship* (Cambridge: Cambridge University Press, 2008), and Charlotte Scott, *Shakespeare and the Idea of the Book* (Oxford: Oxford University Press, 2007).

12 See Stephen Booth (ed.), *Shakespeare's Sonnets* (New Haven: Yale University Press, 1977), p. 172. See also Patrick Cheney, '"O, let my books be . . . dumb presagers": Poetry and Theater in Shakespeare's Sonnets', *Shakespeare Quarterly*, 52 (2001), 222–54, revised and reprinted in *Shakespeare, National Poet-Playwright*, pp. 207–38, in particular pp. 220–5; and Lukas Erne, 'Revisiting Shakespearean Authorship', *Shakespeare Studies*, 61 (2008), forthcoming.

13 Jonas Barish, '"Soft, here follows prose": Shakespeare's Stage Documents', in Murray Biggs et al. (eds), *The Arts of Performance in Elizabethan and Early Stuart Drama: Essays for G. K. Hunter* (Edinburgh: Edinburgh University Press, 1991), pp. 32–48, 34, quoted by Helen Smith (p. 73 above).

14 I quote from John Milton, 'L'Allegro', line 134, in John Carey (ed.), *Complete Shorter Poems*, 2nd edn, Longman Annotated English Poets (London: Longman, 1997); and Alexander Pope, 'The First Epistle of the Second book of Horace, Imitated' (1737), in John Butt (ed.), *Imitations of Horace, The Twickenham Edition of the Poems of*

Alexander Pope, vol. 4, 2nd edn (New Haven: Yale University Press, 1953), p. 199.

15 See Cheney, *Shakespeare's Literary Authorship*.

16 E. K. Chambers, *William Shakespeare: A Study of Facts and Problems*, 2 vols (Oxford: Clarendon Press, 1930), vol. 1, p. 267.

17 For a fuller version of the present argument see my 'Print and Manuscript', in Patrick Cheney (ed.), *The Cambridge Companion to Shakespeare's Poetry* (Cambridge: Cambridge University Press, 2007), pp. 54–71, in particular pp. 64–9. Another recent article which stresses the importance of 1594 as marking 'a watershed in Shakespeare's composition' (p. 14) is Bart Van Es's 'Company Man: Another Crucial Year for Shakespeare', *Times Literary Supplement*, 2 February 2007, pp. 14–15. While Van Es also singles out *Richard II* as 'probably the first work written by an established member of a stable and successful acting company' (pp. 14–15), he is concerned to show how Shakespeare's new status as in-house playwright, writing for a group of actors with whom he was closely connected, shaped the dramatic make-up of his plays.

18 Erne, *Shakespeare as Literary Dramatist*, pp. 192–244.

19 Ibid., p. 218.

20 See Ibid., p. 218.

21 See Andrew Gurr, 'Maximal and Minimal Texts: Shakespeare v. The Globe', *Shakespeare Survey*, 52 (1999), 68–87, and Andrew Gurr (ed.), *The First Quarto of King Henry V*, The New Cambridge Shakespeare: The Early Quartos (Cambridge: Cambridge University Press, 2000). See also Stephen Orgel, *The Authentic Shakespeare and Other Problems of the Early Modern Stage* (New York: Routledge, 2002), p. 22.

22 Note that Richard Dutton argued as early as 1996 that 'in writing plays which were in some respects unplayable . . . [Shakespeare] was effectively writing for a readership no different in essence from that of his sonnets and epyllia', and that 'Shakespeare had readers in mind too, however much practical theatrical applications must also have shaped his thoughts' ('The Birth of the Author', in R. B. Parker and S. P. Zitner (eds), *Elizabethan Theater: Essays in Honor of S. Schoenbaum* (Newark: University of Delaware Press, 1996), pp. 71–92, reprinted in Dutton, *Licensing, Censorship and Authorship in Early Modern England: Buggeswords* (Basingstoke: Palgrave, 2000), pp. 90–113 (pp. 111–12)).

23 Fredson Bowers, 'The Publication of English Renaissance Plays', in Fredson Bowers (ed.), *Elizabethan Dramatists*, Dictionary of Literary Biography, 62 (Detroit: Gale, 1987), p. 414.

24 Alan H. Nelson, 'Shakespeare and the Bibliophiles: From the Earliest Years to 1616', in Robin Myers, Michael Harris and Giles Mandelbrote

(eds), *Owners, Annotators and the Signs of Reading* (London: Oak Knoll Press, 2005), pp. 49–73, 70.

25 H. R. Woudhuysen, 'The Foundations of Shakespeare's Text', in *Proceedings of the British Academy: 2003 Lectures* (Oxford: Oxford University Press, 2004), pp. 69–100 (p. 88); see also pp. 74–7, 88–9.

26 H. R. Woudhuysen, 'Early Play Texts: Forms and Formes', in Ann Thompson and Gordon McMullan (eds), *In Arden: Editing Shakespeare*, The Arden Shakespeare (London: Thomson Learning, 2003), pp. 48–61, 55.

Index